PENGUIN BOOKS

ROCK 'N' ROLL

– I GAVE YOU THE BEST Y

'In the spring of 1958 when I took my first tentative steps in the music business as a wide-eyed naïve youngster, I expected my career to last for two or maybe three years, certainly no more. I was out for a good time and music was just part of enjoying myself. Thirty years later – *I am still playing* . . . My career has . . . given me fame, a nice lifestyle, money and all the trappings that follow success. I have travelled the world through my ability to play three chords' – Bruce Welch

ROCK 'N' ROLL

– I GAVE YOU THE BEST YEARS OF MY LIFE

A LIFE IN THE SHADOWS

BRUCE WELCH

WITH
HOWARD ELSON

PENGUIN BOOKS

PENGUIN BOOKS

Published by the Penguin Group
27 Wrights Lane, London W8 5TZ, England
Viking Penguin Inc., 40 West 23rd Street, New York, New York 10010, USA
Penguin Books Australia Ltd, Ringwood, Victoria, Australia
Penguin Books Canada Ltd, 2801 John Street, Markham, Ontario, Canada
L3R 1B4
Penguin Books (NZ) Ltd, 182–190 Wairau Road, Auckland 10, New Zealand

Penguin Books Ltd, Registered Offices: Harmondsworth, Middlesex, England

First published by Viking 1989
Published in Penguin Books 1990
10 9 8 7 6 5 4 3 2 1

Filmset in 9/11 Baskerville
by Centracet, Cambridge

Made and printed in Great Britain by
Richard Clays Ltd, (The Chaucer Press)
Bungay, Suffolk

For my mother Grace and Aunt Sadie

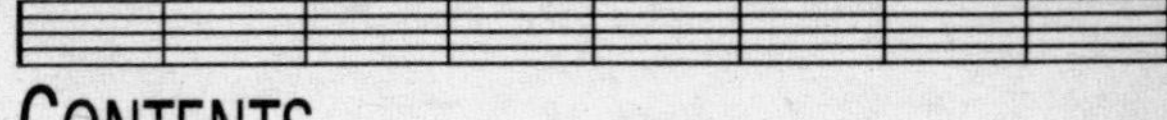

CONTENTS

Acknowledgements

I would like to thank the following people for their assistance and endeavours in helping me with this book: Brian Bennett, Hank Marvin, Cliff Richard; Ray Alan, Brian Berg, Erica Elson, Syd Gillingham, Brian Goode, John Friesen, Larry Page, Laurie Mansfield, Carolyn Whitaker, Brian Southall and Janet Lord, and all at EMI Records.

Bruce Welch
February 1989

Photo credits

Daily Express 9b; *Daily Mirror* 3b; EMI Records 4b, 6b, 7a, 7b; Harry Hammond Collection/Victoria & Albert Museum 5a; Dezo Hoffmann 11b; Dezo Hoffmann/Rex Features 3a; Steve Terrell 14b; John Woodward 13c.

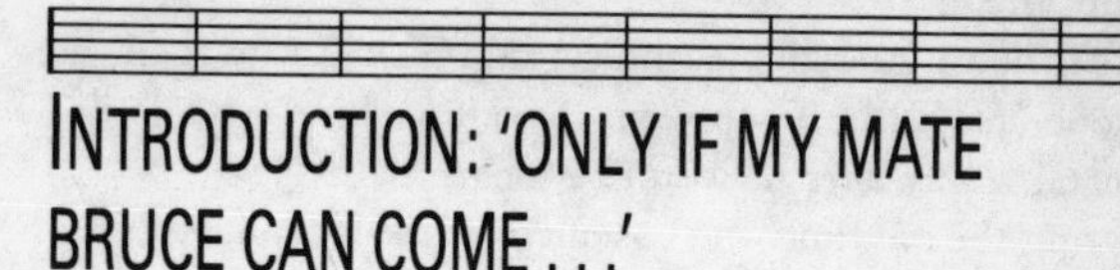

INTRODUCTION: 'ONLY IF MY MATE BRUCE CAN COME . . .'

On an unusually warm afternoon in the last week of September 1958, John Foster, the eighteen-year-old manager of Cliff Richard, the new British singing sensation, caught the Green Line coach number 715A from Hertford to Oxford Circus in the West End of London and headed for Soho.

Only days before, on 12 September, the seventeen-year-old singer had entered the hit parade at No. 28 with his début single, 'Move It', which was now climbing steadily. It was on the strength of this first release that Cliff had been booked to appear on a three-week British theatre tour with the American singing duo the Kalin Twins, who had spent much of the summer at the top of the charts with what turned out to be their one and only hit, 'When'. They were the first set of twins ever to top the British hit parade. The tour was scheduled to start in a matter of days.

Cliff's backing group, the Drifters, had recently lost their lead guitarist, Norman Mitham, who had quit after the rest of the boys had decided to turn professional and chosen the security of a steady job instead. The line-up had now dwindled to just two, with Ian Samwell playing bass and Terry Smart on drums. They desperately needed a replacement before the tour started; Cliff realized that the group was not strong enough instrumentally or musically to tour with such exalted company as the American chart-topping brothers, and dispatched his manager to find a suitable recruit. John Foster already had someone in mind for the role. He had seen Tony Sheridan performing several weeks before at the 2i's coffee bar in Old Compton Street, where he was building a reputation for himself as a brilliant guitarist. John was determined to get this man. When he arrived in Soho, however, he discovered to his great disappointment that Tony Sheridan was not there.

'He'll be in later this evening,' said Tom Littlewood, who ran the coffee bar. 'But if you want to wait for him, why don't you go downstairs? I'm sure he won't be long.'

During the daytime, the basement of the legendary 2i's – which exploded into action each night with skiffle music and rock 'n' roll – was closed to the general public. Only a privileged few musicians were ever allowed downstairs in the afternoon, so John Foster felt honoured to be part of the inner circle and eagerly accepted the invitation. He picked his way down the steps into the dingy cellar and waited. And waited.

There was no sign of Tony Sheridan, although several other musicians drifted into the tiny venue from time to time, strummed a few chords, and drifted out again. It was that kind of place.

When Hank Marvin arrived, John was getting anxious. Time was moving on, and he was now facing a dilemma. What to do? The last Green Line coach back to Hertfordshire, which he had to catch if he did not want to be stranded in London for the night, was due to leave shortly. He didn't want to leave the 2i's empty-handed, but Tony Sheridan still hadn't shown. Maybe he should come back tomorrow? While John decided his next move, Hank started to rehearse for the evening's performance. He ran through a couple of Buddy Holly numbers, and practised some devastating lead solos he had picked up from Ricky Nelson singles. The whole cellar reverberated to the sound of his guitar.

Hank Marvin was much admired by his fellow musicians in Soho for his prowess on the guitar. His technique was quite outstanding for one so young, and the more John Foster heard him play, the more certain he became that the young beanpole of a man would be a valuable asset to the Drifters, if only he would join them. It was worth a try.

When he had finished playing, John sidled up to the guitarist and introduced himself.

'I'm John Foster,' he said, 'Cliff Richard's manager,' and held out his hand.

Hank laughed. He thought John was joking, and told him so in no uncertain terms. But the manager persisted, and eventually convinced him that he was genuine.

'Have you heard Cliff?' he asked.

Hank nodded. 'I love "Move It",' he replied. 'I heard it on the radio this morning. It's a great record – great guitar work.'

'Well,' said Foster, 'we're looking for a guitarist to join Cliff's backing group for a tour with the Kalin Twins. It starts next week. Are you interested?'

Hank nodded again. His eyes lit up, and John outlined more details of the tour – how long it would last, who was appearing, what was required.

'What do you think?' he asked when he had finished, and glanced at his watch again. He was in luck, there was still time to catch the last bus.

The Geordie boy looked thoughtful for a while. 'I'll do it,' he said, and smiled, 'but only if my mate Bruce can come along as well. He plays rhythm guitar.'

John Foster was relieved. He nodded his agreement and shook Hank's hand.

'Okay. It's a deal.'

A few days later John took Hank and me across the road to a tiny tailor's shop in Dean Street, where upstairs Cliff Richard was being fitted for the shocking pink jacket he was having specially made for the forthcoming tour, and we were introduced for the first time. Cliff, dressed immaculately even then, eyed us up and down slowly – the greasy hair, the pimples, the scruffy, tight trousers and the crêpe soles – and thought we looked like a couple of yobs.

1

'THERE'S NO PEOPLE LIKE SHOW PEOPLE . . .'

Bastard.

It is strange, but in today's so-called permissive and enlightened society, where almost anything is acceptable as far as morals and standards are concerned, there is still a stigma attached to that word and everything it stands for. It even sounds soiled and distasteful.

I was born a bastard – and the shock of discovering the truth at the age of seventeen and into adolescence has left its mark and given me, it seems, a permanent chip on my shoulder. It hurt like hell at the time – but it is something that has been with me now for most of my life and I am still coming to terms with it. Ever since I found out about my birthright I have suffered bouts of depression that can hit me at any time, which has sometimes made me very difficult to live with. There have been lengthy periods in my life when I have been wrapped up totally in my own self-imposed sadness to the detriment of everything else around me, and that has led to many problems over the years, both with the group and in my relationships with women, including the break-up of my second marriage in 1988. It has also left me with an almost obsessive desire for perfection in everything I do. I am convinced that psychologically it harks back to my childhood. I can't seem to shake it off.

I found out that I was illegitimate by accident in 1959, when I applied for a copy of my birth certificate to enable me to get married. I had not realized that my parents had never been married, but had just had an illicit affair. I was stunned, and the revelation really hurt. I couldn't believe that no one had ever bothered to tell me – and I felt cheated.

I never really knew Grace, my mother. She died when I was just five years old, and I was brought up by her sister, Sarah – Aunt Sadie – who told me very little about the past. She kept everything from me to protect me, I guess, although it was in fact over-protection.

I have absolutely no recollection of my mother before she died, and I can't even picture her face in my mind without looking at photographs. I can never say with conviction that I can remember holding her hand or sitting on her knee. I can't recall her hugging or kissing me, or telling me she loved me. Obviously I must have blacked out the early years in my subconscious: I have no memories at all – and that worries me.

I didn't have any kind of relationship with my father, either, and when I have had to face major problems in my life – and I have had a few heartaches over the years – I have never had anyone close to turn to for love and encouragement, or simply for a shoulder to cry on. Most people have a family to call on for solace and support – their mother, father, brother or sister – but I have never had anyone (somehow Aunt Sadie wasn't quite the same), and have always tried to cope with things on my own.

It is only since Aunt Sadie died in 1987 that I have been able to piece together a few details about my mother and her family. It is silly, I suppose, but in many ways I am still looking for her. I even took her family name for my own in 1958, when Hank and I decided that we needed to change our very ordinary names to ones that sounded at least slightly American and that would be more in keeping with the raw aggression, energy, drive and image-consciousness of rock 'n' roll. I had actually been christened Bruce Cripps, taking the surname from my father, Stan Cripps. But I wanted a link with my mother, so I adopted the name Welch instead. To be fair, 'Bruce Cripps' didn't really capture the imagination. It didn't reek of rock 'n' roll, and it didn't sound anything like as good a name for a musician as those of Elvis Presley, Johnny Ray, Marty Wilde or Tommy Steele; their names had strength. On the other hand 'Bruce Welch' had a distinct ring to it. At one stage in my career, though, I very nearly became *Buddy* Welch, after Buddy Holly.

Hank's real name was Brian Robson Rankin, but he had been nicknamed 'Hank' at school because he was bandy-legged and walked a little like a cowboy. The school also seemed to be overrun by Brians, so some other form of identification was needed to single out the individuals. The name stuck; endearing and unique to this lovely, affable character, it really suited him, but it wasn't until the spring of 1958 that he made it official. At that time the British hit parade had been dominated by a song called 'Whole Lotta Woman', by a singer with the even more unlikely-sounding name of Marvin Rainwater. He was a Cherokee Indian, and his real name was Marvin Percy; by coincidence, he also took his mother's maiden name for his own when he started recording.

'Whole Lotta Woman' had topped the British charts through April and May, and it became a huge juke-box hit, too. Hank and I used to sit together practising the number for hours on end. It was a great song for the times, with a spectacular guitar introduction which Hank, bless him, could play perfectly. With rock 'n' roll gripping Britain in those days, we were very much swept up by the music and everything it stood for, particularly American culture. Hank decided to borrow the singer's name, mainly because it sounded *American.* He also retained the initial 'B' from his own real name, Brian, and this emerged as Hank B. Marvin, which definitely sounded like a rock 'n' roll name if ever there was one, and a great one at that. Actually, there was just a possibility that he might become Hank *Rainwater*, which was far too contrived and pretentious. But it was in with a chance!

The Welch family came from Ferryhill in County Durham, a close-knit mining community. King Coal was very much part of everyone's life in that area of Britain, and in many families it was coal-dust that flowed through their veins instead of blood. My grandfather, like so many generations before him, was sent down the mines as a young boy. Later, he and my grandmother raised a family of five: four girls – Mary the eldest, Peggy, Sarah, and my mother, Grace – and Billy, the only son. They were brought up strictly but fairly, to fear God, to show respect for their elders, and to be true to the often archaic Victorian values and principles of their parents.

My mother was still very young when she married an Irishman, William 'Topper' Meehan, in the Catholic church at Ferryhill. (It is ironic that the name 'Meehan' would feature so strongly in my life years later.) It seems, unfortunately, that the marriage was beset with problems; in the end Grace could stand it no longer and walked out on her husband. To avoid the shame which would follow in such a small town, she left the area completely and, with my grandmother and Aunt Sadie, moved south and went to live on the coast at Bognor Regis. My grandmother went into service and became housekeeper to an elderly gentleman called Mr Scardon, who owned a large residence in the West Sussex seaside resort, while my mother took a job at the Royal Norfolk Hotel on the seafront. It was here that she eventually met a young soldier called Stan Cripps, who was serving with the Royal Artillery.

Britain, like most of the world, was in the grip of war when they met, and many soldiers, who could not be sure where their next posting would take them, or if indeed they would ever return home, lived each day at a time and took everything in their stride without making too many plans for the future. Grace and Stan had an affair, and on Sunday, 2 November 1941, I was born. It was a pretty eventful year. Yugoslavia finally capitulated to the Nazi invaders in April; the so-called invincible German battleship *Bismarck* was sunk in May; the Japanese attacked Pearl Harbor in December; and Britain continued to take an aerial pounding from marauding German bombers.

My mother was twenty-seven and still married to William Meehan when I was born. To avoid any kind of scandal in such a respectable family, my Aunts Mary and Peggy and my Uncle Billy, who by now were all married with children of their own, were not immediately told of my arrival. In fact it was quite some time before they learned the truth. It would have brought tremendous shame to the family name if news of Grace's illegitimate offspring had ever leaked out in gossip. Peggy's husband died in 1987 without ever knowing me, and remained ignorant of the fact that his sister-in-law, Grace, had given birth to a son. I only found this out by accident, many years later. After the Shadows had made it in a substantial way, I bought my Aunt Sadie a bungalow in the charming residential area of Whickham, overlooking Newcastle upon Tyne, and whenever the group were playing in the city or close by, I always made the time to go and see her. On one occasion in the early sixties we were booked to appear at Newcastle City Hall, so that afternoon I made my usual pilgrimage across town to visit Sadie. I hadn't been back for some time, and I was looking forward to seeing her again. By now the group was established and earning a lot of money, enough to afford me the luxury of a Rolls-Royce of my own which I wanted to show off to Sadie. I was elated. It was an impromptu visit and nothing special had been arranged. But as soon as I arrived, Sadie was fidgety and irritable. Something was troubling her deeply. She didn't greet me with her usual warmth and affection and seemed strangely distant. It was easy to sense that there was a problem.

'Something's wrong,' I said innocently. 'What's happened?' I wanted to know – maybe I could help. I certainly wanted to try.

She looked at me sheepishly. 'I'm sorry, Bruce, but you can't stop,' she said by way of explanation. 'You'll have to go.'

'But I've only just arrived,' I stammered. 'I haven't seen you for ages. How's . . .?'

'You must go,' she interrupted quickly. She started to panic. '*Please*. Your Aunt Peggy and Uncle Jimmy are coming to tea. They'll be here at any moment. They mustn't find you here. Please go.'

'But why?' I searched for an answer. I was shocked, and suddenly felt like an outcast. Why me?

Then, to my utter amazement, Sadie told me the whole story: that Jimmy, Peggy's husband, had been told nothing about me and that it would be too great a shock for him after all this time to find me there now. The circumstances of my birth had been deliberately kept from him to avoid any possible trouble or repercussions because, I learnt later, Jimmy and William Meehan, my mother's legitimate husband, had been the best of friends, indeed almost inseparable. If Meehan had ever found out the truth, well . . . as Sadie said, it didn't bear thinking about what might have happened. There was no point in telling Jimmy now, all these years later. They were in too deep, and there was no knowing how he might react to the news that he had been deceived by his own wife and her family for over twenty years. It was better left alone.

It was an extremely delicate situation, but there was nothing I could do except continue with the charade and leave the house quickly to avoid any further embarrassment to my aunts. I felt very sad and upset, but I respected my mother's memory too much to bring her shame.

I spent the first three years of my life in Bognor Regis, by which time the war was kicking its heels towards a final conclusion, and the bombing raids on Britain's industrial cities by the Luftwaffe had given way to sporadic but nevertheless deadly attacks by the VIs – the flying bombs, the dreaded doodlebugs – and the VII rockets.

When Mr Scardon eventually passed away, there was nothing to keep us in Sussex any more. The ties with the north-east were still as strong as ever, so my grandmother, Aunt Sadie, my mother and I turned our backs on the south coast and headed north. We settled in Chester-le-Street, one of the oldest towns in Britain; founded by the Romans in 1 AD, it lies just a handful of miles north from the city of Durham and directly south of Newcastle upon Tyne. We moved into a picturesque semi-detached house at 15 Broadwood View, in a little terraced street overlooking the cemetery at the bottom of a hill off Ropery Lane. My mother could see the graveyard from the upstairs room where she slept, and always insisted that when the time came she wanted to be buried there, under a tree and within sight of her home. Sadly, the time would come a lot sooner than anyone realized.

Not long after we arrived in Chester-le-Street she became ill with tuberculosis, and for the next two years she fought bravely against the debilitating illness. These days it can be completely cured, thanks to modern drugs, but in the mid-1940s such medicine was still in its infancy. Then it was looked upon as a potential killer, and some of the methods of treatment employed by hospitals seem positively brutal now. Once the disease had taken a firm hold, Grace was taken into a sanatorium in Bishop Auckland where TB patients often slept outside on a balcony, exposed to all the elements, as part of their treatment. It was the severe winter of 1947, and it proved fatal for her. She grew progressively weaker, and died on 7 February at the age of thirty-two. Her wish was granted a few days later, when she was buried under a tree in the little cemetery overlooked by our house in Broadwood View. Tragically, I can't remember her passing away, nor can I even recall attending her funeral.

Before she died, Aunt Sadie had promised her sister that she would look after her young son and raise him as her own. Had she refused my mother's plea, I would probably have been taken into care and put into a home, as all contact with my father had been lost. As far as Sadie knew, he was still living in Bognor Regis; as far as I was concerned, he didn't exist at all – I had been told nothing about him and I was never encouraged to ask questions. I didn't even know of his existence until I was eight years old. One morning, without any explanation, Sadie asked me to dress in my best Sunday clothes and told me we were going on a journey. She took me to Newcastle Central Station in Neville Street for a special meeting. I was totally bewildered. What was happening? When we arrived I was introduced to a kindly-looking man who seemed very eager to please, and was told that he was my father, which didn't mean a great deal to me. How could it? There was no tearful reunion with hugs and kisses, just a stark introduction and a polite handshake. He seemed pleasant enough to me, but we were complete strangers.

My father and his new wife, Ann, took me on holiday with them. We went by train to Berwick-on-Tweed, where Ann's parents came from, and spent most of the time fishing the River Tweed at a place called Red Rocks. We were away for two weeks in all, which was the longest time I ever spent in my father's company. But it was a sad time, on reflection, and a very false relationship developed. We were both trying so hard. There were no fond memories to look back on together, just stilted observations and chit-chat to pass the time. We should have been so close, we should have shared a very private and special friendship – the bond of father and son. We both tried in our own ways, but we were worlds apart and very wary of each other. Had there been a stronger emotional tie, who knows what might have happened? I might have gone to live with him and my life would have changed completely. But it was not to be, and I returned home to Chester-le-Street to live with my grandmother and Aunt Sadie once more. I never saw my father again, apart from a very brief encounter in London when I was seventeen. I know nothing about his background, I never met any of his family except for his wife, and I obviously wasn't accepted . . . or maybe my existence had been kept from them, too? For a young, impressionable boy, it was a traumatic and very confusing experience.

From the age of five, I was sent to Red Rose Primary School, which was just a short walk from my home in Broadwood View. It was a delightful little school. By now Sadie had become the mother figure in my life, and in the early days she used to take me to school and pick me up afterwards. Miss Selkirk, the headmistress, was always kind to me; indeed, all the teachers were very warm. They would have known about my family background, but I was never singled out for real preferential treatment.

I wasn't particularly mischievous at school at the time. I had plenty of spirit and was quick and bright in class, and I made friends easily. I tended to finish my lessons ahead of my classmates, and while I waited for the others to catch up, I would often do little chores for the teachers. It was at Red Rose Primary that I fell in love for the first time with a girl called Anne Usher. We were both eight years old, and our romance blossomed in the playground and out on the swings. I looked up to her and admired her tremendously. She seemed so elegant and charming, and what's more, her house had its own garage, which at that time was a great status symbol and impressed me no end. Our love, however, came to nothing. Perhaps it was only the thought of the garage that had moved me so.

Besides Anne, there was another great love coming into my life – music – and one of my most vivid early memories was of dancing and prancing around the school hall (with all the other lads, I hasten to add) to the strains of 'In the Hall of the Mountain King' from Grieg's *Peer Gynt Suite*. That is my first recollection of ever consciously listening to music. Music was all around me, and like many children I took it for granted, but from that moment onwards it started to enter my life with ever-increasing intensity. I also spent many happy hours watching the Saturday morning picture shows at the Palace cinema in the town, where for a mere sixpence you could see Superman saving the world and Jungle Jim and Flash Gordon. There were cowboys and Indians, gangsters, cops and robbers and cartoons, in a great big fantasy factory where cars could fly and rockets could land on the moon and animals could talk. It was a happy escape from the mundane things in life like growing up. I was spellbound. I adored the cinema and felt particularly drawn towards cowboy films – Roy Rogers in *Sons of Pioneers*; *The Singing Cowboy*, with Gene Autry; and *Santa Fe Marshal* with Hopalong Cassidy. It was in this kind of film that I discovered cowboys who sang to the accompaniment of a guitar, but although I was being exposed more and more to this sort of music, it did not then give me a conscious feeling that I had to rush out and play the guitar and sing. I was too young anyway. That was to come later.

I was given my first musical instrument at about this time. Sadie had a couple of friends who would occasionally visit the house – I always addressed them as Aunt Minnie and Uncle Norman, although they were not related to us. Whenever Uncle Norman visited the house he would bring his ukelele with him; he used to play it for me, and sing. He could see I was impressed, and eventually he gave me a ukelele of my own, which of course I couldn't play at all. Still, I practised like mad and it made encouraging noises, although nothing that could ever be mistaken for music. A few months later, nature took a hand and put us all out of our misery. One night we suffered a particularly bad storm, which flooded the house and caused a fair amount of damage inside. One of the casualties was the ukelele, which was washed away in the torrent.

Our main source of musical entertainment at home was the wireless – 'steam' radio. I was an avid listener to the BBC Light Programme, as it was then called, which served up a broadcasting diet of music, variety, comedy and adventure serials. They also had a special programme for children at five o'clock each afternoon – *Children's Hour* – while Uncle Mac played musical requests on Saturdays. I much preferred to listen to the comedy series like *Life with the Lyons*, *Ray's a Laugh* with Ted Ray, *Take it from Here* with Jimmy Edwards, *Much Binding in the Marsh* with Richard Murdoch, and *Stand Easy* with Charlie Chester, whose son Peter would later play an important part in my own career. Then there was *Journey into Space* and *Riders of the Range*. *Dick Barton* was a special favourite, and I know many people, including John Lennon and Paul McCartney, whose own childhood was enriched by the escapades of Snowy and Dick. Shortly afterwards *The*

Goons, with Harry Secombe, Peter Sellers and Spike Milligan, broke down all the traditions of comedy shows as they made up their own rules. They were classics and I adored them.

The big musical shows of the day were *Housewives' Choice*, *Workers' Playtime* and *Two-Way Family Favourites*, which went out each Sunday lunchtime and linked families in Britain with their loved ones serving in the forces throughout the world. The idea of the programme was to play record requests and to send out special messages over the air so that servicemen, who were often stationed thousands of miles away, would know that the folks back home were still thinking about them. It was tremendously popular. Even after all these years, I still associate the smell of roast beef and Yorkshire pudding with the show's theme tune – 'With a Song in My Heart'. Cliff Michelmore, Jean Metcalfe and Bill Crozier, who were just a few of the people who presented the programme each week, became household names and were looked upon as friends of the family.

During the early days of 1950 there were no music charts or hit parades in Britain which were based purely on record sales. In America the *Billboard* national pop chart had been in existence since 1940, but the popularity of songs in Britain was still calculated on the number of copies of sheet music each one sold. Successful songs were frequently performed on record by a number of different artistes, and you could never be quite sure which was the authentic hit version. There were many popular songs at the time that were regularly requested on *Family Favourites*, including 'Bewitched, Bothered and Bewildered', 'Tennessee Waltz', 'La Vie en Rose', 'My Heart Cries for You', 'Twilight Time', 'Music, Music, Music', 'If I Knew You Were Coming I'd Have Baked a Cake', and 'Sam's Song', which all went on to sell a million copies and reflected perfectly the wide variety of music that people were listening to and enjoying.

The music industry at the beginning of the 1950s was in a transitional period. The dominance of the Big Band sound, which had prevailed from 1937 to the end of the 1940s, was slowly coming to a close. That era was over, giving way to crooners and solo singers, who in many cases had started their own careers with the Big Bands and moved on – Frank Sinatra being a prime example. A new breed of star was also emerging, like Patti Page,

Frankie Laine, Teresa Brewer and Guy Mitchell, to stand alongside such well-established artistes as Eddie Arnold, Perry Como, Nat King Cole, Vaughn Monroe, Fats Waller, Louis Armstrong, Billy Eckstine and Ella Fitzgerald.

One of the biggest stars of the day, however, was Johnny Ray – nicknamed 'the Million Dollar Teardrop', 'the Prince of Wails', 'the Cry Guy' – who every time he appeared on stage broke down and wept through the sheer emotion he put into the songs he was singing . . . and people loved it. His audience was made up entirely of women of all ages, from schoolgirls to grandmothers. It was phenomenal. Johnny had tremendous magnetism, but he was an unlikely star. He was partially deaf (he made no attempt to conceal his cumbersome hearing aid), lean and scrawny, with an almost tuneless voice. He slid into the notes at the second attempt. Yet he had some remarkable hits – 'Just Walking in the Rain', 'Cry', 'Such a Night' (which was banned in America for 'its sexual suggestiveness'), and 'Little White Cloud That Cried' – and it was rumoured that he had been taught to sing the blues by LaVern Baker, one of the great American rhythm 'n' blues singers. When Johnny Ray first toured Britain in the early 1950s he was mobbed by unprecedented crowds of women everywhere he went. He was screamed at, besieged at the theatres, his clothes were ripped from him and his hair was pulled out at the roots, long before rock 'n' roll, or Beatlemania, had arrived. It was the most intense reaction to a singing star ever seen in Britain at that time, and, as many people have said, the hysteria he created was unequalled *anywhere* during the entire 1950s. One night, after a show at the London Palladium, he was forced to serenade a vast crowd of several thousand fans from the roof of the theatre after they made it obvious they would not leave until he had given them an encore.

In the States in particular, the age of the dark, good-looking, macho, second- or third-generation Italian–American stereotype singer was also beginning to establish itself through artistes like Tony Bennett, Dean Martin, Vic Damone, Tony Martin and Al Martino, who had the distinction of being the first person ever to top the British hit parade, with 'Here in My Heart', when the music magazine *New Musical Express* published the very first official list of best-selling records on 14 November 1952. The chart was made up of just fifteen records at the time, including 'Feet Up' by Guy Mitchell, 'Somewhere Along the Way' by Nat King Cole, and 'You Belong to Me' by Jo Stafford. Our own Vera Lynn had no less than three records in the listing – 'Forget Me Not', 'Homing Waltz' and 'Auf Wiedersehen'. She was a huge star, along with Ted Heath, Anne Shelton, Donald Peers, Frances Day and Max Bygraves.

Movies were also a vast market-place for selling records and promoting songs. That particular year, the multi-selling 'My Foolish Heart', by Billy Eckstine, 'Be My Love', by Mario Lanza, and 'The Harry Lime (Third Man) Theme' (which the Shadows recorded almost thirty years later) by Anton Karas with his famous zither, were all featured in big box-office film successes. 'Mona Lisa' by Nat King Cole picked up the Oscar for the best film song of the year. Another great movie musical was *Annie Get Your Gun*, starring Betty Hutton and Howard Keel, which I saw at our local picture house. It featured the song 'There's No Business Like Show Business', which hit me straight between the eyes when I first heard it. The lyrics were magical and made a great impression on me, especially the line 'There's no people like show people, they smile when they are low', and almost immediately I could identify myself with the people in the song. I was all of nine years old, and thought that these were the people I wanted to be with for the rest of my life. Nothing seemed to upset them, they smiled through all adversity. This was the life for me – but Aunt Sadie had other ideas.

1950 was a bleak year for the Welch family and for Bruce Cripps. My grandmother, the matriarchal head of the household, who owned our home and had lived with us since we returned from Bognor Regis, died, leaving my aunt and me alone. Sadie, who of course inherited the house we lived in, shortly afterwards met a Pakistani trader called Nazam Din, and fell in love, I guess. I never liked him. Within two years, she decided to set up home with him, which of course went totally against the strict Victorian upbringing her parents had tried to instil in her.

The move was a complete upheaval, and meant swopping the much slower-paced, almost parochial, way of life in Chester-le-Street for a far more frenetic existence in Newcastle, eight miles away. My aunt sold our house in Broadwood View, which had been a happy home, and invested the money she received in a three-bedroomed flat above the fish and chip shop her boyfriend owned at 126 Elswick Road, in a sleazy, run-down and neglected part of the city. In the summer of 1965 when the Animals sang about 'This dirty old part of the city, where the sun refused to shine', they could well have been describing Elswick Road. Reluctantly, I had to move as well, but I continued to go to school in Chester-le-Street for the next few months. It was a big adventure for a ten-year-old to travel to Red Rose Primary by bus. I felt very important and very grown-up. After school I was brought down to earth again in Nazam's presence, and I soon became an unwilling and unpaid worker in the establishment downstairs, peeling and chopping up potatoes and gutting fish. Its particular smell never seemed to leave me – or my clothes – and remains in my nostrils to this day.

Newcastle was a grey city in the early days of the 1950s, dull, drab and almost devoid of all colour, as if the very life-blood had been drained from it. Everywhere seemed to be in sad decline. Instead of dragging itself into the future, dusting itself down and starting all over again after the ravages of the war, Newcastle appeared content to stand still and feel sorry for itself. It wasn't alone; most of Britain's cities were suffering the same hangover at the same time.

Tynesiders are fervently partisan, and have always referred to their city as 'Canny Newcassel', meaning pleasant and orderly. Yet in those first few fitful years after the war, it was confused. Hitler had certainly left an indelible mark wherever you looked. There were bomb sites around every corner, scarring the landscape even more with dust and desolation, each one a potential deathtrap. But they provided exciting ready-made adventure playgrounds for every inquisitive schoolboy for miles around, and doubled up as pirate ships on the high seas, craters on the surface of the moon, or lost cities of the Aztec Indians to our vivid young imaginations, oblivious as we were to any lurking dangers. Still, it was a long, hard and expensive process to clear them all away and rebuild the heart of the city. For the time being, at least, the falling-down buildings and city slums I passed each day on my way to school had to remain, but they fostered hopelessness, depravity and bitterness. The Scotswood Road, running parallel with the River Tyne, was probably the most notorious area of Newcastle at that time and was highly volatile, regularly providing a backdrop to terrible scenes of violence. It was only a few hundred yards away from where we lived in Elswick Road.

Our new home was on a main bus route into the city centre, so the fish and chip shop was never short of customers and seemed to be a lucrative business. The flat itself had an outside toilet and a back yard where we kept the machine for peeling the potatoes and stored the fish, which was delivered in large blocks of ice. In the winter months the work was extremely difficult, and the rigid fish used to freeze to my already frozen fingers. As I got older I was promoted to help inside, and served in the shop itself.

Nazam was a Muslim and refused to eat pork, so bacon and eggs and black pudding were definitely out. Instead, I was brought up on a diet of fish and chips, chapattis and curry – every kind of curry imaginable. Its pungent aroma hung permanently in the air in every room of our house; we, of course, didn't notice it, but for anyone visiting the flat it must have been overpowering. Nazam was very strict in his religious beliefs and thus was also forbidden to eat any meat he had not killed himself, so on occasions our back yard became a temporary residence for chickens and goats, which he slaughtered by slitting their throats. It was a pretty wild experience in the heart of Newcastle upon Tyne. Sometimes the animals did not die instantly and thrashed frantically around the confined space with their throats slashed, spreading blood everywhere in a frenzied, uncontrollable death spasm. I hated it.

Nazam was an arrogant man who had come to England from Kashmir. He was illiterate and signed his name by making his mark with a cross. He was very volatile, and despite being unable to speak much of the language of his adopted country, he would shout and curse almost incessantly in his pidgin English or his native Urdu whenever his friends or relatives came to visit. I used to go out as much as I possibly could.

Nazam was also violent. He and Sadie used to bicker and row persistently, and there were times when he would punch and beat her and slap her around. She would frequently have to hide bruises on her face with make-up. She was a big lady, but no match for him. He used to cuff me a lot too, and resented my presence in his house. As I grew older, I grew to dislike him intensely. I hated the way he treated my aunt, whom I felt he had tricked into living with him in the first place, and I could see that he made her work terribly hard, as if he owned her. But I suppose she must have loved him deeply for despite all the bitterness and the beatings she stayed with him for nearly thirty years. Even when I asked her to leave him and to move down to London and live with me, she refused and stuck by her man. They were still together, and still working together, when he died of a heart attack on Christmas Day, 1980. They never married, for Nazam already had a wife and family back home in Pakistan.

I'm sure Sadie suffered in other ways as well through living with Nazam and sharing his life. Racism was beginning to creep into Britain at that time, as more and more Commonwealth immigrants arrived from the West Indies, Africa and the Indian sub-continent to set up homes and make new lives for themselves in inner city areas, particularly in London, where the Notting Hill riots of the late 1950s helped to highlight and publicize a burgeoning problem. It wasn't as bad in Newcastle, but being black in the north-east was still not easy. Indians and Pakistanis started to populate the cheaper and seedier parts of the city, their presence barely tolerated. At times it proved extremely difficult for my aunt mixing socially with Nazam's circle. Happily, there were never any racial taunts or threats from my school mates, perhaps because I could take care of myself.

Besides owning the fish shop in Elswick Road, Nazam was also a wheeler-dealing market trader and a very sharp one at that. He always appeared to have business ventures on the boil. He sold 15-denier nylons from a stall, and would buy up job-lots of imperfect stockings in all shapes, styles and sizes, then make me sit up for hours on end trying to match them into pairs so that he could sell them at a fancy profit at the market the next day. He dealt in blankets and table-cloths as well, and in any other household goods he could lay his hands on; he bought them cheaply in bulk direct from factories in Leeds or Leicester, and transported them back to the north-east by means of an antiquated and unreliable Commer van that had seen better days. (Every subsequent van he owned had seen better days long before it came into his possession.)

Nazam and Sadie worked extremely hard together, and it paid dividends in terms of money. Before long they were operating four or five different stalls at each of the markets they worked during the day, as well as running the fish and chip shop in the evening. It was a tough existence, though. They were up at dawn and within two hours were setting up their stalls wherever they were needed. They worked seven days a week, visiting all the local markets in Chester-le-Street, Morpeth, the Quayside in Newcastle, Stockton, Berwick-on-Tweed and South Shields. Business proved so good at one stage that they employed my Aunt Mary to run one of the stalls for them, while I helped out the so-called family firm at weekends. It was an unpaid position, although Sadie would give me a few pounds for my endeavours whenever Nazam was not around to see her. He would have been furious if he had caught her frittering money away on me, and would certainly have beaten her for it.

He seemed to make a lot of money from his enterprises, and at one stage bought three houses in Westmoreland Road, another squalid and unsavoury area of Newcastle in the 1950s, which he rented out. It was my job to go round and collect the rent money for him each week. He had an inbred dislike of banks, and kept his money locked firmly away at home. Despite his income from various sources, Nazam consistently bemoaned the fact that he was broke and that money was tight. We certainly didn't live well or enjoy the fruits of it all. Far from it. It was a pitiful existence really, living in a slum which we also shared with mice and vermin. But Nazam had other commitments, and sent most of the money that he and Sadie worked long and hard to make together back to Pakistan to support his wife and family.

To my great surprise and delight I passed my eleven-plus examination at Red Rose Primary, which enabled me to move on to grammar school. In September it was a vulnerable and very nervous young schoolboy who took his first tentative steps through the gates of Rutherford Grammar School for Boys in Newcastle, not really knowing what to expect, but with butterflies fluttering in his stomach in anticipation. On that first morning, as the new boys – each resplendent in a sparkling new black blazer and cap and neatly pressed grey trousers – shuffled through the playground, looking among a sea of faces for a friendly smile to help share this ordeal, I bumped into another equally worried newcomer. He was a strange-looking boy, extremely thin and scrawny in his regulation school uniform, topped by a pair of National Health spectacles. He was wiry and awkward, and when he smiled I noticed that one of his front teeth was chipped. We exchanged friendly nods and polite conversation, eyeing each other inquisitively. He was older than me by six days, lived in Stanhope Street and had been put in class 1D. I was in 1B. His name was Brian Rankin, and I found out later that his friends called him Hank.

2
'WE'VE GOT TO GET OUT OF THIS PLACE'

Rutherford Grammar School in Bath Lane was in the heart of Newcastle city centre, a short distance from Central Station and a mile and a half from Elswick Road. It was an imposing Victorian building, although by now the school had entered into a state of gentle decay and disrepair. Yet it still retained an air and graciousness of its own and a special kind of smell that only schools seem to possess – a mingling of ink, chalk dust and cheap corporation disinfectant.

The classrooms were large and spacious, with high ceilings and tall windows that could be opened only by a long wooden pole with a special hook attachment at the end. Most of the rooms contained desks and benches that looked like a throwback to some previous century, each one ingrained with dirt and with years of now meaningless graffiti, a few choice swear words and the carved initials of dozens of former occupants. Even then, schoolboys were creatures of strange habits. Like young tomcats marking out their territories, each one of us customized and personalized the desks we inherited for the duration of our stay there.

The corridors were old and impersonal. At regular intervals each day, at the sound of a bell, they echoed with the sound of feet as hundreds of pupils pounded their way up and down the well-worn stone stairs from lesson to lesson, babbling away endlessly to each other despite the roars of 'Silence, boys!' from any teacher who happened to be in the vicinity.

It was in the school toilets, commonly referred to by schoolboys everywhere as 'bogs', for some reason now long forgotten, that I discovered smoking. A few illicit drags on a damp and well-fingered cigarette made me feel instantly sick. I hated it, and I have never touched a cigarette since. I could never understand what all the fuss was about.

When I arrived at the school as a wide-eyed eleven-year-old, Rutherford Grammar's time was running out. It had served its purpose admirably over many years, and had tried in its own way to educate at least some of the sons of the city of Newcastle. Fortunately, within eighteen months of my passing the eleven-plus examination, we were all transferred to a brand new purpose-built school up at Westgate Hill, some three miles away to the north-west of the city with room to breathe, as Newcastle started the first stages of its post-war redevelopment. Here, for the first time, we were able to enjoy the luxury of having our own playing fields – soccer and rugby pitches – which we had not had at the building on the old site, so close to the city centre. They were a great attraction; I enjoyed all kinds of sport and developed into quite a useful runner. Rugby was a speciality of mine, and under the careful coaching of the games teacher, Mr Nimmo, I eventually made my way into the school first team; but an eye-watering, stomach-churning kick in the crotch from an opponent put me off the game for good.

I tolerated academic lessons, did well in most subjects, and got quite acceptable grades for my efforts, certainly for the first two or three years. But we had a motley collection of teachers, some of whom had a basic inability to teach their chosen subject while others spent most of their time putting fear and trepidation into the hearts of their young charges. 'Slasher' Grant, who taught art, was one master everyone feared. He had a terrible reputation, although Hank, who excelled at the subject, had a special rapport with him. I think Hank enjoyed playing the archetypal Bohemian student, and went round the school dressed in a scruffy blue duffle coat and a coloured scarf, similar to those of most of the undergraduates at Newcastle University. Many years later, when the Shadows appeared in the city, Mr Grant wrote to us and asked if he could come and see our show and meet us backstage afterwards. We were delighted to hear from him again after all those years, though both Hank and I fully expected to meet the man we had left behind at school and were slightly apprehensive at the prospect. Even thirty years on, his reputation was still awesome. Instead, we were introduced to an elderly gentleman who was absolutely nothing like the man we remembered. The striking figure who had terrorized the third form had gone, to be replaced by a very distinguished and charming old man. He *was* human after all. Or perhaps it was we who had changed?

Pa Brown, our French master, was an exceptionally gifted teacher who had the ability to communicate his subject to the boys with ease. Everyone listened when he spoke; everyone learned – and because of this influence I was particularly good at the language. My respect for him deteriorated when I was fourteen, however. One afternoon, completely by accident, I fell asleep in his lesson, only to be awakened abruptly by the sound of his bellowing voice.

'*Cripps!*' he ranted. 'Your mother must have dragged you up to have such appalling manners, boy.'

I was shocked. I was fairly thick-skinned and could take any kind of taunts or jibes thrown at me by the teachers or the other boys, but when he started maligning my mother, I saw red. In a split second, as outrage welled up inside me, I lost control. My emotions took the upper hand and I hit him. I was well built for my age and very strong, so the impact of a crashing blow from my left hand must have hurt him. Of course it was the wrong thing to do, I knew that immediately I'd thrown the punch, but I couldn't help myself. I wouldn't draw back. When it was over I expected the worst, and thought that at least I would be suspended or even expelled. Instead I was taken to the headmaster's study and soundly thrashed across the backside with a fearsome strap of webbing by one of our teachers, who seemed to enjoy the task.

I suppose in a way that was my first encounter with homosexuality which was very much in the closet in the 1950s, suppressed and driven underground. It was also illegal. When I went down to London in 1958 and started working at the 2i's coffee bar in the heart of Soho, I sometimes saw men kissing each other in secluded doorways in Old Compton Street or Wardour Street or Dean Street. I didn't give it much thought, it seemed part of London night life, and I was very young and naïve. I knew as much as I could know about homosexuality at that time. It wasn't talked about at all, and to the vast majority of people it didn't exist. I learned later, however, that there was a thriving rent-boy business around Piccadilly even then. I got one of the biggest shocks of my life several years later when I was out dining with friends at the Lotus House Chinese Restaurant in Edgware Road, which was a favourite haunt of show-business celebrities during the sixties. To my amazement, I witnessed one of the biggest pop stars of the day kissing and canoodling in public with a teenage boy. I was horrified that he was so indiscreet and felt thoroughly uncomfortable.

Music at school leaned very much towards the classical. We sang folk songs and hymns in assembly, but nothing more adventurous than a Negro spiritual. My own classical knowledge was limited to Tchaikovsky's *1812 Overture*, or the kind of lighter music that tended to be played as record requests on the radio at the end of *Two-Way Family Favourites*, to bring the Sunday lunchtime programme to a rousing finale before handing over to the *Billy Cotton Band Show* at 1.30 pm. I wasn't particularly interested. It all sounded very much the same to my young ears.

There was a young teacher at Rutherford called James Moody, who also taught French, but spent a large proportion of his lesson time talking to us about music. When he casually mentioned that he was the proud owner of a banjo, Hank, as cheeky as always, stepped in smartly and asked if he wanted to sell it. By now Hank was becoming more and more interested in jazz. Benny Goodman, Sidney Bechet and Monty Sunshine, all very accomplished clarinet players, were his great musical idols, and he wanted to play the same instrument so that he could eventually form a jazz band with some school friends. However, when he discovered just how much a new clarinet, and a course of lessons, would set him back, he had second thoughts. A banjo sounded an ideal substitute. The trouble was, he couldn't play it, though he had studied piano for three years from the age of eight and obviously had a good solid grounding in the technicalities of music. Still, Hank was determined to get the instrument and after much bartering came to a serious arrangement with the young teacher. For the sum of £2 10s (£2.50p), which the fourteen-year-old promised to pay in instalments of 2s 6d (12½p) a week from his pocket money, the five-string Windsor G banjo changed hands. Hank spent the next few weeks trying to tune it, with very little success, and eventually bought himself a manual and taught himself to play. He had a natural talent, and he became a very gifted musician once he had mastered the finer points of tuning.

For several years Hank had been fascinated by New Orleans and Chicago jazz and had listened to it with an avid devotion. He was a traditionalist, and very much influenced by Leadbelly and Negro folk roots. When he wasn't in school he spent a lot of his time hanging around the specialist record shops in Newcastle which sold that type of music, or reading jazz journals. He was a great collector, too, clipping newspaper cuttings about the musicians he admired, such as Fats Waller, Jimmie Rodgers, Woody Guthrie, Jack Teagarden, Baby Dodds and Lonnie Johnson, into a school exercise book that doubled as a scrap book, which he lavishly illustrated himself. He also started going to concerts and traditional jazz shows at the City Hall, where he saw George Melly, Lionel Hampton, Humphrey Lyttelton and Chris Barber. At that time the most influential jazz purist in Britain was Ken Colyer, who stuck rigidly to the concept of New Orleans jazz from the turn of the century. Legend had it that at recording sessions he put a biscuit tin over the microphone, to enable him to get an authentic echoing effect resembling the bustle of a New Orleans nightclub. His band, which also featured Memphis blues, folk blues and classic blues in its repertoire, had a marvellous pedigree and attracted the very best of British jazz musicians to its ranks, including at one time Chris Barber and Monty Sunshine.

Being a university city, Newcastle was a hotbed for jazz, mainstream and modern as well as traditional. In the main, university students have always tended to latch on to older musical cultures rather than modern trends, for example, all the derivative forms of jazz from boogie-woogie and cajun blues to ragtime. It is as if the more intellectual students embraced the obscure music of the past in order to reject the present. They had to be different, and besides, it was far more romantic and had to do with the struggles of the Negro race against oppression, out of which the music was born. There were many thriving clubs in Newcastle that satisfied this demand for all kinds of jazz music. The Vieux Carré, down by the River Tyne, was a favourite with musicians. If a band had been playing in the city, the chances were that they would find their way to the club afterwards to unwind and relax, to sit a while and talk about music. It had a great atmosphere and was the kind of place that encouraged any would-be musician to get up on stage and have a blow, so impromptu jazz sessions among sidesmen were just a small part of its attraction. The club was run by Pete Deuchar, who lived in a caravan nearby and played the banjo. It was Pete who helped teach Hank to play the instrument. It didn't take too long. Another friend, John Tate, taught him to play the guitar.

Unlike Hank, I had very little spare time of my own after school. Nazam saw to that. He worked me so hard in the evenings that I didn't even have a spare moment to do my homework, although I didn't need an excuse to get out of that. Most times I managed to catch up and do the work the following morning on the bus on my way to school, or copied it from one of my classmates who was exceptionally clever and didn't particularly relish the thought of being beaten up. Occasionally, before Nazam and Aunt Sadie arrived home from whichever market they had been working during the day, I would meet a crowd of my friends and we would play football or cricket – depending on the season – along the back lanes behind the houses. Sometimes we would congregate in packs outside nearby shops to while away an hour or two talking aimlessly. We rarely bought anything; after all, we needed money to buy sweets and that was in very short supply. Later at home I would indulge myself in a sugar sandwich; thick doorstep slices of bread and butter filled liberally with spoonfuls of sugar. I adored them.

Alternate Saturday afternoons in the winter were sacred. They were spent worshipping on the terraces at the shrine of St James's Park football ground, roaring on the mighty Newcastle United – 'Howay the Lads' – the famous Magpies' all-conquering team of the fifties which made local heroes out of such players as George Robledo, Joe Harvey, Bobby Mitchell, Vic Keeble and Jimmy Scoular, and created a national legend out of Jackie Milburn. *Wor Jackie*. We revered them all. I dreaded the summer holidays when I had to help Nazam on one of his market stalls. He had no time for football and it wasn't part of his culture anyway. That wasn't my problem. I had other things on my mind: I was growing up.

Ten years after the world emerged bleary-eyed and shell-shocked from the second great war, vowing never to let it happen again, vast social changes were taking place among its youth. A generation of war babies, whose lives had been shaped by the effects and aftermath of war, yet who had never directly participated in it, were reaching adolescence, and a whole new youth culture was being born which had begun to question the values and ideals of parents and of previous generations. Teenagers craved their independence, and needed something that was entirely of their own making, free from parental influence. They also wanted a say in their own destiny. Until then, teenagers the world over had been trapped in an adolescent no-man's-land, waiting impatiently to grow up from childhood and into adulthood, and that took time. Through the pressures of society, they became scaled-down versions of their parents, following the same conventions, adopting the same tastes in fashion, and listening to the same music their mothers and fathers enjoyed. It was a 'do as I do' society.

Instead of responding to the birth of the new youth culture in a positive way, encouraging it to grow, society's immediate reaction was one of disapproval, which in turn fuelled a fire of rebelliousness. The generation gap was emerging. It manifested itself initially in 1954, through films that explored the teenage explosion like *The Wild Bunch*, with Marlon Brando, which was banned in Britain for several years because local authorities were convinced its screening would incite riots, and *Rebel Without a Cause*, which launched the brilliant but all too brief career of James Dean.

James Dean became an idol of the young, a most unlikely movie star but one with whom every teenager could immediately identify. We tried to emulate him – we shared his dreams of independence and imitated his speech, his attitude to life and his arrogance. He was mean, moody, magnificent. His charisma on the big screen was riveting. In his first movie role he became a victim of parental misunderstanding, all too close to our real world, which was a point in his favour. He represented contempt for authority and two fingers to the establishment.

He was the first teenage cult hero . . . and we all wanted to be just like him.

Elvis Presley was the second.

Then there was the music.

Teenagers wanted a music all of their own, not something handed down from their parents' generation. It had to be raw and raucous, stinking of sweat and sex, a music suitable for dancing which also expressed exactly how we felt about life. And it had to be so outrageous that adults wouldn't like it.

We found it in rock 'n' roll. It dictated its own fashions and trends, and liberated teenagers everywhere. The music had been developing for a long time in America. As far back as the 1920s, popular music had advanced almost sedately through jazz and the blues to bebop and Big Band swing. It exploded in the fifties.

Rock 'n' roll was a hybrid music, a synthesis of many forms of black and white musical influences, although channelled through two main streams. The first of these was rhythm 'n' blues, which had emerged from Negro spirituals, various styles of the blues (the term rock 'n' roll was often used in blues songs to describe love-making), Dixieland jazz and swing. It was the music of the poor American blacks. The second was country-and-western, with its origins in blue grass music, hill-billy and European folk songs, although there was nothing in the slightest way European about it. This was the music of the poor American whites.

Nobody can be certain when rock 'n' roll actually started, but it made its headway on a completely regional basis in America and steadily gained momentum. It was brought to the attention of an unsuspecting world in 1955 through a movie called *Blackboard Jungle*, which featured Bill Haley and His Comets playing 'Rock Around the Clock' over the titles. The song had been written two years earlier as 'a novelty foxtrot' by Jimmy De Night and the sixty-three-year-old Max C. Friedman, and when it was recorded by Sonny Dae for Arcade it sank without trace.

Blackboard Jungle highlighted the growing problems between pubescent teenagers and the older generation. The film revolves around adolescent tensions in a New York high school, with Glenn Ford playing a young teacher, Richard Dadier, who is desperately trying to communicate with his violent and near-delinquent students of various colours and nationalities. One memorable scene stands out, in which Glenn Ford tries to win his pupils' respect by bringing in his prized collection of jazz records for them to play in class. He hopes that music will give them a common interest and cement a better relationship between them. Instead, the students show only their contempt for the man and the authority he represents by smashing the records to pieces.

The film caused a riot everywhere it was shown, and by the end of the year 'Rock Around the Clock' had topped the best-selling charts on both sides of the Atlantic. It was the forerunner of greater musical things to come.

I can remember seeing *Blackboard Jungle* at the Regal cinema in Kenton, a suburb of Newcastle. It was rated an X certificate, which meant I had to be at least sixteen years old to see it, and at that time I still had a year or so to go, even though I was a big lad for my years. But no matter. I managed to persuade one of my friends, who had reached the magic age, to come with me, and after he had legitimately bought a ticket and gone inside, he made his way to the toilet, carefully opened one of the exit doors at the back of the theatre, and let me in for nothing.

The film made a tremendous impact on us all. As soon as the music played, everyone in the cinema stood up and cheered. The excitement it generated was unprecedented. It was so different from what anyone expected. 'Rock Around the Clock' became the great anthem of teenage culture, while Bill Haley, the former country-and-western singer turned local radio disc jockey, became the unlikely champion of the teenage cause. One American newspaper described him and the Comets as 'the nation's rocking-est rhythm group'. Only a few months earlier, he had made the British hit parade for the first time with 'Shake, Rattle and Roll', an old Joe Turner number which had originally been recorded for the minority black audience in the USA. Haley cleaned up the racy and suggestive lyrics, and re-worded the song himself. It marked the beginning of the 'white cover versions', which saw a spate of white American singers recording the music of black American artistes to bring it to the attention of the much wider audience of middle America. Several years later many British rock 'n' rollers created whole careers for themselves by recording cover versions of American material, black and white, and the vast majority of the public knew no difference. Strangely enough, Haley's first British single in 1953, 'Crazy, Man, Crazy', was covered by Billy Cotton and His Band.

Music in the States at that time was still segregated, and most of the early rock 'n' roll material was created by black artistes like Chuck Berry, Fats Domino, Little Richard, Joe Turner, Bo Diddley and Larry Williams. Yet because they were denied exposure to the mass white audiences, many of their classic songs were exploited and recorded by less aggressive, wholesome, white 'teen' idols. Pat Boone, who recorded Fats Domino's 'Ain't That a Shame' and Little Richard's 'Tutti Frutti' and 'Long Tall Sally', was a prime example. His sanitized versions of such belting numbers – the scaffold on which rock roots were constructed – made the charts around the world.

Despite the odds being heavily stacked against them, however, black artistes persevered; eventually they did establish themselves on an international scale, and their music gained the reputation it deserved. In that way rock 'n' roll helped to break down the barriers and desegregate music for the first time, and brought about the long-awaited acceptance of black musicians who had been totally ignored in their own environment in the past.

For someone who did so much to pioneer rock 'n' roll and inspire so many teenagers, Bill Haley was not an influential figure in musical terms – he was merely a vehicle for its evolution. By the time 'Rock Around the Clock' became a gigantic hit all over the world, Haley was already thirty and almost old enough to be the father of many of the teenagers he was liberating with his music. The members of his backing group, the Comets, were even older, and at that time it was a crime to be old. No one tried to copy Haley or his style because, quite simply, he was ageing, cross-eyed and overweight. Nonetheless, when he arrived in Britain in 1957 at the start of a lengthy and highly publicized tour, 5,000 screaming fans turned up to welcome him at Waterloo station. There was mass hysteria as Britian went wild with Haleymania, and his tour was a complete sell-out. But his popularity didn't last once his middle-aged spread was exposed.

The advent of rock 'n' roll was accompanied by the emergence of the Teddy boy, particularly in Britain, although similarly styled teenagers could be found in most parts of the world. They were conspicuous by their clothes, favouring Edwardian style draped jackets with velvet collars, boot-lace ties, brocade waistcoats, drainpipe tight trousers, brightly coloured luminous socks, and thick crêpe suede shoes which were nicknamed 'brothel creepers'. Most had silver or gold laces and it was possible to buy shoes with guitars emblazoned on the sides. The outfit was completed by hair greased back in the shape of a trunk at the front, a DA (duck's arse) at the back, and long sideburns. Teddy boys had a reputation for violence, and crowds of them often roamed the streets of the major British cities looking for rival gangs on whom to vent their anger and frustration. They carried flick-knives, cut-throat razors, knuckle-dusters and bicycle chains as weapons, and as gangs clashed there were some scenes of quite horrendous violence, which were eagerly reported by the national press. In some cases fights, or rumbles, as they were called, were pre-arranged; rival leaders would get together to fix up the place where the fight would occur and the time when hostilities would commence.

When *Rock Around the Clock*, a cheap-budget, no-plot, rock 'n' roll movie starring Bill Haley, was produced in a hurry to cash in on the runaway success of the record, there were unbelievable scenes in cinemas all over Britain where the film was screened. Teddy boys and their girlfriends jived and danced in the aisles of the theatres, and clapped and chanted in time to the music. Many were ejected, but continued dancing in the streets long after the film was over. Others went berserk, let off fireworks inside cinemas, and ripped or slashed the theatre seats to pieces with their flick-knives.

When I returned home from school one afternoon sporting a Teddy boy haircut, Sadie went absolutely mad and tried to pull my hair out in her rage. She thought I had become a delinquent and joined a gang. She didn't realize that I had done it only for the music and *that* alone. It was part of the teenage image. Like most parents, Sadie didn't understand.

Most of our fashions came from movies. In 1956 Jayne Mansfield, Tom Ewell and Edmund O'Brien starred in another cheap rock 'n' roll picture called *The Girl Can't Help It*, which featured many of the current big names in the music business, including Fats Domino, Little Richard, Eddie Cochran and Chuck Berry. Several of the musical groups that sang in the film wore ill-fitting zoot suits, which soon became popular in Britain. One such outfit was the Treniers, whose choreographed dance movements and routines on stage as they played their songs later inspired Hank and me to develop our famous Shadows 'walk' for our own live performances.

Movies like *The Girl Can't Help It*, *Shake, Rattle and Roll*, and *Don't Knock the Rock* helped rock 'n' roll to reach a vast untapped international audience. Yet in its own back yard of America, it was radio that played the crucial role in its development and popularity. Without it, music as we know it today would certainly not exist. Radio was that vital link with the people.

The radio boom in the USA had actually started tentatively in 1920, when the first commercial broadcasts were initiated on a limited scale by the *Detroit News*, using the identification call sign WWJ. In the same year Radio KDKA opened in Pittsburg, followed by WJZ in Newark, New Jersey.

Within two years there were 500 radio stations across America, and yearly sales of receivers had reached a massive 60 million dollars. During the same year the first sponsored programme was broadcast on WEAF, New York, by a real estate company, the Queensborough Corporation, giving rise to the first radio commercial. Four years later when the first radio network – the National Broadcasting Company – was formed, there were over 1,000 stations broadcasting coast to coast. By 1930 radio had emerged as a multi-million-dollar industry with annual sales heading for the 1,000 million dollar mark, while 12 million American homes owned radio sets. Within a handful of years, radio had become the fourth largest industry in the country, and 30 million people listened daily. The medium created its own stars, like Bing Crosby, Gracie Allen, Amos 'n' Andy, Jimmy Durante and Rudy Vallee, besides giving the world the 'soap opera' – a daily diet of protracted romantic serials sponsored by soap manufacturers and aimed directly at women listeners.

By the early 1950s there were literally thousands of local radio stations operating throughout America, catering for all tastes of music. Most stations were small, with a limited budget and limited broadcasting range, often under fifty miles, but they tailored their output and their advertising to their audience. At the same time, black minority stations started to grow to prominence, featuring only black music in their scheduling – boogie-woogie, the blues, rhythm 'n' blues, and gospel. Although the music was aimed at a specific black audience, and indeed the station's advertising was geared to sell its products in the same Negro market-place, once on the airwaves it became public property and non-discriminating. Anyone could tune in and listen to what was on offer, including young white teenagers, who suddenly discovered black music and took a great liking to it. They adopted it as their own, particularly rhythm 'n' blues, and they also borrowed the hip, jive-talking language of the station disc jockeys and their strange vocabulary, which used words like 'dig', 'cat', 'flip', and 'cool'.

It was Bill Haley who later exploited this 'be-bop' phrasing in many of his songs, including, 'See You Later Alligator', 'Crazy, Man, Crazy', 'Go Man Go', and 'Cool Man'. It was through being exposed to music of this kind that white teenagers helped to shape the course rock 'n' roll would take. In Memphis, Tennessee, Radio WDIA was one of the first to adopt an all-black music policy, changing from a country-and-western station as early as 1947. No radio station in history had ever exerted a greater impact on musical tastes. It became one of the first Negro networks to win a large audience among white folk, who listened to a daily programming of black recorded music. One of the station's most avid listeners was a young boy of thirteen, who tuned in to the radio in the cab of his father's truck so that he could hear the music. His name was Elvis Presley.

As the output of music increased on radio, disc jockeys and presenters found themselves having a very definite effect on the development of music. They were in a powerful position as arbiters of popular tastes, and were often able to dictate trends and influence musical progression. They were also open to bribery and corruption and there were many spectacular scandals, the most famous of which was the 'payola' affair in 1960, which brought to an end the illustrious career of Alan Freed – the man who, legend had it, had coined the phrase 'rock 'n' roll'. Freed was found guilty of taking large bribes in return for playing certain records, and was given a suspended prison sentence.

In Britain, however, we were not in the same league. Radio, although extremely popular throughout the country, was very staid and relied on just three national channels, controlled by the BBC. Of these, the Light Programme was for 'light' entertainment and music, although very little rock 'n' roll was ever played. Indeed, Chuck Berry's 'Maybelline', one of the first records to pioneer the music, was banned by the BBC because the lyrics to the song made reference to a V8 Ford car and a Cadillac, which was against the Corporation's charter. The BBC banned Gene Vincent's 'Woman Love' for its 'sexually suggestive' lyrics, while the Coasters' 'Charlie Brown' was kept off the air for three weeks because the song contained several American slang terms that could be interpreted as obscene.

But the popularity of rock 'n' roll eventually forced the BBC to change its programme ideas. Within a year, shows aimed more towards teenagers began to creep into scheduling. One of the first was *Skiffle Club*, which was broadcast each Saturday morning. But the biggest impact made by radio in Britain at the time, and for many years in the future, came from the independent commercial station, Radio Luxembourg, which broadcast from the Grand Duchy of Luxembourg itself each night between the hours of 6 pm and midnight, and had been operating an English language service since the early 1930s. In 1948 it launched one of the very first best-seller music charts to be based on sales of records alone rather than of sheet music. The programme, *The Top Twenty*, went out on air each Sunday evening and was required listening for any teenager who wanted to keep up with his friends.

Radio Luxembourg's programmes were a combination of quizzes, variety shows, music and adventure serials, and the station relied on advertising and sponsorship to operate successfully. Shows especially synonymous with the early 1950s were *Dan Dare*, sponsored by Horlicks, and the *Ovaltinies*, while Hughie Green presented *Double Your Money* and *Opportunity Knocks* for the first time on Luxembourg before both transferred successfully to television. I will always associate the station with Horace Batchelor, the man who had developed a so-called foolproof system for winning money on the football pools which he marketed and sold through Radio Luxembourg from an address in a town called Keynsham, just outside Bristol. Whenever the name of the town was read out on air, it was accompanied by the inevitable announcement 'spelt K-E-Y-N-S-H-A-M'. Happy memories. I never did win the pools.

Almost two-thirds of Luxembourg's air time was licensed to the big four British record companies, EMI, Philips, Decca and Pye, who bought and sponsored their own special programmes and played all their latest releases and back catalogue.

As rock 'n' roll spread across the Atlantic, Radio Luxembourg's policy changed. It was a surprisingly slow process. American radio stations had realized that if rock 'n' roll attracted an audience, it made good business sense to play the music as often as possible. With Luxembourg it took a little longer. The BBC took longer still. Slowly but surely, Radio Luxembourg established itself as the most important music station in Europe, playing all the latest imported sounds from the USA as well as British records. Because of its late-night programming, it was Luxembourg that everyone tuned in to in bed, snuggled down under the sheets with the radio pressed hard against an ear to try to eliminate the incessant continental interference that plagued the station. It served the double purpose of keeping warm and muffling the noise.

Apart from radio and, of course, juke-boxes, there was another major outlet for the exploitation of rock 'n' roll to the public in Britain – *fairgrounds* – which are rarely given the credit they deserve for helping to popularize the music. Fairgrounds were a vital medium for the development of rock 'n' roll because they were patronized by young people out for a good time. We even dressed up in our best clothes to go to the fair.

Every June in Newcastle on the Town Moor there was a large fair known locally as the 'Hoppings'; it was always exciting, and we knew the music would be good. Another great attraction was Spanish City, a permanent funfair sited at Whitley Bay, six miles outside the city centre on the North Sea coast. It was here that all the great American rock 'n' roll records could be heard blasting out from large clapped-out loudspeakers, above the noise of the droning and chugging generators, as we whirled around on the Carousel, flew through the night sky on the Big Wheel, or pretended to live life in the fast lane behind the wheel of a dodgem car. There was something strangely romantic about that heady combination of flashing multi-coloured light bulbs, the smell of axle-grease and diesel oil mixed with a warm aroma of candy floss and rancid onions from the hot dog stall, and the incessant beat of rock 'n' roll music. The records sounded magnificent – 'Yes,

Tonight, Josephine', by Johnny Ray, which was the nearest he ever got to rock 'n' roll, 'Be-Bop-A-Lula' by Gene Vincent, and Paul Anka's classic 'Diana', which sounded absolutely amazing in the confines of the fairground out in the open air, but seemed to lose a lot of its compulsion and impact when it was played anywhere else. Much later, Del Shannon's 'Runaway' emerged as another masterful fairground attraction – the organ solo seemed to float on the air for ever. It was Spanish City that much later provided the backdrop and the inspiration for Mark Knopfler to write one of his brilliantly expressive songs, 'Tunnel of Love'.

The rock 'n' roll boom in Britain, however, did not catch on in any great strength until the spring of 1956, with the emergence of Elvis Presley in the charts. Then it opened the floodgates for others to follow. Bill Haley had sown the seeds; now Presley would reap the harvest. In two years there were eight principal acts in the world who originated this new sound. They were all American, and all different: the Everly Brothers, Jerry Lee Lewis, Buddy Holly, Fats Domino, Bill Haley, Chuck Berry, Little Richard . . . and Elvis.

Britain's own burgeoning music industry was still very parochial. Irish singer Ruby Murray had the distinction of having no fewer than five records in the Top Ten in the spring of 1955. She was discovered by EMI's A & R man, Norrie Paramor, who within three years would be recording Cliff Richard and the Shadows. Other artistes who regularly appeared in the charts included Dickie Valentine, Alma Cogan, Jimmy Young, Joan Regan, the piano-thumping Winifred Atwell, and the trumpet-playing Eddie Calvert. David Whitfield, a former concrete worker from Hull who was discovered on Hughie Green's *Opportunity Knocks* radio show in 1950, became the first British male singer to have a million-selling record in America with 'Cara Mia'. But in the main the British charts were dominated by American records, and in February 1956 US artistes held every position in the British Top Ten, with Lou Busch at No. 1 with an instrumental called 'Zambesi'. New and exciting things were happening, however. British music was on the move.

My own life changed dramatically at the beginning of 1956. I had just turned fifteen, and the course my future career would take started to fall into place the first time I heard Lonnie

Donegan on the radio singing 'Rock Island Line'. Like thousands of other teenagers, I couldn't believe what I was hearing. I was bowled over by the music. It was so different from anything else I'd heard before. Skiffle had arrived with a vengeance.

Lonnie Donegan had been the guitarist and banjo player first with Ken Colyer's band and later with Chris Barber. It was with Barber's jazz band that I had first seen him performing on stage in Newcastle a few years before. His real name was Tony Donegan, but he changed it in 1952 in homage to blues man Lonnie Johnson after they had appeared together at London's Festival Hall during the American's first visit to Britain. Two years later he made an album with Chris Barber called *New Orleans Joys* for Decca, on which he was featured solo on two numbers – the old Leadbelly blues 'Rock Island Line' and 'John Henry'. On both songs Lonnie sang and played guitar, accompanied only by Beryl Bryden on washboard and Chris Barber on bass. At the end of the following year, Decca decided to release 'Rock Island Line' as a single by public demand after it had been requested so many times on radio. It was issued under the banner of Lonnie Donegan and His Skiffle Group, without any reference to Chris Barber. By January 1956 the song had become a massive hit in Britain, staying in the charts for six months. It went on to make the American national Top Ten and to sell over a million copies. This was ironic, because Lonnie Donegan – white and British – had taken an obscure indigenous black American music style, repackaged it into a popular and commercial format, and given it back to the country of its origin. It was like taking coals to Newcastle.

However, it was through people like Lonnie Donegan that American teenagers discovered that they had a much deeper musical heritage than they had at first realized, when they found out that the source of his material was right there in their own back yard if only they bothered to look for it. In return for playing on an internationally selling hit record, Lonnie Donegan received the princely sum of £3 10s (£3.50p), the standard musician's session fee for that time *and no royalties*. But it did give him a whole new career. The skiffle craze took Britain by storm almost overnight and turned Lonnie into a huge star.

The name skiffle was a scatalogical term from Chicago, and the music was a strain of country blues, first heard in the USA in southern 'juke joints' and speakeasies, and in the black tenement slums of the northern industrial cities in the 1920s. It took its name from a 1928 Paramount Record Company race record, 'Hometown Skiffle'. 'Race' was a polite way of describing black music at the time. It was the music that black people played at ghetto rent parties when impoverished neighbours got together. They would lay in some homemade hooch and liquor and play a little music together on whatever makeshift instruments they could find – broom handle bass, washboard, fruit jars and liquor jugs – and then they would pass the hat round to collect next month's rent money. Like most blues, skiffle was made up of just three single chords, but the music of the 1950s bore little resemblance to its counterpart from the 1920s: it was an American music, predominantly morose and lamenting, given a British feel and happy-go-lucky style by Donegan.

Despite the success of 'Rock Island Line', skiffle generally failed to make much of an impact as a musical force in America, where it was regarded as too typically British. If only they had known.

Skiffle in Britain had everything going for it. It was good to listen to and, more importantly, it was simple to play. It attracted many hundreds of people who lacked any real musical ability but were sufficiently interested to learn to play the three basic chords around which the music revolved. There was nothing to it. It was get-up-and-go, do-it-yourself music that anyone could play – and it was cheap. You didn't need expensive equipment to make a noise. All that was required was a guitar and the kind of old washboard that was normally used to scrub shirt cuffs and collars. A tea chest placed upside down, with a broom handle inserted into it and a long piece of string stretched firmly between the top of the broom and the bottom of the box, acted as a double bass.

Lonnie Donegan was the unsung hero of British music – his influence was absolutely enormous and far-reaching, and he has never been given the credit he deserves. But time seems to have eroded his impact on the British music scene. In 1977 he made an album called *Putting on the Style*, accompanied by many of the musicians whom he had influenced in their formative years, including Elton John, Ringo Starr, Brian May of Queen, Leo Sayer, and Gary Brooker of Procol Harum. The album was produced by Adam Faith, who put the whole package together at the suggestion of Paul

McCartney. Lonnie was one of the great pioneers of rock 'n' roll in Britain even though he expressed contempt for that kind of music, preferring to be a purist in the blues, and he inspired many of us to start playing. He didn't have an image as such, no one wanted to look like him particularly, but they all wanted to try and match his musicianship and sound like him. For that reason he didn't attract great numbers of female fans, and instead had a large following of males who just liked the music.

It was Lonnie Donegan who inspired Phil Spector to play guitar, and Paul McCartney to become a musician and write songs. John Lennon formed his first group, the Quarrymen, after listening to Lonnie's records. There were many others. Thousands of young musicians all over Britain got their first taste of music through Lonnie Donegan and skiffle. He gave them hope. Years later, Chris Barber claimed that Lonnie Donegan had had a far greater influence on the development of rock music in Britain than the Beatles had ever had. What is certain is that *his* breakthrough was the first of the factors that eventually led to the birth of British rock, which in turn dominated the world.

It was after I went to see Lonnie Donegan and his group performing every single night of the week at the Empire Theatre, Newcastle, that I suddenly realized just how much I wanted to sing and become a musician like him. Music was taking over. It was a thrilling experience to go to live concerts at the Empire, and in a short space of time I saw Charlie Gracie, Slim Whitman and Billy Daniels, from up in the gods of the theatre for 3s 6d a ticket. But Lonnie was the king for the time being. It was the 'no business like show business' syndrome all over again, but this time I wanted to become a part of it. So with a little money I had gleaned from my aunt for working on the stalls, I bought my very first guitar from a sports-cum-music shop. It was an American six-string National with a metal body, and it set me back £4 19s 6d (£4.97½p). I thought it was the greatest guitar in the world. Looking back, it had a terrible action, and once I moved on past the fifth or sixth fret the strings were almost half an inch off the fretboard and cut my fingers to pieces as I tried to teach myself to play the obligatory three chords.

Before I bought the guitar, Sadie had given me a record player of my own that she got from the market. I'm sure she didn't pay for it – she probably came to an agreement with one of the other stallholders, without Nazam knowing anything about the deal. It was an old model, one of the wind-up machines with a handle for cranking and needles that needed to be changed at regular intervals before they scratched the cumbersome ten-inch records. For the first time it gave me the opportunity of hearing records of my own, and I listened avidly to a lot of traditional jazz, particularly Monty Sunshine and Chris Barber, and Lonnie Donegan, of course.

At that time all single records were played at 78 rpm, but they were brittle and extremely delicate and quickly wore out if played too often. Several of mine did just that, as this thing called music became an all-consuming passion.

Even though I hadn't yet mastered the art of playing my guitar, I thought I was good enough to form a group of my own with a friend called George Williams, who also played guitar and had similar aspirations to mine. With Jim Simmons on washboard – plus various other school friends who sat in from time to time – the Railroaders were born. We were just one of hundreds of similar groups that sprang up all over the country in 1956. I was the singer, trying to copy Lonnie Donegan's nasal drawl with a Geordie accent! I guess we chose the name Railroaders because we all met in a café by Central Station. A lot of skiffle songs were written about trains, firemen and engineers – there is something quaintly romantic about railways and the subject has provided inspiration for hundreds of songs over the years – so it was an apt name. Naturally our repertoire was based around the Lonnie Donegan song book, and we featured certain numbers that we had heard the singer himself liked, including material by Lead-belly, Woody Guthrie, Lonnie Johnson, Big Bill Broonzy, Josh White, Muddy Waters, and other American blues artistes. They meant nothing to us, but if Lonnie liked them who were we to argue? We also browsed through catalogues and old files in libraries looking for ethnic material to perform.

We were very dedicated to our cause. The group rehearsed regularly in various bedrooms, although never at my home in Elswick Road. I spent a lot of my time trying to keep on the right side of Nazam, and I don't think skiffle would have gone down too well with his friends.

We soon started to pick up engagements around the city and to enter talent contests. There was a series of competitions held in local pubs called 'Go as You Please', where anyone with an urge to entertain could get up on the makeshift stage, perform before an audience and win a cash prize, and we won quite a bit of money. It was a start, and it made us all more determined to succeed. George Williams was a very go-ahead sort of guy, a bit of a hustler, and got us a fair amount of work.

Across the city in Stanhope Street, Hank had also been smitten by the musical bug and had formed a group of his own which featured a combination of friends – John Tate, Derek Johnson, Mal Malakey and Howard Muir on various cheap guitars, mandolins, and washboards, and his brother Joe, on bass. Hank played banjo. The band was originally called the Riverside Skiffle Group, but when it was discovered that there was already an established group going under the same name, it was hastily changed to the Crescent City Skiffle Group, Crescent City being the nickname musicians gave to New Orleans. They played together quite a lot at a new jazz club that had sprung up in the hall next to the old Rutherford Grammar School site in Bath Lane, and, like us, they entered local talent shows.

As our mutual respect for music grew, Hank and I became good friends, but we had our musical differences. He was very much the traditionalist, exploring the ethnic origins of black American music – the purist who played authentic material like 'Go Down Old Hannah', 'Stack O'Lee Blues', 'Midnight Special', and 'John Henry'. I just wanted to make music. Officially we weren't allowed to take our instruments to school but, whenever possible, Hank brought along his banjo and I took my guitar, and we spent our break periods together playing. He had this rare ability to pick out single notes from the guitar solos he'd heard on records and on the radio. He was very talented and dedicated even then. I was still struggling with the basic three chords. If a song required to be played with a D7 chord or an E flat, I was stumped and had to find someone who could show me where to put my fingers on the fretboard. It took hours of practice and several sore fingers to get it right. I never had any formal training and found it difficult to play guitar with any fluency at first.

With music dominating my life, my school work began to suffer and gradually took a nose dive. Academically, I wasn't interested any more. I had other things to occupy my time which seemed far more important. I thoroughly enjoyed playing with the group so everything else took second place, including girls, though this, I'm happy to say, was only a temporary situation.

Music was very important to me in that I saw it as a way out. If I could make it happen, if I could become successful, I could leave everything I didn't like in Newcastle – Nazam, my way of life – behind me. Music was my escape. Going to school, to sit through tedious lessons like chemistry and maths, became a chore. I began not to bother to go at all, and took to playing truant regularly. I had the perfect opportunity. Nazam and Sadie left the house an hour before I had to leave for school, and didn't return until long after I got back myself, so they had no idea of my movements during the day and naturally thought I was safely engrossed in my school work up at Westgate Hill. I covered myself by getting my friends to write sick notes for me. I had never been so ill, or so often, in my life.

I spent my illicit days at home practising the guitar, or wandering aimlessly around the streets of Newcastle with no particular place to go. Nothing was planned. In the afternoon I often went to the cinema just for something to do with my time. I can honestly say that it was one of the first periods in my life when I can recall feeling troubled within myself. I can't explain it; I was confused, and even though I was skiving off school, I wasn't having a great time. I was terribly unhappy and could never settle at home. One day off school would lead to two or three, and spill into a whole week. Then I would become too scared to go back, take the coward's way out, and stay away even longer. A week's absence turned into a month. Eventually I was taking so much time off that my seemingly foolproof plan was discovered by the school inspectors, who called round to Elswick Road one evening to see Sadie and find out what was going on. I had put her in a compromising situation. She was totally unaware of what I was doing and was devastated when the full story was revealed. She was very upset and angry, and with great reluctance I went back to Rutherford Grammar, but I realized that my days at school were numbered.

3

'THE SINGER'S GOING TO BE AN ABSOLUTE GIANT'

In April 1956 Britain felt the first rumblings of a phenomenon called Elvis Presley, with the release of 'Heartbreak Hotel'. Nothing would ever be quite the same again. The song was issued as a single over here by HMV (His Master's Voice), a subsidiary of EMI who had an agreement with the American recording giant, RCA-Victor, to put out their product in Britain. The label manager was Wally Ridley, who had a good, solid track record behind him after discovering such British talent as Max Bygraves, Donald Peers, Alma Cogan and Frankie Vaughan. He'd also had great chart success in the past with a stream of American singers, most notably Perry Como and Eddie Fisher. He was well respected in the record industry, such as it was at the time, and his judgement was sound.

One morning in the spring of 1956 a package arrived on his desk containing acetates of a new American singer; it had been sent by Steve Sholes, who with Chet Atkins was head of A & R for RCA-Victor in Nashville, Tennessee, and was the man who signed Jim Reeves, Hank Locklin and Hank Snow to the American label. The package contained a note: 'I know you probably won't understand a word, and you probably won't know what on earth the records are all about, but you *must* release them. The singer is going to be an absolute giant.'

The singer was Elvis Presley and, to Wally Ridley's mind, Steve Sholes was perfectly correct – he couldn't understand a word of them, but he took the American's advice and put out 'Heartbreak Hotel'. It was Elvis Presley's first single release in Britain. It reached No. 2 and was prevented from making the top spot by a combination of Pat Boone's 'I'll Be Home', Lonnie Donegan's 'Lost John', and 'No Other Love' by Ronnie Hilton. By the end of the year, Elvis had enjoyed no less than seven hits in the British charts.

Without doubt, Elvis Presley was the greatest rock 'n' roll star the world had ever seen, and his impact in Britain was immediate. I heard 'Heartbreak Hotel' on the radio, and felt compelled to go out immediately and buy it. It cost me 5s 7d (28p). When I put it on my wind-up gramophone, it was as if someone had hit me over the head with a hammer. This was the 'King of rock 'n' roll', there was no one else. Bill Haley paled into insignificance behind him. Elvis had such an expressive voice, and it was enhanced on record by the addition of echo, giving it a haunting appeal. It was certainly different, and it left Lonnie Donegan standing. (Lonnie, however, went on to have another twenty-five British hits.) Skiffle was still exciting to listen to and great to play, but *this* was something else.

Elvis had everything going for him. He had a superb voice and was often described as having a black voice in a white body. He looked amazing, too – the black hair and sideburns; the dark smouldering eyes and sparkling white teeth; and a well-formed and very photogenic face that seemed always to have a slightly sneering and arrogant expression. That was the image he was creating, and it added to his magnetism. The raw material was all there, and the fact that he could wiggle his legs and shake his pelvis was a bonus. He oozed sex appeal, and took the James Dean look a stage further to become the definitive teenage cult hero. He was what rock 'n' roll has based itself on ever since.

I can remember the *Daily Mirror* carrying a double-page spread on Presley under the headline 'The New Sensation'. A few weeks later, when 'Blue Suede Shoes' came out, shoe shops all over the country were besieged by teenagers all wanting a pair just like Elvis's. The passion for brothel creepers was cooling. In America 'Heartbreak Hotel' went on to top all the known national charts within four weeks of its release, and resulted in Elvis appearing on network television's *Ed Sullivan Show*, which was the most popular TV programme in the USA, with massive viewing figures. However, he was given an ultimatum and only allowed to perform on the show if he wore a dinner jacket. To be absolutely safe, the camera shot him from the waist upwards in case the sight of his hip swinging gyrations offended some of the viewers.

As Elvis became more successful he also came in for criticism from the older generation, who loathed him and the effect he was having on teenagers. They couldn't quite understand what all the fuss was about but resented his appeal nonetheless. One Baptist minister in the USA called him 'morally insane', while another critic labelled him 'obscene' and prayed for his salvation. A third described him as 'unspeakably untalented' and a 'vulgar young entertainer'. His impact, not only on music, but on life and society in general, was enormous. When his movie *Love Me Tender* was shown in Britain, the cinemas were packed to the rafters. Girls screamed at the screen whenever he appeared and, at the end of the film when the character he is playing is killed, they wept uncontrollably for their idol. The guys, too, felt slightly choked.

In the space of a year Presley's impact was felt the whole world over, as hip-shaking, voice-quivering Elvis look-a-like imitators sprang up everywhere. Some faded into obscurity, others carved out useful careers for themselves. In Britain we had Terry Dene, Vince Taylor and Marty Wilde. Even in America singers copied Elvis Presley's style. When I saw Eddie Cochran in the film *The Girl Can't Help It*, I thought I was watching Elvis Presley singing 'Twenty Flight Rock'.

If Lonnie Donegan had inspired me to play the guitar, to get up and make music of my own, then Elvis Presley gave me the drive and determination to play rock 'n' roll, and slowly I introduced more numbers into the Railroaders' repertoire. I dreamed of becoming Elvis and, like thousands of other teenage lads, I stood in front of my bedroom mirror, wiggled my hips, snarled, and sang 'Heartbreak Hotel', 'Blue Suede Shoes' and 'Hound Dog', just like him. However, you could get an even better echo on your voice if you sang in the bathroom.

Elvis's early records featured great guitar playing, and for the first time I started to take an active interest in the music being played behind the vocals, instead of accepting it as a whole. I began to notice the solo breaks and pick out the musical phrases I liked. There was some superb guitar work on 'Mystery Train' and 'I Don't Care if the Sun Don't Shine', and I wanted to find out more about the musicians involved, for example Scotty Moore, who played lead guitar on all of the early Elvis Presley singles, Hank Garland, and James Burton. On Gene Vincent records it was the guitar playing of Cliff Gallup that stood out; Chuck Berry and Bo Diddley had their own individual styles. I suppose it was inevitable, with rock 'n' roll sweeping the world, that Britain would try to create its own rock stars in the wake of Bill Haley, Elvis and Gene Vincent. That same summer of 1956, Britain's first rock 'n' roll group emerged in the unlikely shape of Rory Blackwell's Rock 'n' Rollers, hastily followed by Tony Crombie's Rockets, for whom Jet Harris later played double bass. It was Crombie, one of the country's finest jazz drummers, who introduced Jet to the electric bass guitar, and he became the proud owner of the first instrument of its kind in this country. Neither of these groups gained any kind of following. It was left to a former merchant seaman from Bermondsey in South London by the name of Tommy Steele to lead the domestic assault, and before long he became Britain's first teenage idol.

Tommy Steele was on leave from the merchant navy when he was discovered playing and singing in the 2i's coffee bar in Soho by John Kennedy, a journalist cum publicity agent. His real name was Tommy Hicks, and he worked as a steward on the cruise liners to New York and often got up to entertain on board ship using the name Chick Hicks. On leave in America, he had discovered rock 'n' roll music and returned home to England with his bag full of records which had yet to be released in Britain. He promptly learnt several of the songs and performed them live in London clubs and coffee bars. He sang 'Heartbreak Hotel' long before anyone over here had ever heard it. John Kennedy could see his potential, and by using all his professional expertise as a press agent and former newspaper man, he set about launching his new star on to the unsuspecting British public. He did it through the media.

In the mid-fifties the British media was far less sensationalist than it is today. There was really only one popular newspaper that attracted a mass circulation, the *Daily Mirror*, which did a great job in keeping us all informed about the current trends in music. There was little else. Unlike America, which published a whole series of magazines and specialist papers devoted to music of all kinds, such as *Billboard* and *Cashbox*, Britain had just three music magazines: *New Musical Express*, *Melody Maker* (which was more in tune with jazz) and *Record and Show Mirror*, all published as trade papers for musicians. It was only during the late fifties that they switched allegiance towards the record-buying public instead, as a result of changing musical trends, although *Melody Maker* struck a happy medium and remained loyal to the musicians it served while still catering for public tastes. In 1958 they were joined by *Disc*.

John Kennedy cleverly manipulated his Fleet Street colleagues to create the initial interest in Tommy Steele through a number of carefully stunted newspaper stories along the 'rags to riches', 'working-class boy makes good' line. The first story featured Tommy performing at a high society débutantes' party, which Kennedy had carefully laid on himself. A Sunday newspaper took the bait, and headlined the following morning: 'Rock 'n' Roll Has Got the Debs, Too.' There were several other stories, and each one helped to perpetuate the carefully marketed image. When his first record, 'Rock with the Caveman', written by Lionel Bart and Mike Pratt and featuring a young session guitarist called Bert Weedon, was released in October 1956, Tommy Steele's name was already known and the public were expecting great things. He didn't disappoint them. He was guaranteed a big hit success when he appeared on BBC Television's only popular music show of the day, *Off the Record*.

'Rock with the Caveman' was a huge hit, much to the chagrin of George Martin, who would later emerge as the most famous record producer of the 1960s through his work with the Beatles. George had actually turned Tommy down and dismissed him as 'just another coffee-bar yodeller'.

In November 1956 Tommy embarked on his first nationwide tour of the Moss Empire theatres. The only outlet for new musical stars at that time in Britain was through the old music-hall circuit as part of a variety bill, and Tommy worked with a series of speciality acts on tour, including comedians Mike and Bernie Winters. There were no specialist venues for rock 'n' roll and no specialist impressarios. The men booking these new music acts were all old-fashioned theatrical agents with staid and dated ideas.

One of the first cities the tour visited was Sunderland, where I got a first glimpse of what all the fuss was about. Tommy caused a riot. The girls went wild, and he was mobbed everywhere he went. The music seemed to be of secondary importance to them. Within two months Tommy Steele had become a household name. His second single, 'Singing the Blues', which we thought was an original number, not realizing until later that it was a cover version of a Guy Mitchell song, topped the charts and gave him his biggest hit of all time.

The great danger with covering established American hits, however, was that there was always a possibility that the original record would be released in Britain to compete in the market-place with the domestic version. Indeed, Guy Mitchell also enjoyed the same kind of success with 'Singing the Blues' that Tommy Steele had, and, like the Londoner, he too topped the charts. It also happened to a man who later became a good friend of mine. Larry Page, the 'Teenage Rage', who was possibly the *worst* singer I have ever heard, had been a record packer for EMI when he was given the opportunity to make records. He often packed his own product on the conveyor belt, though most of his early offerings were appalling. In 1957 he was given the chance to make a cover version of an American song called 'That'll Be the Day', written by Buddy Holly. Larry's producer assured him that the American version of the song would not be released over here because, as he put it, 'It's terrible.' So the 'Teenage Rage' went ahead and recorded Holly's song, with the Geoff Love Orchestra and the Rita Williams Singers, who had the distinction of being featured regularly on radio's *Billy Cotton Band Show*.

It was quite dreadful! Larry called it 'the biggest load of crap you ever heard'. Still, he was the first British artiste ever to cover a Buddy Holly song, and his picture appeared on copies of the sheet music. Yet only a few weeks after Page's record had reached the shops, the original version of 'That'll Be the Day', by Buddy Holly and the Crickets, was brought out and went on to top the hit parade. Larry's rendition sank without trace.

Much later, Larry Page went into management and handled some of the biggest groups of the sixties, including the Kinks. He also managed and produced the Troggs. Reg Presley, the group's lead singer, had read somewhere that one particular rival band had taken over three days to make a single, which was an outrageous amount of time to record a number. There was a lot of rivalry between groups at that time. They were all suspicious and jealous of each other's success. If one group had broken new ground in the recording studio, all the others wanted to copy them immediately for fear of being left behind. When the Shadows and the Beatles put strings on their singles, every group wanted to use strings, and when another band recorded a concept album, all the others wanted to follow. So Reg Presley was fired by the idea of spending more time in the studio to make a single and called for a meeting with Larry Page.

'How long can we have in the studio to record our next single then, Larry?' he asked, and outlined exactly what he'd read in the newspaper.

The 'Teenage Rage' looked quizzical. 'How long does the song last?' he inquired.

Reg thought for a while.

'About three minutes,' came the reply.

'Well . . . that's how long you've got!'

Although Tommy Steele had been discovered by John Kennedy, he became the first British rock 'n' roll star to be managed by Larry Parnes – 'Mr Parnes, Shillings and Pence' as he was affectionately called. Hailed as the godfather of British rock 'n' rock, Parnes went on to form a rock dynasty and to control the careers of many of Britain's burgeoning pop singers, most of whom were cloned in the image of Elvis Presley, like Marty Wilde, Vince Eager, Billy Fury, Dickie Pride, Duffy Power, Johnny Gentle and Terry Dene.

Tommy Steele himself was acclaimed as 'Britain's answer to Elvis', which Parnes refuted as rubbish. He believed Tommy to be a better stage performer than the American, and claimed that Presley never toured Britain in the early days because of the threat Steele posed to him. He figured he would be shown up as a 'one-dimensional performer' in the face of such opposition. In truth, I think Tommy realized early in his own career, after he'd seen Elvis Presley perform on film and on television, that there could be no comparison between the two of them. He knew there was only one Elvis and always would be. He couldn't compete on the same level, and why should he?

When the hit singles ran out in 1961, Tommy Steele had

diversified his talents and was still as big as ever. His contribution to the music industry must never be overlooked or dismissed out of hand. Tommy Steele was the *first* British rock 'n' roller and served as the prototype for those who came after him. Even so, I can honestly say that Tommy never inspired me musically. Elvis Presley was my mentor. Tommy's influence helped me in other directions, however.

When we were sixteen, Hank and I decided it was time to leave Newcastle for good and escape its grimy clutches. We'd had enough and wanted to get away. I remember that Tommy Steele had once been to sea with the merchant navy, which seemed to me an ideal way of escaping the grim reality of Tyneside. So we, too, looked towards careers as merchant seamen, and I was even mercenary enough to find out that the Norwegian merchant navy paid the best rates for sailors. With very little to hold us back, we signed eagerly on the dotted line and waited for a ship to dock that would take us on our big adventure. When we discovered we would be fishing off the freezing northern coast of Norway in the Arctic Circle, and the weather looked decidedly stormy, we got cold feet and never reported for duty.

In the summer of 1957 Hank's band, the Crescent City Skiffle Group, split up and he joined Jim Simmons, George Williams and me in the Railroaders. Despite the fact that there were many other similar groups in Newcastle, we slowly started to build a reputation for ourselves and became quite well known locally. We were often featured in the *Newcastle Evening Chronicle* and rated very highly. We were working regularly now, two or three nights every week in socials and working men's clubs, and making money, sometimes as much as £6 or £7 a week each.

At first I had a difficult job persuading my school friend to make more of his undoubted talents and to broaden his outlook on music, to play rock 'n' roll. Hank was still very much the musical purist at heart. I persevered, and eventually we compromised and started playing a combination of material by Elvis Presley, Lonnie Donegan and Fats Domino, and more ethnic songs like 'O Mary Don't You Weep' on which we all sang harmony.

We learnt most of the songs we featured in the act from records or from the radio, but we didn't write the music down. Hank simply sat down and worked out the guitar solos, copying note for note the lead breaks of American guitarists like James Burton and Scotty Moore. He tried to reproduce the sound of the guitar that he heard on American rock 'n' roll records. It differed dramatically from the sound of British records – the Americans' were far superior – but it was a combination of the guitars themselves, the amplification, the echo chambers, the strings, the recording techniques, and of course the feeling in the way the notes were played. It was easy to Hank, even though at the time he couldn't hope to perfect the ideal 'American sound'. We all learnt by listening to other artistes, there really was no other way. I stuck to playing rhythm guitar – it appealed to me. I was too lazy, and simply not good enough to play lead.

Initially Hank Rankin played banjo in the Railroaders, but for his sixteenth birthday, in October 1957, his parents gave him a Hofner Congress cello-bodied guitar, which cost sixteen guineas. Later he added an electric pick-up and borrowed a friend's tiny amplifier, which was no bigger than a cornflake packet. Hank said it sounded like one too.

Not long after he joined the group, we were booked to appear in a week's variety at the Newcastle Palace, which was a major engagement for a band like ours. On the Monday we were due to open, Hank spent much of the time available rehearsing, being the new boy in the group and still feeling his way around. He was on stage when he managed to touch a live microphone with his electric guitar and very nearly electrocuted himself. There was a blinding blue flash, an almighty bang as sparks flew from the guitar, and a singer standing next to him on stage was thrown into the orchestra pit by the explosion. They were both lucky to be alive. Hank's guitar strings were sheared through. Had he been touching them at the time, he might well have been killed.

As we added more and more to our repertoire, Eddie Silver was brought into the group as an extra musician. A lot older than the rest of us, he had a terrific voice and was well known on the local club circuit. Besides singing, Eddie played guitar and owned a magnificent black American Vega which Hank later bought from him and used on our first tour in 1958. He eventually sold it to me and I still have it! I often give it a friendly pat when I happen to pass it. At the same time that Eddie joined the band, George Williams switched to play bass.

I suppose I should have been happy with the way things were progressing with the group. We had a settled line-up, the music was good, and we were earning a little money. But my life at home was becoming unbearable.

Sadie and Nazam had always had what seemed to me a volatile relationship since they had first started to live together in 1950, and I was forced to accept it. As I grew up I could see just how badly he was treating my aunt, hitting and slapping her for no apparent reason. When I pleaded with her to leave him, she refused. 'It will improve,' she would say. 'It will get better.' It never did.

One evening I lost my temper completely when I found Nazam punching Sadie. I turned on him. He tried to defend himself and lashed out towards me with his hand. I stepped to one side, hit him hard, and bodily threw him down the stairs, charging after him shouting abuse, threatening him. 'If you hit her again,' I screamed, 'I'll kill you.' He was a big man, crumpled on the floor at the bottom of the stairs, and he glared back at me more in shock than in fear, not appearing to be hurt physically. He had obviously not expected me to react so strongly or with such violence. All the bitterness and anger towards Nazam that had been pent up inside me over seven years came out in that one blow.

After that incident it was impossible for me to go on living under the same roof as him. It was Nazam's house, and he could easily have thrown me out. He didn't. Instead, I went to live in one of the flats he rented out in a property he owned in Westmoreland Road, and fended for myself. I was fifteen years old. Sadie was upset by my decision, but she knew he couldn't hurt me any more, and I still saw her every day.

At last I had my freedom, and now I could enjoy all the food I wasn't allowed to eat at Elswick Road, like eggs and bacon and black pudding. My first sexual activities began in earnest shortly after I moved into the flat, with one of the other residents, the daughter of one of the lodgers. She was slightly older than me, already very experienced in the ways of the world, and she taught me well. It was a very physical relationship. I was also very much attracted to another girl called Edna at the time, who lived nearby. We held hands and went for long walks around Elswick Park, a very romantic but purely platonic affair which soon ended.

I was becoming very single-minded as far as music was concerned. I had no ambitions other than to succeed as a musician, and after I saw Jim Dale at the Empire Theatre in Newcastle, my mind was made up. Jim, who later became an actor and appeared in many of the *Carry On* movies, and scored an enormous triumph on Broadway in the leading role in the musical *Barnum*, had recently enjoyed a substantial British hit with 'Be My Girl' when I saw him, and as soon as he walked out on stage the whole place erupted. Wow! The audience was amazing and the atmosphere in the theatre was electric. I thought to myself, if one man can do all this, I have got to be in show business. I started to make plans.

Tommy Steele was still Britain's biggest star, and when I read somewhere that he had started his career in the 2i's coffee bar in Soho, I decided I just had to go to London and see for myself. I wanted to find out if everything they said about the club being a hotbed for young musicians was true.

So towards the end of the year I made the trip south and spent a weekend at the YMCA hostel at Tottenham Court Road.

Soho was alive, teeming with excitement. There was a superb camaraderie about the whole area. It was ablaze with neon lights, giving an almost surreal atmosphere that reminded me very much of the fairground back home. The streets were seething with people, falling in and out of restaurants, pubs that never seemed to close, and coffee bars. From the doors of each establishment came the pulsating sounds of music – jazz, skiffle, rock 'n' roll – and laughter, as groups and singers peddled their musical wares, or juke-boxes burst into life in subterranean cellars. I was spellbound. I had never experienced anything like this before in my life. Suddenly Newcastle seemed light years away, dead and buried by comparison. London was the place we had to go to if we were to have any chance of making it in show business, of that I was certain, and I returned home to convince the others. I didn't expect to be back in London so quickly.

George Williams saw it first. He was browsing through one of the music magazines when he came across an advertisement for a talent contest to be held at the Granada Cinema at Edmonton in North London. It seemed just the opportunity we were looking for.

Fortunately our entry for the competition was accepted, and on a cold and misty Friday evening we made our way by train from Newcastle Central to London's King's Cross, wide-eyed and excited. We were also very apprehensive. Weeks before, we had been turned down by the BBC after auditioning for the Saturday morning radio show *Skiffle Club* – which later became *Saturday Club* – so our spirits were pretty low. We were also worried that we might not be good enough to appear in such exalted company. What were our chances? London groups were bound to be good.

But we were better, and to our great delight, after performing two numbers in our heat, we won our way into the semi-finals.

After our success in North London we spent most of the night in the West End, sampling the many wonders and delights Soho had to offer. In the Nucleus Club, off Shaftesbury Avenue, we saw Robin Hall and Jimmy McGregor performing live on stage, and later came across a group of transvestites, which to young, naïve Geordie lads was a real eye-opener. We thought they were girls; when we realized our mistake we left the club in a hurry.

Back in Newcastle, I realized that it would be far better for all concerned if Rutherford Grammar School and Bruce Cripps parted company permanently. I decided to leave during the Christmas holiday period without sitting my O-level examinations – I could see no point in it anyway, and I never returned for the spring term of 1958. I didn't go to work either. In fact I have never had what some people call 'a proper job' in my life. I lived off the money I made from the group and a few hand-outs from Sadie.

For our semi-final appearance in the London talent contest in January, we changed the group around. The tea-chest bass was replaced by a real, upright double bass which George played, and Jim Simmons switched from washboard to drums. I got a better guitar, trading in my National for a Framus acoustic. It was an inspired change, too, because we managed to come out on top again and headed for the final at Easter. We celebrated by appearing for a couple of nights at Chaquito's, a real live London coffee bar in Hanway Street, off Tottenham Court Road. It felt like a second home.

We returned to our real home in the north-east full of confidence for the forthcoming final, and opened our own club in a hall in a village on the outskirts of Newcastle. We called it the Six Five Club after the television series *Six Five Special*, which had been shown on the BBC since the previous February. We charged an entrance fee for anyone who wanted to come in and see us play. Even then we were developing into young entrepreneurs, all of sixteen years old.

Two months after I left school Hank followed me, much to the disapproval of his parents. They had high hopes for their eldest son but, like mine, Hank's dreams and aspirations lay firmly in a musical career. We both wanted to turn professional. Hank's mother and father had other ideas and insisted he get a job, otherwise they would make him leave home immediately. Hank took their warning to heart and started working as a delivery boy. For the sum of £2 10s (£2.50p) a week, he spent the best part of each day cycling around Newcastle delivering electrical parts and components. He was employed for precisely two weeks.

We had other things on our minds. We planned to go down to London for the final of the talent contest on 6 April, and then – win or lose – come back to Newcastle.

But we changed our plans, and Hank and I never returned.

4 'LIMP, YOU BUGGER, LIMP'

On 24 March 1958, two weeks before the Railroaders were due in London for the final of the talent contest we hoped would make our name, Elvis Presley reported to the draft board in Memphis, Tennessee, at the start of a two-year spell in the American armed services. The man known the world over as 'Elvis the Pelvis' became plain Private Presley, E. A., US53310761, on a salary of twenty dollars.

It was to prove the beginning of the end in some respects. John Lennon said later that Elvis died the day he went into the army, and in terms of relevance to rock 'n' roll he was right. When Elvis was demobilized and came out of uniform two years later, the hard edge had gone. The great rebel and leader of the teenage pack had been tamed, to move into the realms of wholesome family entertainment. Someone suggested that maybe it had been carefully stage-managed. Going into the army gave Elvis the time, and an ideal opportunity, to break away from his image as a teen idol and appeal to a much wider and much more lucrative audience. I suppose Colonel Tom Parker, his manager, reasoned that Elvis could reach far more people by making movies and appearing on television than he ever could on tour. And by then the great halcyon days of rock 'n' roll were gone.

For us five young Geordie lads from Newcastle, Private Elvis Presley was the last person on our minds as we headed for the Granada Cinema in Edmonton again after spending the weekend in a bed and breakfast hotel in Victoria. We had an appointment with destiny, and we were all aware that it could change our lives overnight if we were lucky in the competition. We had read about it happening to other people in show business – Tommy Steele was a prime example – and we had every reason to believe that this time we could go all the way. Confidence is a great stimulant.

There were several other groups taking part in the competition besides ourselves, along with a variety of acts. During rehearsals we were very taken with an outfit from Palmers Green called Errol Hollis and the Velvets, and thought they could be our main rivals for the first prize. Hank and I were very impressed by the group's drummer, who had exceptional talent, with a great style and a sound reminiscent of Buddy Holly's drummer, Jerry Allison. It was the first time we ever met Brian Bennett. Another drummer we befriended before the competition started was Pete Chester, son of the famous comedian Charlie Chester and leader of a group called the Chesternuts, who also looked a good bet for a prize.

The final of the talent contest took place on Easter Sunday, 6 April 1958, and much to our dismay we discovered that the winner was to be determined by a panel of so-called experts, and not by audience reaction as we had hoped. Still, it was up to us to show them just how good we were. We went down very well indeed with the theatre audience, but not sufficiently well with the judges, who voted us into third place at the end of the evening. It was a big let down; we had expected much more and were very disappointed to have travelled all this way to come only third. We were pipped on the final run in by a Malaysian opera singer and a traditional jazz band, their names lost in the mists of time. Neither made it in show business.

Coming third was a very respectable achievement, but it effectively marked the end of the Railroaders. Our drummer, Jim Simmons, needed to get back to Newcastle. He was a miner and had to go to work the following morning. Eddie and George went with him, George later becoming Eddie Silver's manager. Hank and I decided to stay in London to see if the streets really were paved with gold as the *Daily Mirror* had once reported. We knew that if we were ever going to make it in the music business, this was the place to start. There was a slight problem; we had nowhere to stay and very little money.

The manager of the Granada Cinema was a robust and kindly Scot called Livingstone, and during the previous heats of the competition we had become good friends. I guess he liked us because, being Northerners, we were kindred spirits far from home in what appeared a big, unfriendly city. Despite its size, bright lights and general hustle and bustle, London can be a desperately lonely place. He solved our problem immediately with a telephone call to a landlady he knew in Finsbury Park. Mrs Bowman, like us, was a Geordie – I'm sure that's why we got on so well together. She owned a large house in Holly Park, near King's Cross, which she ran as theatrical digs, renting out rooms to people in show business. She was a delightful lady, everyone's favourite aunt and very kind to us, proving to be our salvation on many occasions. Fortunately for Hank and me she had an attic room available if we wanted it. It was only a temporary arrangement, one night or two, and then if we wanted to stay in London we had to find something else.

We arrived at the Bowman house exhausted, and were shown into our tiny room at the top of the building. It was sparse, with twin beds and a gas fire in the corner which was operated by means of a meter that seemed to devour shillings at a frightening rate – when the fire was turned on full blast it burnt out eyes. We had to find our own food.

We shared the house with an ever-changing assortment of thespians; actors, theatrical folk, singers, and dancers. Leapy Lee, who had a sizeable British hit with 'Little Arrows' in 1968, rented a room opposite us.

The two nights we originally intended to stay in Finsbury Park turned out to be over a year. But for the first six months of our existence in London, from April to October, we almost starved.

We had very little money, and what we did manage to get together went to pay the rent, which was always overdue. Sometimes we went for weeks on end without paying Mrs Bowman, who was very generous towards us and understood our predicament. The only things we owned were our guitars and the clothes we stood up in. My Aunt Sadie regularly sent me down a registered envelope containing a £5 note, or sometimes £10, which she managed to fiddle on the market stall even though Nazam watched her like a hawk. I think she would have been horrified to see how we were living. She never stood in my way when I told her I wanted to go to London to become a musician and seek my fortune, and she was happy that I was trying to make something of myself, even though I knew she was petrified for me. I wrote to her as often as I could, just to reassure her that everything was going well, but my letters belied the situation I was in. If only she had known. Had it not been for Sadie's money and Mrs Bowman's patience and generosity, I do believe Hank and I would have gone under very quickly.

Food, or rather lack of it, was the big problem. When we became desperate to eat, we would tiptoe downstairs from the attic and raid Mrs Bowman's fridge, relieving it of a pint of milk, some eggs, or anything edible. There was an art to our late-night raiding parties. Mrs Bowman's dogs slept downstairs, so it was essential not to disturb them – one bark and we would be caught red-handed in the act of petty larceny. It didn't happen very often. Of course, next morning when our landlady told us that food was missing from the fridge and asked us if we knew anything about it, we shook our heads sheepishly.

'Oh no, we didn't get in until 2 am and we went straight to bed,' we chorused. 'It couldn't have been us.'

When it became impossible to attack the fridge by night, we turned to the apple trees in the back garden, which became a great source of sustenance when the fruit was ripe enough to be picked. Hank and I once lived for two days on a single apple, which we split between us. It was always a question of survival. Some days we stayed in bed so that we wouldn't have to worry about finding food. We reasoned with ourselves that we could not possibly get hungry if we were asleep. Most times hunger kept us awake. We were desperate, but we were driven on by a blind faith in our ability as musicians; we were certain that one day we would eventually make it. Starvation was only a temporary setback.

On other days we spent our time listening to authentic American rock 'n' roll records in our room. One of our fellow lodgers had a collection of old Sun classics he had brought back from America, featuring Elvis Presley, Jerry Lee Lewis, Carl Perkins and Charlie Rich, which we played incessantly. The whole house reverberated to the sound.

We had only been in London a few weeks when we teamed up with Pete Chester, whom we had first met at the Edmonton talent show, and became permanent members of the Chesternuts, joining Gerry Furst, who sang and played harmonica, and Neil Johnson on bass. Pete played drums. We travelled as often as we could from Finsbury Park to the Chester home in East Finchley, to rehearse in Pete's bedroom, not through any great devotion to the music we were playing, but because it meant we would get a meal after we'd finished practising. I think Dorita, Pete's mother, could see we were undernourished and took pity on us.

It was with Pete Chester that we started to write songs, which developed out of rehearsals. Pete had a talent for writing, which must have come from his father, who was a very fine songwriter in his day. Charlie Chester wrote several best-selling songs, including 'The Old Bazaar in Cairo', 'Forget-me-not-Lane', and 'Primrose Hill'.

Buddy Holly was the inspiration for us to write our own material, and we tried to evolve our own style by listening to his records. He was one of the first singer-songwriters – he wrote most of the songs he recorded, and did the arrangements as well. They were great songs, too, an endearing testament to the melodic, romantic side of rock 'n' roll. He wrote lyrics which teenagers could relate to and understand. We started to think about the words to our own songs because of his influence.

Buddy Holly wrote his songs for his own style of guitar playing, a distinctive combination of rhythm-and-lead that blended perfectly; a chunky sound that carried the songs, and around which the melodies were constructed. The introduction to 'That'll Be the Day' sent shivers down my spine every time I heard it. The instrumental breaks to 'Peggy Sue', 'Oh Boy', and 'Maybe Baby' were infectious and made you want to get up and dance and enjoy yourselves. Holly was unique in the music industry at that time, for it was almost unheard of for artistes to write and record their own material. It had been an unwritten rule for many years that the music publishing houses in what was affectionately called 'Tin Pan Alley' supplied singers with the songs they recorded, and a whole industry had grown up on the strength of it. Bill Haley didn't write his own songs, neither did Elvis Presley or Jerry Lee Lewis; there were a few exceptions, such as Chuck Berry, but Buddy Holly started to change it all. Ironically a few years later the Shadows did exactly the same thing, writing for Cliff Richard, and then the Beatles – themselves influenced by Buddy Holly –

came along and turned the whole songwriting business on its head.

It was Buddy Holly who inspired John Lennon and Paul McCartney to start writing together. 'John and I used to slag off school and go to my house and just try to write songs,' Paul McCartney once told me. 'We'd put on a Buddy Holly record, then after we'd listened to it several times we'd sit around with our guitars and try to write something like it.' Hank and I did exactly the same thing. However, John and Paul's songs were deliberately written in the key of A, not because it was the key in which they preferred to sing but because they believed Buddy Holly wrote his songs in A.

We admired Buddy Holly not only for his marvellous songs, which are as fresh today as they were when he first wrote them, but for the way he sang them, in that unusual, jerky, hiccuping style, with his childlike phrasing. He just sounded like no one else. Then there was the guitar. It was Buddy Holly who introduced us to the magnificent Fender Stratocaster. We'd seen nothing like it before – it looked like a spaceship and was way ahead of its time. It became the distinctive symbol of rock 'n' roll. This was the elusive sound we had been hearing on all the early American rock records; this was the sound we had been desperately trying to reproduce. It was no wonder British rock 'n' roll records sounded so shallow. Unfortunately at that time there was an import ban on American instruments coming into the country, so Fender guitars were not available in Britain unless you were lucky enough to pick one up second-hand that someone had brought back from the States, or that maybe an American serviceman had sold over here. It was our dream guitar.

Buddy Holly's appeal went even further. He destroyed the myth that *image* was everything. Buddy really wasn't a particularly good-looking guy, like Elvis, Eddie Cochran or Ricky Nelson. He was lanky and awkward, and whoever heard of a rock 'n' roller wearing glasses? Yet he gave hope to millions of ordinary-looking guys who wanted to get involved and play rock 'n' roll. He showed us the way, the rest was up to us. His career was far too short, and during it he recorded less than 100 titles and never appeared in films. For all that, he became one of the most important figures in the history of music.

I cried when I heard of his death. I was stunned. I was walking to catch the Underground at Finsbury Park station when I saw the front page of the *Daily Mirror*. 'TOP ROCK STARS DIE IN CRASH' screamed the headline, and there was a picture of Big Bopper at the top of the page and a smaller one of Buddy Holly below. I couldn't believe what I was reading, that he had been killed in a plane crash. 3 February 1959 was one of the tragic days for rock music. Years later, in his song 'American Pie', Don McLean called it 'the day the music died'.

From out of our first tentative efforts at writing, most of which seemed terrible by comparison to Buddy Holly's, Pete came up with a respectable little song called 'Teenage Love', which was very much in the style of the Crickets, with the slight Latin rhythm and flavour to it that experts predicted would be the next big sound in music, while Hank chipped in with a number about one of his former girlfriends, 'Jean Dorothy'.

In our previous group, the Railroaders, we had worked whenever we could but the Chesternuts made only a handful of public performances. We spent most of our time together writing and rehearsing. We did manage to make a memorable appearance at a charity concert at Stoke Newington Town Hall, where we backed Benny Hill, who treated the audience that night to the first-ever performance of a new song he had recently written, one that was to become a big hit for him three years later, called 'Gather in the Mushrooms'. I couldn't believe it. We had come down to London to play rock 'n' roll; we were starving for our art, struggling to survive, and here we were playing comedy songs. I certainly wasn't laughing. Yet from that one engagement, we ended up in the recording studio a few weeks later making our first single.

Leslie Conn was an impresario and record plugger who ran the British end of the American Carlton label. He was in the audience at Stoke Newington that night and was very impressed with our performance despite Benny Hill's comedy. Leslie decided that what we needed was careful handling and exploitation, and encouraged us to write more of our own material. He was at least ten years older than us, but it was not only for that reason that we listened to what he had to say; we also had a lot of respect for the man. He knew his business and had seen the impact Buddy Holly was making as a songwriter.

I think Leslie was seriously hoping that we would emerge as a British version of the Crickets. Nevertheless, he showed his great faith and belief in the group by arranging some recording time for us. We were to make a record at the Philips studio in Stanhope Place, behind Marble Arch, and Leslie paid for this session himself, splashing out £40. We were scared stiff at the prospect. We had no idea what to expect, as none of us had made a record before – even Pete Chester, who had been brought up in a show-business family, was apprehensive. The large, imposing studio that greeted us was awe-inspiring, but we kept telling ourselves that we were professionals and should remain calm and collected.

We had a few hours in which to record our two songs. It was a one-track studio. Over-dubbing facilities had yet to arrive in Britain, and it meant that if we made a mistake in the middle of a song we would have to stop, start all over again, and play the number right through until we got it right and the engineer was satisfied with our performance. Three hours later we emerged with our finished product, very disappointed. Hank and I, who both sang on the session, had never heard ourselves on record or tape before, and we expected to sound exactly like the Everly Brothers. We didn't. What we failed to realize was that the reason Don and Phil Everly sounded so good was that, because they were brothers, they possessed a rare tonal empathy in their voices that made them blend together perfectly when they sang. Their harmonies were magnificent, and the results came quite naturally because they were related.

Hank and I were still learning. We were very inexperienced, and at that time we were not very proficient musicians either. Still, Leslie Conn was very pleased with the results and leased the tapes to EMI, who released the two numbers on a single on Columbia Records. 'Teenage Love' became the A-side, coupled with 'Jean Dorothy'. And on the strength of this one record, Leslie, through another series of contacts in the business, managed to secure an appearance for us on the biggest TV programme of the day, *Six Five Special*, which went out live early each Saturday evening from the BBC studios in Lime Grove, Shepherd's Bush. Remarkably, I never saw *Six Five Special* on television until I appeared on the show myself. In fact it was only when I went to London that I saw television for the first time in my life.

Rock 'n' roll on British television in the first few months of 1958 was almost non-existent. The TV stations, like their counterparts on radio, were slow to realize its potential. Independent Television, the commercial channel which had started broadcasting three years earlier at the same time that rock 'n' roll was beginning to take root, had made some concessions to the growing musical craze as early as 1956, with the introduction of a fifteen-minute late-night music programme called *Cool for Cats*. It was hosted originally by Ker Robertson, who was later replaced by Kent Walton, and the following year it was extended to half an hour. The show featured artistes miming to their latest record releases, although just occasionally some performed live in the studio. There was also a resident dance company, led by Dougie Squires, which included in its ranks a very young Una Stubbs, later to appear in several of the early Cliff Richard movies.

BBC television responded with the introduction of *Six Five Special*, which had been devised by two young producers, Josephine Douglas and university graduate Jack Good, and hit the screens in February 1957. The idea for the name came from Lonnie Donegan's hit 'Midnight Special', and the opening title sequence featured an express train hurtling towards the screen. The show had no definite policy and featured a random selection of music across the board, from rock 'n' roll to jazz, skiffle and ballads. Regular guests included Tommy Steele, Jim Dale, Mike and Bernie Winters, Johnny Dankworth and Tony Osborne and his Orchestra. Trombone-playing Don Lang led the resident group, the Frantic Five.

Whenever Wee Willie Harris appeared on the show, he had his hair dyed a different colour especially for his performance, even though these were the days of black and white television. He wore a huge, outsized jacket that looked as if it still contained the coat-hanger, and a vast polka-dotted bow tie. He was a better showman than he was a rock 'n' roll singer. His TV appearances subsequently led to questions being asked in the House of Commons, as MPs accused the BBC of promoting 'teenage decadence'.

The show itself was presented by Josephine Douglas, Pete

Murray and the former world light-heavyweight boxing champion, Freddie Mills, who looked wooden and out of place, like an embarrassed scout leader. When he retired from the ring, Freddie turned towards television for a career and also got involved in a series of business ventures, eventually owning a West End nightclub. In the summer of 1965 he was found shot dead in Soho in mysterious circumstances.

Six Five Special gave rock 'n' roll its first voice on television, albeit in small doses, and it later spawned a big screen movie of the same name, starring Lonnie Donegan and Dickie Valentine and all the regular features from the BBC series, produced by Anglo Amalgamated. The TV show proved the forerunner to all the rock and pop programmes that followed it on television. Certainly its format of staging the programme live in a bare studio, with cameras and lighting gantries on full display to the viewers, technicians and floor managers walking in and out of shot, and the audience milling around the cameramen – then a revolutionary step forward in TV terms – was the same technique used on other shows in the 1960s, notably *Ready, Steady, Go*.

Producer Jack Good, who pioneered this style of instant free-form television, left the show at the end of 1957 and went on to the independent channel, where the following September he started his own half-hour series, *Oh Boy*. This was something completely different again: it was Britain's leading rock 'n' roll show and unique for its time – fast-moving, non-stop, uninterrupted wall-to-wall music, with acts set against a backdrop of moody lighting and screaming girls. It was screened live from the stage of the Hackney Empire in London, with a strict formula of resident artistes mixed with special guests. Among the residents were the Vernons Girls for back-up vocals – the Dallas Boys were often featured as well – and the 'house' orchestra, Lord Rockingham's XI, a fit-up band of mainly session musicians. It was through their exposure on television that they started to make records on their own, and in 1958 they topped the charts with 'Hoots Mon'. *Oh Boy* embodied the realization that rock 'n' roll was all about one thing, *image*, and Jack Good became an image-maker extraordinary.

It was Good who took away Cliff Richard's guitar and made him shave off his sideburns, in an effort to move him away from the moody, snarling Elvis look-a-like mould and into something that was essentially his own. He turned him into a sensual performer – 'the quiet smoulderer' – and it was through *Oh Boy* that Cliff emerged a star. Jack gave Johnny Kidd an eye-patch to camouflage a nasty squint, and it opened up a whole new career for him. Jack was also responsible for putting Gene Vincent into the black leather which became his trademark, for an appearance on his follow-up series *Boy Meets Girl* in 1959. It was this show that helped to revive Vincent's rapidly faltering career.

Vincent was handicapped by a withered leg and wore irons, which Good exploited to the full by turning him into the personification of Richard III, sinister with evil overtones. It was an apt description, since Vincent was not one of the world's most warm and wonderful human beings. Good dressed him in black, with leather gloves, and draped a cloak over his shoulders like a shroud. To gain even greater impact, he arranged for the singer to make his stage entrance by walking down a flight of stairs which could only help to emphasize his limp and set the overall scene. It was perfect, or so Jack Good thought, but as Vincent started to descend the staircase, in full view of the audience, he delicately picked his way down the steps, trying to negotiate each obstacle in turn. Jack was horrified. In a flash he left the production room from where he was directing the show, and raced around the back of the set screaming: 'Limp, you bugger, limp.'

In 1959 the BBC launched a new show to compete with *Oh Boy* in the shape of *Drumbeat*, but it didn't last. However, the Corporation had produced a modest record review show that was to outlast all the early pop programmes and claim a regular Saturday evening viewing audience of over 14 million: *Juke Box Jury*.

Within two months of arriving in the capital, Hank Rankin and Bruce Cripps had made a record and appeared on national television. We couldn't believe our luck, and by now it really did seem that the *Daily Mirror* had got it right for once and the streets of London *were* paved with gold. However, it wasn't to be. Our appearance on *Six Five Special*, which was introduced by Pete's father, Charlie Chester, wasn't one of the memorable moments in British pop history. It certainly did not help to sell any records either, and the single in which we had so much confidence failed to make any kind of impact in the charts. I was more disappointed that my Aunt Sadie never saw the show after I had written to tell her we were appearing. She was working in the market at the time and Nazam certainly wouldn't have let her go home early just to watch a TV show.

Not long afterwards we faced up to the grim reality that we *weren't* going to make it as recording artistes – well, not for the time being – and the group drifted apart. Gerry and Neil went off and found proper jobs (Gerry became a chemist). Pete Chester persevered with his writing and later emerged as a prolific songwriter, penning, among others, 'Don't Be a Fool with Love', 'Lonesome Fella', and 'Left Out Again'. We remained good friends. I think we were attracted by the large helpings of egg and chips his mother piled in front of us when we arrived at the Chester home.

Both Hank and I collaborated with Pete on a number of compositions. With Hank he wrote 'I Live for You' and 'Saturday Dance', which became the Shadows' very first single release in 1959, while Pete and I were responsible for 'Tell Me', 'It's You', 'First Lesson in Love' (which Cliff recorded), 'True Love Will Come to You', 'Now's the Time to Fall in Love', and 'Please Don't Tease', which gave Cliff Richard one of his biggest successes and topped the British charts for two weeks in 1960. We found writing easy, though we invariably stuck rigidly to the standard formula of three chords around which to build our songs.

In order to eat regularly and pay the rent, which was a secondary consideration, we had to work. If we didn't work, we starved, it was as simple as that. There was a limit to the number of meals we could scrounge from friends. The only way we wanted to earn a living was by playing, and the only place where we knew we might stand a chance of achieving that ambition was at the 2i's coffee bar at 59 Old Compton Street – but we weren't alone in our thinking. Soho had become a Mecca for hundreds of young musicians who drifted into London from Manchester, Liverpool, Birmingham, Glasgow and Newcastle, their only possession a guitar, all hoping to get work in the many coffee bars along Wardour Street, Frith Street, Dean Street, Rupert Street, Greek Street, and the alleyways in between, and praying that they would be discovered by the proverbial man in the suit with a fat cigar. We all shared the same dreams.

Soho was like a beacon to us all. It was the Bohemian centre of London, where musicians and writers, artists and artisans congregated each night to talk together, drink together and generally have a good time. Soho was all about good times. It was awash with colour and colourful characters, a cosmopolitan village within a city where an old-fashioned form of urban life revolved around French, Italian and Greek bars, restaurants, snack bars and delicatessens; where English was just one of many languages that might be heard, long before pornography got its grubby hands on the place. What strip clubs and peep shows there were seemed to blend in as part of the scenery, and no one took them seriously. It was exciting, unusual; a place where you could belong. Rich smells of coffee beans, mingled with salami, pastrami and pasta, hung on the air at all times. The atmosphere was warm and good-humoured, but it was full of contrasts. People always greeted you cheerfully, while it was a notorious vice area – prostitutes plied their trade from dinghy street doorways (young French models, who invariably lived on the second floor), and villains carried out their business in darkened back streets. Jack Spot was just one of the infamous gangland characters who, rumour had it, controlled the Soho streets. Ironically, his daughter was an avid member of the 2i's crowd. Despite the presence of the underworld connection, the wide boys and the wheeler-dealers, Soho was not a sleazy or sinister place. There was never any overt hint of violence, at least we certainly didn't see any, but we were probably trying to have a good time and earn a living. It seemed to be safe not only to us two Geordie lads, but to thousands of people who flocked to the area each day to sample its delights, to drink good Italian espresso coffee, and to listen to British rock 'n' roll.

For a whole week every summer this tiny area of no more than a square mile took on a completely different air. It was turned into one vast street party – a miniature Mardi Gras – for the Soho Fair. Ornately decorated floats paraded through the streets to the accompaniment of skiffle groups or jazz bands. Music was everywhere. People danced in the streets from dusk to dawn; buskers entertained on the corners as the carnival came to town. Old

Compton Street was closed off to traffic and hosted some memorable events of merriment, the highlight of which was the annual waiters' race. Employees from each of Soho's restaurants and eating houses competed against each other in a straight race over a measured distance. They had to run in their full waiter's regalia and carry a tray containing a bottle of wine and glasses. It was a great spectacle and all added to Soho's quaintness and charm.

Just why the coffee-bar craze should explode in the 1950s is hard to understand, but it certainly became part of the new teenage culture of liberation and rock 'n' roll, and provided a much more acceptable alternative to pubs and as social meeting places for teenagers, many of whom were under eighteen years of age and were forbidden by law to enter such premises. It was also much cheaper to drink coffee than alcohol and, coffee bars not being restricted by licensing laws, they operated throughout the day and could stay open longer at night. We all felt they provided a far more inspiring atmosphere in which to congregate, and girls found it much easier, and far less intimidating, to go into coffee bars on their own than into pubs. Also, unlike public houses, coffee bars were not frequented by parents – something that was all-important. The music was a bonus, although in the end it was the music that became the great attraction. Coffee bars became a vital outlet for musical expression, and without doubt the birth of British rock 'n' roll took place in the coffee bars of Soho.

Soho's first in the new breed of espresso coffee bars opened in Frith Street in 1953 and was called the Moka. It became the first of many, and each one helped in its own small way to pioneer British rock and see it develop, either by featuring new and exciting musicians playing live, or by pumping the music out at high volume on the obligatory juke-box in the corner. There were some famous clubs whose names will always be synonymous with the new musical revolution that was taking place, most of them located below street level in small, dimly lit basements, which all added to the atmosphere.

Russell Quaye's Skiffle Cellar in Greek Street was where I saw the Worried Men for the first time. They were fronted by a devastatingly good-looking singer from Acton by the name of Terry Nelhams. He had striking blond hair and high cheekbones and resembled James Dean, but he sang like Buddy Holly with a catch in his voice as if he was laughing all the time. However, he only established himself as a recording artiste after he left the group on the advice of Jack Good and changed his name to the much more identifiable Adam Faith. The very first time I saw him, I realized he was going to be a big star. Even though he was raw and undisciplined, he had tremendous charisma in front of a microphone.

Chas McDevitt, one of the doyens of British skiffle, opened his own club on the corner of Berwick Street and Noel Street and called it, appropriately, Freight Train, after his monster hit single. We had met him a few months before when he had appeared in Newcastle, and on the strength of that friendship he occasionally asked Hank and me to play together at the club. Another great den for skiffle music was Studio 51, where Ken Colyer was a regular. In 1956 Rory Blackwell transformed it into London's first rock 'n' roll club. Others quickly followed: the Partisan in Carlisle Street, the Top Ten in Berwick Street, next door to the house of Sam Widges, which was run for a while by singer and Elvis Presley look-alike Vince Taylor, the Gyre and Gimble, off the Strand, and the Good Earth in Gerrard Street.

The Nucleus, in Endell Street, was a modern jazz club that stayed open long past 4 am. Some nights we would go there instead of heading back to Finsbury Park. I wasn't particularly fond of jazz, but the club had a great atmosphere and attracted a whole variety of musicians, all eager to talk music and swop stories, which was fascinating to a sixteen-year-old just starting out in the same business.

It was here that I had my first encounter with drugs. Jazz clubs were notorious hives for dope. Most musicians who frequented the Nucleus rolled weird-shaped cigarettes and puffed on them greedily, the smoke having an unusually sweet and pungent aroma. It seemd to float on the air and to hang around far longer than normal cigarette smoke. I found out quickly that they were smoking 'hash' or 'marijuana', which they referred to affectionately as 'jazz woodbines'. Hank and I were invited to indulge on a number of occasions, and we took great pleasure in politely refusing. My smoking days had ended after a few experimental puffs back at Rutherford Grammar School.

Many years later I was asked to produce an album for a famous group who had enjoyed some sizeable chart success in the mid-seventies. We were in the studio one day when the session was interrupted by the arrival of a man whom I can only describe as the 'drug doctor'. He had a briefcase with him from which he took out a quantity of white powder and placed it on top of the organ. Obviously it was cocaine, but it looked like talcum powder or chalk dust to me, which irritated my nose. In the next moment I gave out an almighty and uncontrollable sneeze and blew the whole lot all over the floor. There was cocaine everywhere. It must have cost a fortune, and I wasn't very popular!

Cyril Davies, one of the legendary British blues singers, opened the Skiffle Centre above the Roundhouse public house in Wardour Street in the early fifties. In 1955 he joined forces with guitarist Alexis Korner, a former Chris Barber sideman who had originally replaced Lonnie Donegan in the band, and together they converted the premises into the first London club to specialize in the music of the blues; they renamed the venue the London Blues and Barrelhouse Club. Over the next few years, until it was closed down for being too noisy, the club became a hotbed for the blues and attracted many visiting American performers to its tiny stage, names we had only read about in such specialist music magazines as were available, for example Memphis Slim, Little Brother, Jimmy Cotton, Roosevelt Sykes, Big Bill Broonzy, Muddy Waters and Otis Spann. Alexis Korner's career had started in a coffee bar on the outer limits of the Soho boundary called the Breadbasket, in Cleveland Street, which also saw the musical birth of Wally Whyton and the Vipers, who played there in 1956. It was to the Breadbasket that Paul Simon came in 1965, hoping to launch a solo career for himself as a singer.

As the craze continued to gain momentum, club owners and coffee-bar proprietors had to keep coming up with fresh ideas and new gimmicks in order to attract customers. There were several spectacular attempts. The Heaven and Hell coffee lounge at 55 Old Compton Street operated on two levels. Upstairs was Heaven, a relatively straightforward coffee bar, while downstairs, in almost total darkness and lit only by the red-eyed devil masks on the wall, was Hell, where the music was loud and the heat – due to lack of ventilation – was unbearable. A club in Meard Street went one better. Le Macabre, as its name suggested, was a spooky establishment where skeletons and bones hung from the walls and the basement ceiling. Customers sat at coffins, which were used instead of tables to give the whole place a sinister, almost evil air. The kids loved it.

But the most famous coffee bar of all, and the one that put British rock 'n' roll on the map, was the 2i's. It needed no gimmicks to bring in the punters. Its reputation alone was enough to pack the place to bursting point night after night.

It was an unpretentious place, and from the outside looked like any ordinary snack bar. There was nothing special about the décor, apart from the huge shining juke-box strategically placed in the window, close to the entrance. A simple neon-light hoarding above the door proclaimed: THE WORLD FAMOUS 2i'S COFFEE BAR, HOME OF THE STARS.

But it was downstaris, in the tiny basement, where all the excitement really took place each night, and 200 sweating bodies – the place couldn't take any more – danced to the heady music of rock 'n' roll, jammed together like sardines. It was minute, to say the least, no more than thirty feet in length and ten feet wide, and when it was crammed with people the whole place throbbed. Jet Harris called it 'the black hole of Calcutta'. It was an apt description. The man responsible for decorating the cellar was a budding young songwriter and spare-time washboard player called Lionel Bart, who had painted two large eyes along one wall that stared at you, unseeing. He was a regular at the coffee bar, a real Bohemian, dressed in a duffle coat and wearing thonged sandals.

To reach the basement, customers had to descend a flight of steps and turn right into the narrow room at the bottom, where to the right again was a tiny stage opposite another almost vertical set of stairs that came out at street level. At the back of the room was a Coca Cola machine and another for dispensing orange squash. There was no air-conditioning; two flaps to the street were opened to let the air in from outside.

The premises had originally been owned by three Iranians – the Irani brothers – who called it the 3i's. It became the 2i's when one of the brothers pulled out of the partnership. It was not a successful venture, and in April 1956 the lease was taken over by two Australian wrestlers, Ray Hunter and Paul Lincoln, who installed a juke-box in the place and started evening skiffle sessions in an attempt to breathe new life into an ailing business. For the first few months the music was free and all part of the service. Then along came Tommy Steele and turned everything upside down. The Bermondsey boy's success brought the 2i's unlimited publicity. It was featured in national newspapers and magazines, and the BBC even screened *Six Five Special* live from its cramped cellar.

When Paul Lincoln realized his customers were spending all night in the basement listening to the music, and only purchasing a single cup of coffee and maybe a cheese roll for an evening's entertainment, he acted swiftly and introduced an entrance fee of 1s (5p) which rapidly doubled. At the same time, Lofty became the very watchful doorman. He was a great character, a 6ft 3in matchstick of a man who determined who could go into the coffee bar and who should stay outside. Tom Littlewood was brought in as manager, and most evenings he sat by the door of the basement collecting the admission money.

In January 1956 Wally Whyton and the Vipers were lured away from the Breadbasket to become the 2i's resident group. They were not paid, but were allowed to pass the hat round the audience on three occasions during the evening. When, through the sheer weight of numbers packed into the room, this proved an impossibility, Paul Lincoln agreed a weekly wage. The Vipers followed Tommy Steele into the charts.

Within twelve months the catalogue of young musicians who had made it into the hit parade or on to national television after being given their first strike at stardom in the 2i's coffee bar was formidable: Adam Faith, Marty Wilde, Terry Dene and Wee Willie Harris (who were both managed by Paul Lincoln), Vince Eager and Billy Fury.

There were more to follow. Lincoln's policy of 'giving kids the opportunity to show just what they could do', as he was reported in a national newspaper as saying, had a double effect: the 2i's became a haven for agents, managers and impresarios on the look-out for new talent to discover. It also brought over 5,000 teenage hopefuls flocking in his door each year for that opportunity. If they were lucky, they were auditioned and given a booking; if not, they moved on to the next coffee bar or club, and there were plenty of them around. Hank and I were two of the lucky ones, and we were booked to play at the 2i's for three nights each week. We worked well together as a singing duo, performing Everly Brothers material and Buddy Holly songs. Hank, with his horn-rimmed glasses, bore more than a passing resemblance to the American singer, and he could play all Buddy Holly's lead breaks and guitar solos, which he had religiously learnt from the record.

It was uncanny.

Two years later, in February 1960, during Cliff Richard's first tour of America, we appeared in Holly's home town of Lubbock, Texas, just a year after he had been killed. Ten thousand people packed into the arena to see the show. By now Hank was playing a Fender Stratocaster guitar and when this lean and lanky figure with the guitar and the horn-rimmed glasses bounced out on stage, the whole place went silent. From the auditorium, and in the distance, Hank looked exactly like Buddy Holly. It was an unnerving experience and a very weird feeling. After the show, Buddy's father Laurence Holley (Buddy dropped the 'e' from his surname after it was misspelt on his first recording contract) came backstage to meet us all. He was a lovely man and quite taken with Hank.

Right from the start of our association with the coffee bar, Hank built a strong reputation for himself as a very competent guitarist, which was acknowledged by all the musicians who worked the clubs in the area. By now our voices were blending well together and we were able to handle intricate harmonies. We also complemented each other on guitar and soon became known to regulars as the Geordie Boys.

We were required to appear for four hours each night, usually from 7 till 11 pm, but even we couldn't play for anything like that amount of time on our limited repertoire. We usually performed for half an hour before we were joined on stage by any musician who happened to be in the audience, and frantic jam sessions ensued. People just appeared from the throng and started to play. It was a party atmosphere – nothing was planned. In a sense we were like buskers, and the place attracted musicians like a magnet.

The whole coffee-bar scene was alive and thriving. Regulars included our old friend Pete Chester, a country-and-western singer called Rick Richards, Mickie Most, and Tony Sheridan, who like Hank was a brilliant guitarist. When Tony failed to make any headway in England he moved on to Germany, where he made a name for himself in the sleazy clubs and beer cellars. It was here, in 1961, that he had the distinction of recording eight songs for producer Bert Kaempfert with a group of unknown Liverpool lads who went under the name of the Beat Brothers. From that session a raucous version of the traditional Scottish song 'My Bonnie' coupled with 'When the Saints', featuring Tony on lead vocals with the group providing harmony back-up, was released by Polydor under the group's real name of the Beatles. This led directly to their being discovered by Brian Epstein. However, Tony missed out on fame and fortune once again.

We all thought Vince Taylor was American. Whenever he played at the 2i's he was immaculately dressed in a tailored white jacket, black trousers and white buckskin shoes. He looked like Eddie Cochran and sneered when he sang, and he became a real moody rock star down in the basement. That was his attraction. Years later, after Vince had carved out a new career for himself as a singer in France, we discovered that he wasn't in fact from America after all, but from Hounslow.

We met Jet Harris in the 2i's. Like most musicians he dropped in from time to time when he was not working, and got up on stage to lend a hand with the musical proceedings. He wanted to be James Dean. He dyed his hair blond and used Vitapointe to make it shine. He was one of the best musicians I had ever come across, an accomplished bass player and one of the innovators of the electric bass guitar. He was extremely versatile and could play in any kind of musical style that was required (I certainly couldn't – it was hard enough trying to play what I knew), and I think we were a little in awe of him because of his outstanding talent. Jet was very much in demand as an instrumentalist and toured regularly. If anyone needed a bass player, Jet was their man. He appeared in variety with Wee Willie Harris on the Moss Empire circuit, alongside a bill that featured jugglers, acrobats, singers, dancers and speciality acts of all kinds, and he worked with many other budding stars, including Don Lang and Terry Dene. At one point he briefly became a member of the Vipers.

Early one evening during the summer of 1958, on one of the

rare occasions that Hank, Jet and I appeared together on stage at the 2i's, a pale-faced, jaunty youngster breezed into the basement to watch the show. After a few minutes, and prompted by a friend, he nervously asked if he could sit in on drums. There was a kit permanently set up at the back of the tiny rostrum for just such eventualities. We hadn't seen him in the coffee bar before and we were naturally a little apprehensive about him joining us, as he couldn't have been more than fifteen years old. (We were old men at sixteen.) We agreed to give him a chance, and he surprised us all. Even with our limited musical experience it was easy to see just how good a drummer he was. His name was Tony Meehan, and although we had no way of knowing, it was the first time the group that would eventually become known as the Shadows ever played together.

Tony was still at school, but on the strength of that one performance he was spotted by an agent and asked to join Adam Faith's former backing group, the Worried Men. From there he became a regular on the circuit – which was a confusing and ever-changing network of musicians who would often play with three or four different backing groups at the same time, their allegiances going to whoever paid the most money. In September, Hank took part in the musicians' shuffle when he joined a newly reformed Vipers, along with Tony Meehan and Jet Harris, for a series of engagements on the road. It could easily have meant the end of the Geordie Boys partnership, but Hank lasted a week before he returned to London. After seven days in Birmingham, he realized he didn't fit in.

Brian Bennett, the drummer from Errol Hollis and the Velvets, who had so impressed us at the Edmonton talent contest, was an old hand on the scene. He had been playing at the 2i's as part of the Tony Sheridan Trio, with Brian 'Licorice' Locking on bass, long before we arrived in London. He was one of the best drummers to come out of the 2i's; another was Bob Woodman, who played with Vince Taylor. In the space of two years, Brian backed a variety of artistes including Vince Eager, Vince Taylor and the Red Peppers.

He worked regularly for Larry Parnes, who was a frequent visitor to the basement club on the look-out for talent. Larry was revered by everyone who came into contact with him, and whenever he walked into the coffee bar a buzz of excitement went round the place. Quite simply, he was the most successful manager in the rock 'n' roll business and had the power to make or break a new act. He often organized his entire concert package tours around the musicians he came across playing in the 2i's, forming backing groups and fit-up bands, which usually included Brian on drums, to accompany his growing stable of teenage protégés like Dickie Pride, Duffy Power and Johnny Gentle.

By 1959 Brian was touring regularly with Larry Parnes's discovery Marty Wilde, as a member of the Wilde Cats, one of the few British bands that could hold their own against any of their American counterparts. The band featured Licorice Locking on bass and 'Big' Jim Sullivan on guitar. The following year he joined the ill-fated Gene Vincent–Eddie Cochran tour that ended in tragedy when Cochran was killed in a car smash a few miles outside Chippenham in Wiltshire.

Money was the great motivator for us all. Hank and I earned 18s (90p) for our nightly performance at the coffee bar, which we thought was a fair return. After all, it wasn't hard work and we enjoyed ourselves. Some acts received nothing. According to Tom Littlewood, an appearance at the 2i's was still looked upon principally as a chance to be seen in a showcase for new talent. When Harry Webb and the Drifters appeared there, they were given just 10s (50p) between them.

Years later we found out that we should have been paid £1 per session. Tom Littlewood, who handed the money over at the end of each evening, deliberately took 10 per cent from each musician's wage packet for himself by way of commission and as an agent's fee. He was a powerful man who determined whether you worked or didn't, so we tried to keep in with him and not upset him too much. We wanted to eat. And we wanted to succeed.

When we got to know Tom Littlewood better he allowed us down into the cellar in the afternoons to rehearse. We jumped at the chance because it gave us somewhere to go during the day, when time tended to drag. It was far better than moping around our Finsbury Park bedsit, or staying in bed all day. Inevitably other such privileged musicians would drop in for afternoon music sessions.

On the nights when we weren't required to play, Tom Littlewood paid us to work the orange machine downstairs, so we were always near the hub of the action. The 2i's manager had a unique system of accounting. He worked out how much orange juice had been sold, and subsequently the takings for the evening, by counting the number of paper cups that had been used. He thought it was a foolproof method. What he didn't realize was that by re-using the discarded cups several times over, we could actually charge the same amount for each drink and pocket the money ourselves before anyone found out. We got our friends to bring their cups back to us once they had finished with them, so that we could recycle them until they were soggy and falling apart. At the end of the evening the number of cups issued matched the amount of money taken and Tom was happy.

Besides owning the coffee bar, Paul Lincoln had continued his career as a professional wrestler, fighting under the awesome title of 'Dr Death'. In the ring he wore a black mask, and his identity was a closely guarded secret from the fans. Few of the punters who walked into the club at night knew of his alter ego, although it was well known that he was in the fight game. Paul was a charming man, we all liked him, but we were all scared stiff of him, too. He also staged and promoted his own bouts in venues across London, and employed me to help erect the wrestling rings. It was sheer murder. I was well built and fairly strong, but it was physically exhausting. Still, I would do almost anything for money in those days.

When things were really tight and we hadn't even enough money to get back to Finsbury Park, we would try to get out of paying our Underground fare by ducking under the barrier, or promising the collector we would pay at the other end. Hopping on and off buses without buying a ticket was another ruse. If that didn't work we had to look for somewhere else to sleep. Euston station became a favourite spot. Before it was modernized, the booking hall contained several huge, old-fashioned iron radiators that provided a lot of warmth and a little comfort. If we were lucky we could literally climb on top of one of the radiators to sleep until 5 am, when the tea bar opened. Invariably we were rudely awakened and told to move on by the railway police, despite our impassioned pleas that we were only waiting to catch the 5.30 am train to wherever we could think of.

At other times I stayed overnight with Jet in a basement flat in Eccleston Square, Victoria, owned by Johnny Booker, one of the Vipers. I slept on the floor.

Jet kept a monkey called Elvis in the flat as a pet. Elvis had the complete run of the apartment, and used to relieve himself from either end with amazing regularity whenever he felt like it. It was an absolutely horrendous experience waking up the following morning to the acrid, overpowering stench of monkey shit everywhere. It was a wonder that none of us was struck down by some dreadful tropical disease. It put me off monkeys for life.

The 2i's was the perfect place to meet girls. Wally Whyton maintained that it was the easiest venue in London for 'pulling the birds', as he so delicately put it. But he was right; they seemed to stack them up in the basement, and on most nights the girls in the audience outnumbered the men quite considerably. Lofty, on the door, would rarely turn away a pretty face. It was in the 2i's that Brian Bennett met a young nurse called Margaret who was to become his wife, and where I met the girl who was destined to become Mrs Bruce Welch.

Anne Findley was a charmer. She lived in Peabody Buildings, a council block in Westminster, and worked for a linen company in the posh part of Bond Street. Her father had been a sailor and had served on HMS *Hood* during the war. He was on shore leave when the British battleship was sunk in the Atlantic by the German warship *Bismarck*. Only a handful of his 1,421 shipmates survived. Anne had come to the coffee bar for a night out and very nearly ended up knocked out and in hospital, when one of the speakers fell off the wall and hit her on the head. As usual the basement was packed to capacity, and the continual vibration from the loud music, dancing and stomping around must have shaken it free from its mounting. When I saw what was happening, I rushed to help her. We got to know each other better over a cup of coffee upstairs and soon started going steady. After that we met all the time and, because she was working, Anne used to support me by donating 2s (10p) each day to enable me to buy a bowl of soup and a bread roll, and ward off the pangs of hunger which were never far away.

In those days, long before the introduction of the Pill, you were expected to marry your steady girlfriend, and it was traditional that you asked the girl's father for her hand in marriage. So on Saturday, 29 August 1959, a year after we met, Anne and I were married at St Stephen's Church, Westminster. It wasn't forced upon us, and ours certainly wasn't a shotgun wedding as so many of them were at that time. We were as in love as any two seventeen-year-olds could be. I believed that getting married would be a steadying influence, giving me the one thing I had lacked all my life and wanted so desperately – the love and security of a family unit of my own. Someone to share my life with, to enjoy the good times and overcome the bad together. It was during the preparations for the wedding that I discovered that I was illegitimate.

My best man at the ceremony was Cliff Richard, and the church was besieged by thousands of girls trying to get a glimpse of their rock 'n' rolling idol. After the ceremony we had to rush off and record a programme for BBC Television, so a honeymoon was out. I spent my wedding night in the flat I now shared with Hank in East Finchley, and my Geordie friend came along, too. Anne and I had not been in bed long when our amorous goings-on were interrupted by a terrible pounding on our front door accompanied by cries of 'let me in, let me in'. It was Hank and his girlfriend Billie, who had forgotten the key. I should have ignored him. So much for friends.

I had first seen Cliff Richard one night in the 2i's back in the summer of 1958, while I was working the orange machine. For some reason Hank had stayed at home in Holly Park and I was on my own. Cliff was a revelation. Even raw and inexperienced as he was then, he was an exciting performer, and you could see he was in a different class. He had a very young-sounding and appealing voice. I had heard a lot of singers at the 2i's over the last few months, and I knew immediately that he was way ahead of them all. The audience loved him, too. He looked amazing – olive-skinned, dark haired, moody – the very essence of what rock 'n' roll was all about. I was impressed. Back home at Mrs Bowman's, Hank quizzed me about the evening.

'Many in tonight?' he asked, without waiting for an answer. 'Anything special happen? Don't expect so.'

'Yeah,' I replied in answer to his second question. 'There was a guy in who went down a bomb. He gave them the full works. Looked a bit like Elvis. He was terrific.'

'Seen him before?' Hank was interested now.

'No.'

'What's he called?'

'Cliff Richard.'

'Oh!' he paused. 'Anything to eat?'

What we didn't realize was that within a couple of months Cliff Richard would become one of the biggest stars in Britain and we would be a part of his success. At that moment we were too busy wondering where our next meal was coming from.

5

'Let's Have a Riot'

Without doubt, 'Move It' by Cliff Richard was the very first genuine British rock 'n' roll record, and proved that we could at last compete on equal terms with the USA. It was unique to this country, unlike so many other early British attempts which simply copied everything American.

'Move It' borrowed nothing from across the Atlantic and breathed new life and fire into the British music industry, which had stagnated for much too long. Until then our own hit parade had been a pale imitation of the *Billboard* national pop charts in the States. It was swamped by American artistes, domestic crooners, cover versions of American songs and comedy or novelty records. Indeed in the first weeks of September 1958, when Cliff Richard entered the Top Thirty for the first time, the make-up and content of the chart had changed little throughout the year. The great rock 'n' roll pioneers were, as usual, well represented: Elvis was on his way down with 'Hard Headed Woman', the Everly Brothers had just vacated the No. 1 spot (ironically, to the Kalin Twins' 'When') after seven weeks at the top with 'All I Have to Do Is Dream'; Buddy Holly had three songs in the Top Twenty with 'Rave On', 'Early in the Morning' and 'Think It Over'; and Ricky Nelson was climbing with 'Poor Little Fool'. The crooners were out in force too, with Dean Martin ('Return to Me' and 'Volare'), Pat Boone ('Sugar Moon'), Vic Damone ('On the Street Where You Live') and Perry Como ('Moon Talk'), while Britain's only other contribution came from Tony Brent ('Girl of My Dreams'), Michael Holiday ('Stairway of Love'), Marty Wilde, who was Cliff's great rival in the home-grown rock 'n' rolling stakes, with a cover version of Jody Reynolds's 'Endless Sleep' which was even better than the original version, and comedians Max Bygraves ('Tulips from Amsterdam'/'You Need Hands'), Charlie Drake ('Hello My Darlings'/'Splish Splash') and Bernard Bresslaw ('Mad Passionate Love'). Significantly, it was during that same month that 'Rebel Rouser', by Duane Eddy, the first major guitar instrumental record, also came into the reckoning. It was to prove a big influence on Hank and me.

But the song that was to revolutionize British rock 'n' roll was recorded in three takes and had actually been intended for the B-side of Cliff's first single. Producer Norrie Paramor, head of A & R at Columbia, had chosen the Bobby Helms number 'Schoolboy Crush' as the featured side, and the record was issued as such on 29 August. It was only when Radio Luxembourg played the flip-side, 'Move It', instead, that other disc jockeys followed, and it wasn't long before 'Schoolboy Crush' was ignored completely. The Bobby Helms composition paled into insignificance.

Over thirty years later, 'Move It' is still a classic. The song had been written by Ian 'Sammy' Samwell, the Drifters' original guitarist, on the top of a double-decker bus on the way from London Colney to Cheshunt, and given its title by Cliff's first manager, John Foster. The lyrics were based on recurring but unfounded newspaper reports that rock 'n' roll was beginning to fade and go out of fashion. Sammy was in the Royal Air Force at the time, stationed at Hendon, but he was allowed to live at home in St Albans on compassionate grounds because his mother was ill. He was due to complete his national service and be demobilized in a matter of weeks.

Ian Samwell was to play a vitally important part in Cliff Richard's career. He had first seen Harry Webb and the Drifters, as they were originally called, performing at the 2i's, where he realized that the group was badly in need of a lead guitarist to augment the sound, which was good, but could have been better. He told the singer as much during a break and offered his own services. The singer agreed, and Ian became the third member of the Drifters alongside Terry Smart on drums and Norman Mitham on guitar. Sammy appeared with the group whenever the RAF allowed him a night off, although Cliff remembers that 'he seemed to be on continuous leave'. Shortly afterwards when Norman Mitham left the group, Ian switched to bass.

On Thursday, 24 July 1958 Cliff Richard and the Drifters recorded 'Move It' and 'Schoolboy Crush' in EMI's Studio Two in Abbey Road, North London, where four years later the Beatles would begin their prolific recording career. It was here in 1967 that *Sgt Pepper* was conceived and recorded.

Initially Norrie Paramor wanted to record the song using only studio musicians as the back-up group, but after much persuasion he reluctantly allowed Terry Smart and Ian Samwell to play as well. They were joined by two of the country's leading session men, Frank Clarke on stand-up bass, and lead guitarist Ernie Shears, who created the magnificent descending introduction to the song and the question-and-answer lead breaks at the end of each line. Ernie never played anything quite so effective again. For that session he was paid the standard session Musicians' Union fee of £6 10s (£6.50). Both Hank and I would have dearly loved to play on that record – and been in at the start of history in the making. 'Move It' went on to reach No. 2 in the charts in the first week of November.

Like so many of us, Cliff Richard had been heavily influenced by Elvis Presley. 'He was my idol,' he once told me. 'I guess it goes without saying that Elvis, the performer, was about as big an influence as his music. I spent hours in front of the mirror, miming to his records and polishing the movements: the curl of the lip, the hip swivel, the gyrating legs. If there had been no Elvis, there certainly could have been no Cliff Richard. Personally, he mattered that much.' Buddy Holly said the same: 'Without Elvis none of us could have made it.'

Cliff even tried to sing like Elvis when he formed his first group, the Quintones, with a few friends at the local Holy Trinity Church youth club in Cheshunt, where he lived. Shortly after he had left school and started work as a credit control clerk at Atlas Lamps, Cliff joined the Dick Teague Skiffle Group, where he met drummer Terry Smart. The two of them were far more interested in playing rock 'n' roll than skiffle, so within a few weeks they broke away on their own. With the help of an old school friend, Norman Mitham, they formed Harry Webb and the Drifters and were soon playing at local youth clubs and dances. It was at the Five

Horseshoes public house in Hoddesden that they were discovered by a local sewage worker by the name of John Foster, who offered to become their manager. With £10 borrowed from his parents, Foster paid for the group to record a demonstration tape of 'Breathless' and 'Lawdy Miss Clawdy' at the HMV record store in Oxford Street, which he then hawked around all the leading record companies looking for a deal. The first major engagement he secured for them was a week's residency at the 2i's in Old Compton Street, for the grand fee of 10s (50p) a night, which just about paid for the late-night taxi home. While they were appearing at the Soho coffee bar they were booked for a one-night stand in a Derby ballroom, but the manager insisted on a name change. 'Harry Webb,' he said, 'is not a very good name for a rock 'n' roll singer. It'll have to go.'

A meeting was hastily convened in the Swiss public house a few doors along from the 2i's, from where Harry Webb emerged as Cliff Richard, by way of Russ Clifford and Cliff Russard. It was John Foster's idea, but Ian Samwell added the finishing touch when he suggested that the name should be Richard *without* the 's'. He figured that people would be sure to get the name wrong at first and call him Cliff Richards. 'Cliff could make a point of correcting them,' he said. 'Then on radio and television he'll get the name mentioned *twice*.' Ian was already predicting the big time. It was a brilliant piece of strategy and so right.

Sammy also came up with an agent for Cliff and the group in the shape of a former adagio dancer turned impresario, George Ganjou, whose name and telephone number he picked at random out of the *Stage*, the theatrical profession's trade newspaper. Through George, Cliff auditioned for Norrie Paramor, who was sufficiently impressed by his talent to offer him a long-term contract with Columbia records at the age of seventeen.

Two weeks after his first single was recorded, Cliff quit the Atlas Lamp company and turned to music full-time. His first professional engagement followed, entertaining holiday-makers for a short season at Butlin's in Clacton, and when he returned home to Cheshunt, wondering where the next engagement would come from he was signed up for his first British tour with the American singing sensations, the Kalin Twins, for £200 a week.

He couldn't believe it. Until then he had been lucky to clear £10 a week.

It was as a direct result of being asked to go on the tour that Hank and I eventually joined Terry Smart and Ian Samwell as members of the Drifters for a weekly fee of £12 10s (£12.50p) each, out of which we had to find our own accommodation on the road and our food. Still, anything was better than starving at Mrs Bowman's.

On 13 September, Ian Samwell's prediction came true, when Cliff Richard made his television début on Jack Good's *Oh Boy* for ABC Television – ironically, after failing an audition for the BBC's *Six Five Special* – and he was seen by a viewing audience of 5 million people. On screen he looked edgy and nervous, but the raw material for success was there in abundance – the dark and sultry good looks, a superb voice for rock 'n' roll and a tremendous presence for television. The camera liked him; the girls in the studio audience screamed incessantly throughout his two featured numbers. Jack Good could see the reaction Cliff was creating and, sensing the outcome, he was convinced he had discovered a major rock 'n' roll star. 'He sounded like a rock 'n' roll singer,' said Jack, 'better than anything we had.' The forthcoming tour proved it.

Cliff Richard's first British tour with the Drifters, including the two new recruits from the 2i's, opened at the Victoria Hall, Hanley, near Stoke-on-Trent, on Sunday, 5 October. It was headlined by Hal and Herbie, the Kalin Twins, whom we regarded as mega-stars. All recording artistes from America in those days were big news. We admired and respected them even more because they had recently topped the British chart with their single 'When', and we envied them and their success a little, too. They were in fact two very pleasant and ordinary brothers from Washington, DC, who were slightly overawed by the situation they found themselves in and by all the adulation.

The show also featured Eddie Calvert with his 'Golden Trumpet' as special guest star. Earlier in the year he had enjoyed hit parade success with 'Mandy', following his two chart-topping singles, 'Oh Mein Papa' in 1953, and 'Cherry Pink and Apple Blossom White' two years later. It was completed by the Londonaires and the Most Brothers, who in show-business tradition were not really brothers. Mickie Most, whose real name was Michael Hayes, and Alex Murray (real name Alex Wharton) had both been regulars at the 2i's, trying, like Hank and me, to emulate the Everly Brothers, but with little success. To be honest, they weren't very good. Indeed, Mickie once described the duo as being like 'the Everly Brothers with bad harmonies'.

The Most Brothers lasted no more than eighteen months together before they went their own separate ways, which seemed to be the fate of so many British double acts which tried to copy Don and Phil. None of them really made it. Mickie took himself off to South Africa, where he enjoyed a lucrative career covering Cliff Richard records before returning home. Strangely enough, within a handful of years, Mickie and Alex both established their names on the other side of the music industry as record producers. Alex Murray produced the Moody Blues' outstanding single 'Go Now', while his former partner ended up with his own record label (RAK), a publishing company, and a whole stable of stars whom he produced, including the Animals (for whom he produced 'House of the Rising Sun'), Herman's Hermits, Lulu, Hot Chocolate, Mud, Suzi Quatro and Kim Wilde.

Although they were only one of the supporting acts, the Most Brothers carried with them on tour their own backing group, which featured two old friends from the coffee-bar circuit, Pete Chester on drums and Jet Harris on bass. Jet occasionally sat in with Cliff and the Drifters and doubled up with Ian Samwell to give our overall sound extra depth. Cliff paid him £3 a night. After the first night, Mickie and Alex asked Hank to join their line-up too, and by the third night – at the Ritz cinema, Wigan – Hank's guitar technique so impressed the Kalin Twins that they too asked him to play for them, and offered him an extra £5 a week. At the end of the tour, Hank B. Marvin was the busiest musician on the road, and he made more money than anyone else.

That first tour was an eye-opener for me. On opening night the Victoria Hall was packed to capacity. It looked cavernous. Twenty-five years later, Hank and I paid a nostalgic return visit to the theatre to re-live a few memories of that tour. When I went inside I couldn't believe how small and compact it was in comparison to how I remembered it. Another shattered illusion!

But at the time I had never seen so many people jammed into a theatre for a rock 'n' roll show.

Cliff tore the place apart with a truly dynamic performance, which we soon came to expect each night. He took command of his audience right from the start, and had them eating out of his hand. He was still totally inexperienced, but nonetheless had that natural magic and star quality that produces a bond between audience and performer. There was an instant reaction to his singing which has rightly continued unabated for thirty years. We knew he was quite well known from the appearances he made on television's *Oh Boy*, but we had not anticipated anything like this. Screams, chants, squeals, scenes of mass hysteria greeted each number we performed. Every time Cliff gyrated his hips or wiggled his legs, the reaction intensified ten-fold as the screams got louder and more piercing. Hank and I used to encourage him. 'Come on, Cliff,' we would call. 'Let's have a riot.' When Cliff obliged, the theatre erupted even more and the fans stormed the stage.

We had rehearsed the musical content of our act – the five songs we were going to feature on stage – one afternoon a few days before in the front room of Cliff's council house in Cheshunt, but had paid no attention to any kind of stage movements. I suppose we thought we could leave that sort of thing to Cliff, while we concentrated on our playing. However, when we attacked the old Jerry Lee Lewis number, 'Whole Lotta Shakin'', midway through our spot, Cliff decided to have some fun. As the song reached the chorus – 'Shake, baby, shake' – Cliff started to crouch down on stage, each dip of his body accompanied by even more squealing. As he got lower, so too did the volume at which the band played. 'Shake, baby, shake. Shake, baby, shake.' It was an old trick employed to great effect by Bill Haley and the Comets. So Hank, Sammy Samwell and I followed Cliff's lead, until we were all lying flat out on our backs on the stage and still playing. Slowly we increased the volume and the intensity, to build into a dynamic crescendo, and the plan was for all four of us to spring up into the air at the same time. The trouble was, I couldn't get up and play at the same time. It was impossible. I was stuck on the stage floor, staring at the ceiling like an upturned turtle, unable to move. I turned to Hank, who was in a similar prone position. 'I'm stuck. Play rhythm for me while I get up,' I called to him over the roar of the music, and then I tried in a most undignified manner to stand. I couldn't stop giggling, which made things worse. When I finally clambered to my feet, I found I was covered in dust and grime from the stage. The audience loved it, thinking it was all part of the act, and screamed even louder.

I don't think Cliff fully realized what effect he was having on his audience. It was frightening. When we played 'Move It', the whole auditorium exploded in a frenzy of hysteria. We stopped the show every single time, which was the last thing the Kalin Twins wanted because they simply couldn't follow us. We opened the second half of the show each night, immediately before Hal and Herbie's performance. When they went out on stage, unfortunately, the whole atmosphere dropped dramatically. The reaction from the audience was tepid, and they were shouted down most nights with cries of 'We want Cliff! We want Cliff!'

It was embarrassing for everyone, most of all the two Americans. At one point they even asked if we would move to an earlier spot in the programme so that they wouldn't have to follow us. But Cliff refused to budge. 'Our contract said we would open the second half,' he said, 'and we are sticking to it.' Professionally, it was exactly the right thing to do. All the resulting publicity about a new British singer eclipsing one of America's top acts could not have been more timely. When we started touring, 'Move It' slipped into the Top Twenty at No. 19, and three weeks later, on the day we played our final concert, it had reached No. 4.

For twenty-one days Cliff was mobbed every night; the stage door at each theatre was besieged by girls waiting for him after every show. When he celebrated his eighteenth birthday on 14 October at the De Montfort Hall in Leicester, the stage was showered with flowers in his honour and the whole audience rose to sing 'Happy Birthday'. The Kalin Twins didn't stand a chance. That was the only time Cliff was booked as a support act. Even before the tour was completed, the promoter was negotiating for him to headline on his own.

The tour took Hank and me back to Newcastle for a memorable reunion with family and friends at the City Hall. Six months earlier we had left the city penniless, with just a suitcase and a guitar and plenty of dreams. We returned, not exactly in triumph – that was to come later – but we had certainly made something of ourselves, even if it was only temporary. Aunt Sadie came to see the show. She was glowing with pride and pleasure that I was doing something I wanted with my life. I don't think she particularly liked the music, though. Nazam was told to stay away.

The Kalin Twins' tour of 1958 was one of the very first pop package shows in Britain that attempted to cater exclusively for the growing new teenage audience. However, once again we were copying something that had been in existence across the Atlantic for several years. With the emergence of rock 'n' roll, record-buying teenagers created an overwhelming demand to see their favourite singing stars performing live on stage, instead of just hearing them on disc. Yet despite the music's popularity, there were still no specialist places for them to play, and apart from a few independently owned theatres, the only venues open to promoters were the chains of theatres run by the Stoll and Moss Empire circuits, which were heavily booked and very strictly controlled, presenting only *weeks* of variety. So one-off concerts were out. There were so many of these Empires, Palaces and Grands around the country that artistes could tour for thirty-six consecutive weeks and never play the same theatre twice, and they were the life-blood of the British entertainment industry for a long time. It wasn't too long, in fact, before Cliff Richard and the Drifters toured in variety on the same circuit.

However, the kids wanted something different. They wanted non-stop rock 'n' roll without the trimmings of jugglers, acrobats or speciality acts interrupting the music. So a new form of touring show emerged, featuring bills packed with up-and-coming pop stars and established recording artistes, put together by imaginative young entrepreneurs who saw a very lucrative gap in the music market-place. People like Arthur Howes and Danny Betesh, among many others, made names for themselves as pop and rock concert promoters alongside Larry Parnes and some of the more established agents, and helped to pioneer this new form of entertainment. To challenge the stranglehold of the established theatre groups, they turned their attention to the vast, untapped network of provincial cinemas and booked their shows into the ABCs, Gaumonts, Odeons and Granadas for twice-nightly one-night stands. A whole new rock 'n' roll circuit grew and flourished well into the 1960s.

We travelled to each new destination on the tour by coach. A dozen or more young and starry-eyed pop entertainers, herded together like troupes of boy scouts or national servicemen, re-creating the spirit and camaraderie of the concert party of the 1920s, or the American Big Band tours of the 1940s – a different stop every day – under the sole direction of one tour manager. It was his job to make sure the tour ran smoothly and that we all arrived at the venues on time, did the show at 6.15 and 8.30 pm and then duly assembled next morning at a specific time and rendezvous point, to be picked up by the coach and whisked away to our next destination.

What we did in between shows was of no concern to him, as long as we were in the right place at the right time when we were needed. We generally were. The tour manager had an awesome task controlling so many people and, looking back, I am amazed that everything generally ran smoothly. Most tours started in London from Great Cumberland Place or Allsop Place, behind the Planetarium and Madame Tussaud's, off Baker Street, where on many Sunday mornings over the years the cream of British rock 'n' roll assembled their gear, waiting for the coach to pick them up and take them off on another musical extravaganza.

There were no lavatories on board the coach, so we were continually asking the driver to stop for tea and relief breaks. There were no motorways in those days, either, and often travelling from town to town along crowded main roads took several hours. Schedules had to be strictly adhered to. If anyone missed the coach they had to find their own way to the next stop-off point. The bus rarely waited for stragglers and we all knew the rules. To alleviate the monotony of endless hours of travelling, everyone mucked in together, and the impromptu jam sessions and sing-songs were often far better on the bus than we performed nightly on stage.

We all had to carry our own suitcases and equipment, and as soon as we arrived at our next engagement, usually around mid-afternoon, we all trooped out of the band-wagon into the theatre, plugged in the amps and ran through a quick sound-check on stage in the time available. For that first tour we actually had to borrow two amplifiers: a small Selmer 15-watt combination amp and a Vox AC15. Terry Smart carried his own drum kit with him, and we used the house public address system for vocals. The other acts made their own arrangements. It was the only equipment we needed. On some tours, all the acts used a single communal drum kit and shared three amplifiers – plus one spare in case of failure or breakdown – supplied by the promoter. It was very primitive, but it was all there was available to us in the way of musical equipment. We were all serving a valuable apprenticeship and, though we didn't know it at the time, pioneering a whole new industry.

Nowadays, with the advancements in musical technology and such highly sophisticated instruments and equipment, the big tours employ a whole army of technicians on the road to make sure the artistes are staged and presented in the best possible way. There are people to design the lighting and operate the lasers and special stage effects. There are sound engineers; teams to erect the lighting gantries and stages; technicians to tune and maintain the instruments and organize the wealth of equipment which accompanies many tours. There are stage crews and riggers; front of house staff; merchandising operators; accountants, bookkeepers; dressers and hairdressers; make-up artists; publicists; security men; drivers and humpers; movers and removers. People to set the gear up on stage and people to take it down afterwards. There is even a pecking order of personal assistants and their assistants, and separate specialist caterers for the crew and the artistes, to see that no one goes hungry. Gone are the days of stopping off at transport cafés on the road for a ten-minute break for a mug of tea, a plate of chips and a bacon sandwich. These days even the most exotic food is laid on as a matter of course.

When Pink Floyd undertook their massive 1987/8 global tour, which took in appearances in some of the largest outdoor venues in the world, they carried with them a back-up team of 107 stage crew and personnel to look after the equipment and the intricate stage sets, plus sound and lighting technicians, and ten tour managers and assistants. Equipment which generated 800,000 watts of sound was transported in twenty-five custom-built, pantechnicon lorries. The road crew and administrative staff toured separately by plane or executive transport. When Genesis toured the previous year, they carried a road crew of over fifty people with them.

Set against those figures, the Shadows' own current requirements seem minimal. These days we tour with a back-up crew of six people, which includes lighting and sound designers, and technicians to look after and service the guitars and drums. On the stage we use just 100-watt Mesa Boogie amplifiers, which are *never* turned up to full capacity, after years of endorsing Vox equipment. In fact the Shadows' unique sound was fashioned from Vox amplification. We used it on tour and in the recording studio for over twenty-seven years, and only switched to the American amplifiers in 1986. We were just about to start a lengthy British tour when we took an ill-starred delivery of ten brand new Vox amps, and they all broke down in the rehearsal rooms. As an instrumental group, it was far too dangerous for us to take the risk of being let down on stage if the amplifiers failed. So we changed our loyalty. It was a tough decision for us to make, because I felt we grew up with Vox. All our good times had been shared with the British company, and it was Hank who had a hand in the development of the famous AC30 amplifier, which became part of rock 'n' roll history.

He had been using an AC15 for quite some time when he asked Jennings Music, the company that produced Vox equipment, if they would build an amp for him, containing two separate speakers instead of one. It resulted in the creation of the AC30, a 30-watt tube amplifier fitted with two celestion speakers which became a vital part of the equipment for many groups in the sixties, including the Rolling Stones, the Hollies, the Searchers and the Dave Clark Five. The Beatles actually played Shea Stadium, the 56,000-seater arena in New York and home of the New York Mets baseball team, using AC30s alone, although Paul McCartney's bass amp was a Vox AC50. Even today, Brian May gets that wonderfully distinctive guitar sound of his, which has become a feature of all Queen's records, by using a stack of AC30s linked together.

Touring has changed quite dramatically in the ensuing years. Today our own equipment is transported by one large articulated truck, while we each drive ourselves to and from the venues and rarely travel together. The tour bus has long gone, and yet I often wonder if some groups get the same kicks from being on the road as we did. Maybe the fun has gone out of touring; perhaps it has become far too technical; and in my opinion, sometimes the music is forgotten and takes a back seat for many artistes.

When Cliff Richard and the Drifters were booked to appear on tour with the Kalin Twins, the quality of his first record got us the engagement in the first place, and we were paid by the promoter. It wasn't a lot of money but we were paid a fee. Today, a number of up-and-coming artistes actually pay to appear as the support act on tour with major headliners. Record companies with a new act to break will often use part of their promotional budget to buy into a major tour, to the tune of tens of thousands of pounds. But it is money well spent, because the rewards can be spectacular. The prestige value of supporting with one of the world's top-line acts is immeasurable, and they benefit also through the publicity surrounding such a tour. Exposure in this way can lead to millions of record sales. Recently, T'Pau, who supported Bryan Adams, and Wet, Wet, Wet, who toured with Lionel Ritchie, were launched in this way, and it has done them no harm at all.

Back in the fifties, everything was so new. Our main concern after arriving in each new town was to organize digs for ourselves. Usually the stage doorman had a list of likely places to stay which were cheap and cheerful and provided the basic requirements. Some of them, however, left a lot to be desired, and chances were that two or three of us would end up sharing a room together, sometimes even the same bed. All overnight accommodation costs came out of our own pockets, so we went for the cheapest available, and there was great rivalry between us to see who could come up with the least expensive room for the night. On the opening night of the Kalin Twins' tour we shared with an Irishman who had to be up at six the following morning, and he was already in bed when we booked in during the afternoon. After the evening show we had to tiptoe around the room so that we didn't disturb our room-mate.

On another occasion Hank and Tony Meehan were not so fortunate. They had to share a room with one of the tour officials, called Dave, who arrived back at the digs after a gig in an acute stage of drunkenness. It was a wonder he could remember exactly where he was staying. He was senseless with drink, and rolled around the tiny room hitting all four walls as he tried to make out the shape of his own bed in the darkness. As he stumbled over what little furniture there was in the room, he whimpered, and between agonizing bouts of retching he groaned, 'Neveragain, Neveragain,' the words seeming to merge into each other. Hank and Tony had been in bed for some time following the evening's performance, and their sleep was abruptly halted by Dave's ungainly entrance. They watched him stagger around the confined space, as if he was trying to put two feet into one trouser leg, before he collapsed like a beached whale on to the floor. The whole house seemed to shake.

'That'll teach him a lesson,' Hank whispered to Tony, and they both drifted back to sleep.

When they awoke, the room was like a disaster zone. Dave had been sick in virtually every corner. The smell was overpowering, so Hank and Tony did the only sensible thing. They packed their belongings together and left as quickly as they could. They flew down the stairs and into the street. It was fast approaching dawn when they arrived at the theatre where they had appeared on stage the night before. Luckily they found an open window, climbed inside, and slept in one of the dressing-rooms until the coach arrived later in the day. When Dave turned up at the coach, looking none the worse for his experience the night before, he nonchalantly informed the boys that he had told the landlady that *they* were responsible for the appalling mess.

'That's why you left in such a hurry,' he added.

No one ever shared a room with Dave again. It was far too dangerous.

Sometimes when there were no digs available we checked out the local youth hostels and YMCAs, or slept on the coach, parked in some municipal car park, or at the back of the theatre. We even slept in the theatre dressing-rooms when we were desperate. We were desperate quite often.

6

'WHAT DO YOU THINK OF THE NAME SHADOWS?'

As soon as the Kalin Twins' tour was completed, Hank and I were effectively out of a job and back to the old routine. When John Foster had come down to the coffee bar in September looking for a guitarist to join the Drifters and had signed us both up, the agreement we had struck was only for that one tour. We were realistic, and certainly did not expect a long-term commitment. At that time solo singers rarely carried a backing group of their own, preferring to pick up musicians – usually session men – whenever they were needed. Why should Cliff Richard be any different? After our final appearance, at the Colston Hall in Bristol, we returned to our room in Mrs Bowman's house in Holly Park, and within a couple of days the Geordie Boys went back to work at the 2i's – but not for long.

With the success of 'Move It', Cliff Richard became a regular on *Oh Boy*. He was rapidly emerging as one of the biggest rock 'n' roll stars in Britain, to rank alongside Tommy Steele (who by now was establishing his name in other directions in show business, and by the end of 1958 had completed three major films) and Marty Wilde. It was Marty whom Cliff replaced as resident singer on *Oh Boy*, in a blaze of publicity. Ever since the programme started Marty had been its front man: he was the image of *Oh Boy*. When Cliff Richard appeared for the first time, Marty's manager, Larry Parnes, accused producer Jack Good of undermining his artiste by 'developing the career of a virtually *unknown* singer' in direct competition to Marty Wilde, and withdrew Marty from the show after a heated argument. What annoyed Larry Parnes most of all was that he had auditioned Cliff Richard himself a few months before, and had turned him down. By the end of the year the dispute had been resolved and Marty was back in the fold, sharing the limelight and centre stage with Cliff. He went on to host Jack Good's follow-up series, *Boy Meets Girl*, and to enjoy substantial chart success over the next few years, scoring with cover versions of American hits like 'Donna' (originally recorded by Ritchie Valens), 'Teenager in Love' (Dion and the Belmonts), 'Sea of Love' (Phil Phillips and the Twilights) and 'Rubber Ball' (Bobby Vee), while in 1959 he proved he was more than just a cover artiste by writing the song 'Bad Boy' – it reached No.3. He also became the first British rock star to have a teenage magazine named after him. Later in his career, he followed Tommy Steele's lead and started to diversify his talents into other areas of the entertainment industry, including acting, producing and writing. In 1960 he was reported as saying, 'I am approaching twenty-one now, and I think it is about time to branch out. I want to drop most of the rock stuff and do real class stuff like Sinatra.'

Meanwhile, Cliff's performances on *Oh Boy* were coming in for an increasing amount of criticism. The *New Musical Express*, one of the more established of the pop papers, called his act 'the most crude exhibitionism ever seen on British television', and added: 'His violent hip-swinging was revolting . . . hardly the kind of performance any parent would wish his children to witness.' They went on: 'Tommy Steele became Britain's teenage idol without resorting to this form of indecent, short-sighted vulgarity.' The article, which was picked up by several national daily newspapers, had exactly the opposite effect to that intended and simply added to Cliff's popularity. Two months later the same *New Musical Express* voted Cliff Richard Britain's best new singer. There was no stopping him now, and by the end of the year George Ganjou had negotiated his first film role, playing the part of Curley Thompson, the tough-looking leader of a gang of teenage youths, in the movie *Serious Charge*. His co-stars were Anthony Quayle and Sarah Churchill. Cliff had to be on the set early each morning to have his hair specially curled with tongs.

By now it was obvious that Cliff Richard needed the tightness of a backing group, and he became the first British solo singer to have his own permanent band. So the Drifters were back in business and we were put on a wage of £25 a week. However, there was a change to the line-up. Ian Samwell, who realized he was not up to a sufficient standard as bass player, left the group, and Cliff asked Jet Harris to replace him.

Ian was developing into a very useful songwriter and had written Cliff's second single, 'High Class Baby', featuring the same line-up as 'Move It', which was released in November. It went on to reach No.7 in the charts the following month. He had also been approached by a publishing company to work for them on new songs, so his talent as a writer was very much in demand.

The story emerged that Sammy left the Drifters to concentrate on his writing, but I don't think he really wanted to leave the group. I believe he was politely asked to go, and that his limited ability as a bass player was cited as a reason. I know he wanted to persevere, and he was convinced that with time he could have become good enough to continue playing. He wasn't given the time. By comparison, Jet was such a great bass guitarist that he fitted in perfectly and completely enhanced the sound. Ian wasn't left out completely – he worked with the group in the capacity of manager cum road manager cum publicist for several months. He continued writing songs for Cliff, and enjoyed a great amount of success with 'Mean Streak', 'Fall in Love with You', and 'Gee Whiz It's You' – which all made the Top Ten – and 'Dynamite', which made the Top Twenty. He later carved out a secondary career for himself as a producer and was responsible for, among others, Georgie Fame's No.1 hit of 1966, 'Get Away'.

John Foster became another casualty when he was relieved of his duties as Cliff's manager. He was still only nineteen, and realized his own limitations in the music business. He knew he had taken Cliff as far as he could. He could go no further forward, and stepped down a rung to become Cliff's personal road manager. He was replaced by music publisher and song plugger Franklyn Boyd, who had discovered the song 'Schoolboy Crush' and had originally taken it to Norrie Paramor. He was an older man, who it was thought might have more influence over Cliff. George Ganjou might have had a hand in his appointment.

During the next few weeks the Drifters appeared on *Oh Boy* and undertook the odd Sunday concert. Then on 14 November 1958, Jet, Hank and I went to Abbey Road studios to record with Cliff for the first time, which was another experience to savour.

Norrie Paramor had seen us work on stage and liked the sound we presented. Cliff, in turn, wanted to use us for recording purposes, because he felt we created the right kind of atmosphere, which, he hoped, could be captured on his records. So Norrie cautiously booked us for the session, but took the added precaution once again of employing the two session men, bass player Frank Clarke and guitarist Ernie Shears. We were booked for a three-hour session, during which time we were expected to record three songs. It was written into our contracts, and even if they were crap, we still had to lay down three tracks. In 1958 Abbey Road wasn't as famous as it is today; it was just another recording studio, but it was the biggest one we had been to, far larger than Stanhope Place, where we made our first record with the Chesternuts. We were totally overawed by it all; everything was so organized. All we had to do was turn up, set out our gear and play. We were most impressed to see an A & R man, an engineer *and* a tape operator for one solitary session. We just did what we were told to do, and asked no questions.

The first number we played was 'Livin', Lovin' Doll', which was lined up as Cliff's next single, and Norrie suggested that Hank play rhythm guitar while Ernie Shears did all the lead work. Cliff wasn't very happy at that. He felt that Ernie, good as he was, wasn't really into rock 'n' roll, and that while the guitar playing on 'Move It' was just right, the follow-up single, 'High Class Baby', didn't quite come off. He felt that Ernie tended to repeat the same thing on all rock 'n' roll numbers. Anyway, Norrie wanted him, so Ernie played a few fill-ins and the solo, which was exactly like 'Move It' revisited. Cliff wasn't very pleased. He told Norrie he wanted Hank to play lead guitar and eventually suggested that they each do a take. A compromise was reached. In the end Hank's solo was far more original than Ernie's. It had a completely different sound and feeling to it. It was also a better overall performance. Norrie sensed it as well, and agreed to use it. It was the last time he ever booked other musicians when we recorded. We also laid down 'Mean Streak' at the same time, and the entire session cost £82, with £39 going to the musicians.

Hearing our guitars and voices after those first recordings was a revelation. We were really not very proficient at playing, even though the music was so simple and straightforward, but when we heard the tape played back, it sounded really good – there seemed to be so much going on, even though it was all done on one track. We played everything live and there was no mixing or over-dubbing. It was all produced in mono. We really did lag behind the Americans when it came to recording techniques. Their records always sounded fresh, exciting and so well produced. Ours seemed to lack sparkle, and they were into multi-tracking long before we were. EMI in those days had boffins in white coats. They were the maintenance people. At times it seemed more like a scientific laboratory than a recording studio.

American guitarist Les Paul was perfecting the technique of bouncing tracks backwards and forwards between two mono tape machines in the late 1940s, although it was the German company Telefunken that had pioneered the development of modern tape machines ten years earlier. Prior to the outbreak of World War Two, recording techniques had changed little since Edison's day. Records were still made by means of cutting grooves into wax cylinders, or shellac discs, but at the end of hostilities the American armed forces captured several of these German magnetaphon machines, which were taken back to the USA and used to record weekly radio programmes. Further research and development took place in America, and by the end of the 1940s Ampex had begun to manufacture the first single-channel tape decks, which revolutionized the gramophone industry. For the first time, it was possible to edit recordings. Even more important, two tape recorders could be used in tandem to build up a whole series of tracks and form one recording. Part of a song could be recorded on to one tape machine, which was then replayed and another part added, while the whole effect was taped by the second machine. The process – a technique called 'sound-on-sound' – could be repeated again and again to create the stunning effects which most American records seemed to employ. Buddy Holly was a prime example in this area. The basic developments laid down the ground rules for what was to follow, which led to the introduction of stereo recordings, four-track machines leading to eight, sixteen, twenty-four, thirty-two and the forty-eight track machines we have today. It was a slow process and took a long time to get off the ground. In Britain our recording techniques in the late 1950s seemed archaic by comparison.

Three days after our first visit to Abbey Road, we made our début in variety and opened a week-long engagement at the Metropolitan Theatre, Edgware Road, followed by further weeks at the Chiswick Empire and the Empire Theatre, Finsbury Park (which was just around the corner from where we lived), and a series of one-night stands. Cliff Richard and the Drifters topped the bill. Cliff was working harder than ever. During the day he was up at five to start work on *Serious Charge*; he performed two shows on stage at night; while Saturdays were spent at the Hackney Empire rehearsing and appearing on *Oh Boy*. The pressure started to build up on him. It was all becoming too much. One night in Hull he lost his voice completely, but instead of cancelling the show and letting down hundreds of expectant fans, Cliff went out on stage for that concert and gave a superb performance in front of a packed house, without singing a note. While we played, he *mimed*. In the wings Wee Willie Harris provided the voice and gave a near-perfect impression of Cliff Richard. No one in the audience knew the difference. The deafening screams and squeals from the teenage girls in the auditorium helped with the cover-up.

The incident helped to hasten the departure of Franklyn Boyd as Cliff's manager after less than three months in charge. Cliff's father, Rodger Webb, was concerned for his son's welfare and decided to act quickly. Like John Foster before him, Franklyn Boyd was completely out of his depth as a manager. Cliff's success had happened so suddenly that nobody was prepared for the consequences. We were all running before we had even learnt to crawl. Neither John nor Franklyn could handle the situation. I think at one point Cliff's dad was going to take over the management himself, which would have been disastrous. He had no experience in that direction whatsoever. Fortunately I think he realized that it would be wrong for him to attempt the job. Cliff had become a huge star almost overnight, and a highly bankable commodity, and needed to be handled by an expert in the ways of show business. A few weeks later Tito Burns, the former band-leader and now a successful agent, was appointed to take over the reins of Cliff's career. As far as Tito was concerned, the Drifters hardly existed, they were just a backing group.

Towards the end of what had been a very eventful year in all our lives, Terry Smart – the only remaining member of the original Drifters, who had formed the group with Cliff Richard a few months before – stunned us all when he announced he was leaving. He was becoming increasingly restless as a musician and felt that he was unable to keep up the standard that was required; the way the group was developing was beyond his capabililties. He could see a sparkling future for Cliff, yet had reservations about his own commitment as a rock 'n' roll drummer. We all tried to talk him out of his decision, but his mind was made up. After he left the group he joined the merchant navy and spent the next nine years at sea. It was a sad state of affairs. Within two months the original Drifters had disappeared completely and a totally new group had emerged in its place. The friends who had been so close to Cliff at the very start of his career, the guys who had played on 'Move It' with him, had moved on. Tony Meehan, the youngster who had sat in on drums with us one summer evening at the 2i's, took Terry's place. He had already made a name for himself as a very talented drummer, and in the briefest period of time had worked with Wee Willie Harris, Vince Eager, the Vipers, Mickie Most and Vince Taylor, and had also backed Cliff on several radio sessions. When he joined us he lied about his age. He was still only fifteen, but told us he had turned sixteen 'ages ago'. In truth he didn't celebrate his sixteenth birthday until the following March, by which time he had been with the Drifters for three months.

The first official appearance together of Hank Marvin, Bruce Welch, Jet Harris, and Tony Meehan came in January 1959 at the Free Trade Hall in Manchester. The show was compèred by a brash young Liverpool comedian called Jimmy Tarbuck. It was a nightmare evening for our nervous drummer, who managed to knock over his kit during the third number in his eagerness to please and sat there on stage mesmerized, trying to keep a steady rhythm with one hand, while picking up various cymbals and drums with the other.

Even though Cliff was our boss and paid our wages, he was always one of us: it was *never* a 'them and me' situation. We were five lads together, sharing almost everything. We ate together and often met socially together. Hank and I even shared a flat with Cliff when we finally left Mrs Bowman's. Some time before, Cliff and John Foster had taken an apartment together above Sainsbury's at 100 Marylebone High Street, so that they wouldn't have to commute into London from Hertfordshire each day. It was a six-roomed flat with three bedrooms, lounge, kitchen and bathroom. It was ideal for us, too, so Hank and I roped ourselves into the arrangement and shared the twelve guineas a week rent. It became a rendezvous for Cliff's contemporaries, and Marty Wilde, Billy Fury, Vince Eager and Dickie Pride would drop in regularly for a chat, a drink and a bite to eat. Eventually we had to move out, when the fans discovered Cliff lived there and besieged the place night and day. In the end Hank and I moved into a flat of our own in East Finchley, not too far from Pete Chester's home.

Cliff was very proud of us, particularly Hank. He was delighted that his guitar player was so highly regarded by other musicians and artistes. After our first tour together we became the greatest of friends and allies. I think that it was through our friendship that Cliff decided to keep the group together when the tour was over, and he helped enormously by talking to Norrie Paramor about us. He eventually arranged for the group to audition for the Columbia Records producer with a view to a recording contract, and we went along to Norrie Paramor's office at the EMI headquarters in Great Castle Street, off Oxford Circus, where we actually set up our gear in front of his desk and played for him. We performed two numbers, both vocals – 'Feeling Fine', which had been written for us by Sammy Samwell, and 'Don't Be a Fool with Love', one of Pete Chester's songs. On the strength of that makeshift session, Norrie offered us a short-term contract to record for Columbia. We couldn't believe our luck.

The terms of that first contract, which was drawn up on 5 February 1959, stated that the Drifters would record four sides at 78 rpm in the first year, but with no guarantee of release. We would also receive the sum of one penny in royalties, split between the four of us – one farthing each – on 85 per cent of the gross sales, because 15 per cent was taken off immediately for 'breakages, records returned, those damaged in transit, and those used for advertising and promotion purposes'; royalties were paid for only twenty-five years. There was no advance. It meant that even if the cover price of the record increased, we would still remain on a fixed royalty of one penny. That contract was for one year with further options. Cliff was on a similar deal, although his royalty rose to 1½d after the first year. We had yet to prove ourselves. The contract was between Columbia Records and Terence Harris (Jet's real name), because we were under twenty-one, the legal age to sign such documents. Jet was only nineteen himself, so his father had to sign on his behalf. It read: 'Terence Harris, the artiste, is a performing member, and has under his control the group of musicians known as the Drifters.' These days most acts signing a record deal can negotiate their own royalties, and the deal is usually a percentage of 100 per cent – with substantial advances paid. In 1976, when Malcolm McLaren signed the Sex Pistols to EMI, he received an advance royalty for their services of £40,000. A year later, after EMI terminated the contract and forfeited their money, A & M picked up the deal for a further £150,000, while just a week later, after much adverse publicity, the group was released from the agreement, but allowed to keep the advance. Virgin Records finally signed them for a further staggering advance, reputed to be in excess of £90,000. The Drifters received nothing. It didn't matter. We were just so delighted to have signed a record contract.

We recorded our audition songs at Abbey Road studios on 9 January 1959 and they were released as our first single – 'Feeling Fine' was the A-side – three weeks later. Despite an appearance on our own on *Oh Boy* to promote the record, it failed miserably. Jack Good didn't take much notice of us. He obviously didn't think we had much potential. We were just a group with a single, and not a very good one at that. So he simply allowed us to play, without presenting the Drifters in any spectacular way as he did with the artistes he rated.

Oh Boy was a fun show, full of energy and *live*. So if we made a mistake there could be no re-shooting or editing. One of the musicians featured in the resident orchestra, Lord Rockingham's XI, was a brilliant young guitarist called Joe Brown, who was signed up to a management contract with Larry Parnes. Larry had an instinct for new talent and looked after his stable of stars extremely well. Like Jack Good he was an image-maker, and always very careful that his boys created exactly the right kind of look. Out went their normal, everyday names, to be replaced by far more exotic and strong-sounding rock 'n' roll pseudonyms – all devised by Parnes – who looked upon himself as one of the great Svengalis in show business. The history of rock 'n' roll was to prove it an apt title. In that way Reg Smith became Marty Wilde, Ronald Wycherley became Billy Fury, Richard Knellar became Dickie Pride, Ray Howard became Duffy Power, John Askew became Johnny Gentle, and Clive Powell became Georgie Fame. However, when he wanted to christen Joe Brown 'Elmer Twitch', the Cockney musician refused to go along with his manager's ideas. He was proved right, for as plain Joe Brown he went on to enjoy chart success on his own with several Top Ten hits, including 'A Picture of You', 'It Only Took a Minute', and 'That's What Love Will Do'.

Joe Brown was a lovely man and we soon became good mates. We shared common interests in guitars and music. When Gene Vincent first appeared on *Boy Meets Girl*, which was made in the TV studios in Manchester, Jack Good, knowing how much we admired the American singer, invited us over to meet him. Joe Brown was there too, and he asked Hank if he would like to try a new gadget he had recently acquired, to see if he liked it. It was an echo box, which Joe didn't particularly like and for which he was looking for a buyer. Hank tried it out and couldn't put it down. He played around with it, making weird and wonderful effects. He loved it because it gave him that authentic rock 'n' roll echo heard on so many American records. A deal was struck between the two guitarists, and the echo unit changed hands and became Hank's trademark, and very much a part of the Shadows' unique sound in the future. No one else was using echo in the same way Hank was at the time, so it became distinctive. Joe Brown has got a lot to answer for – in the nicest possible way. Like Cliff he went on to become one of the few solo singers to employ his own backing group, the Bruvvers, which set another precedent. Two years later, when we received the demo tape for our new single 'Kon Tiki', it featured Joe Brown playing lead guitar.

The Drifters' second single release of 1959 was one of Jet's own compositions called 'Jet Black', which he had written in the back of the tour coach taking us to an engagement in Grimsby. Our first instrumental, it came out in July with a Hank Marvin composition, 'Driftin'', on the flip side. We'd heard a few American instrumentals at the time, particularly by Duane Eddy, who was becoming very popular – we were intrigued by artistes who were having success with this kind of material, and we thought we could write our own. A young pianist from television's *Billy Cotton Band Show* – Russ Conway – had also made instrumentals popular and had topped the charts earlier in the year with 'Side Saddle' and 'Roulette'. So we decided to give it a go. Unfortunately the song fared only slightly better than our previous effort in the charts stakes. Both numbers had been originally cut in February as part of Cliff Richard's first album *Cliff*, which was a totally live recording. Norrie Paramor liked them so much that he suggested we re-record them as a single. When we got into the studio to tape 'Jet Black', it took many attempts to get it right. Hank was a marvellous guitarist, but so erratic sometimes. We'd record a three-and-a-half-minute song and he'd screw up the last note, which meant doing the whole thing again.

That album was a very clever idea of Norrie's. For several months he had seen just what kind of reaction Cliff was creating up and down the country with his performances on stage, and he was determined to try and re-create the live sound, and the atmosphere it generated, on to that first album. It was a unique concept at the time. However, instead of taping one of Cliff's concerts on the road, which meant transporting all the heavy recording equipment to a provincial theatre where he stood the chance of being dogged by all manner of technical problems, Norrie decided to cheat a little and produce the whole package in Studio Two at Abbey Road, in front of an invited audience of nearly 300 people from Cliff's fan club. Here, at least, he could have more control over the sound. EMI laid on special caterers to feed all the fans, and erected a stage in the studio at the bottom of the staircase leading to the control box. We worked as if we were performing a normal concert, but had the luxury of rehearsing all the material several hours beforehand. Even though we were appearing in front of a live audience, Norrie was able to supervise everything that went on.

We took two evenings to get everything down on tape, but we

were plagued with problems. On the first night, the barriers keeping the kids away from the makeshift stage were positioned far too close to our microphones, which picked up so much screaming and shouting that the whole sound balance was thrown out completely. The following night they were erected in a different place to improve the overall sound, and to try and get a perfect blend between our playing and the audience reaction. It was a minor problem in comparison to the one that affected Cliff. He had gone down with severe laryngitis and was having great difficulty singing. His throat rasped and the infection was very painful. EMI, in their wisdom, refused to cancel the two recording sessions to allow the singer time to recover. On the second evening he could hardly speak, let alone sing. However, the studio had been booked, the kids invited and the food paid for, so the sessions had to go ahead despite our singer's disability. We didn't realize it at the time, but it could have seriously damaged his vocal chords.

It was to give Cliff's voice a rest during the recording session that the Drifters came into their own and were featured on three numbers on the album. Hank and I sang 'Be-Bop-A-Lula', while we all played on the instrumentals, 'Jet Black' and 'Driftin''. Had we recorded the album a week or so later, when Cliff's infection had cleared up, it would have sounded far better. Still, no one seemed to worry unduly. Norrie had captured the excitement and atmosphere of a geniune live concert performance and everyone had a good time. The album came out in April, went on to sell phenomenally well and made Cliff a lot of money in royalties. Hank, Jet, Tony and I were on a session fee of £24, split four ways! The album stayed in the chart for thirty-one weeks, when we were dealing essentially with a singles market.

Nowadays singles are teasers for albums, but it was so different then. The demand for long-playing records at that time was very small, although Cliff and the Drifters helped to change all that four years before the Beatles made such an impact in the album field.

In 1959, teenagers preferred to buy singles and rarely bought LPs. At £1 10s (£1.50p) each, they were too expensive and out of the price range of most kids. Therefore the market was aimed very much at the middle-aged audience. Rock 'n' rollers were slow to latch on to their potential. The very first album chart appeared in

November 1958 when the music paper *Melody Maker* published an initial Top Ten based on LP sales. In fact the long-playing record as we know it had only been in existence for ten years, after American inventor Peter Goldmark pioneered its development. In the main, the early album charts were dominated by movie soundtracks. When the first listing was published on 8 November 1958, the cast album from the movie *South Pacific* was at No.1. It went on to create history by clocking up an incredible 115 chart-topping weeks, including seventy consecutive weeks at the top. It was followed by *The King and I*, *Oklahoma* and *My Fair Lady*. Elvis was represented with two contributions, *Elvis's Golden Records* and the soundtrack album from *King Creole*. The breakthrough for a British rock 'n' roll album came when a compilation long-player from *Oh Boy* hit the chart in December. The album featured Cliff – backed by Lord Rockingham's XI – singing 'At the TV Hop', 'Rockin' Robin', 'High School Confidential', 'Early in the Morning', 'I'll Try', 'King Creole', and 'Somebody Touched Me', alongside songs by Neville Taylor and the Cutters, the Dallas Boys, the Vernons Girls, John Barry, Vince Eager, Peter Elliott, and Cuddly Duddley. It peaked at No.9. For Cliff's third album, *Me and My Shadows*, which came out in 1960, we set a precedent in British music by writing most of the material featured on the sixteen-track set ourselves.

Apart from records, we were kept extremely busy, and spent much of our time out on the road touring on one-night stands or weeks of variety across the country. It was exciting, stimulating and bloody hard work, and we loved it. The adulation Cliff received was absolutely amazing. The country had never seen anything like it before for a British star: there were wild scenes of mass hysteria at every venue, as girls sobbed and screamed and clambered over each other for a glimpse of their 'teenage dream'. He was worshipped and adored like no one before him. Often we could not hear ourselves play on stage because we were deafened by the shrill, high-pitched screaming from the fans. It was frenzied and fanatical. On most occasions we had difficulty leaving the theatres after our shows, which were staked out and under siege by pubescent girls almost tearing their hair out to see Cliff. He was always great with the fans. Whenever it was possible, he would sign as many autographs as he could, and never shirked his responsibilities. Sometimes for our own safety we had to leave the theatre as soon as we had finished our show. We would come running off the stage the minute the last note was played, and leap into the back of a waiting van or limousine before the fans had a chance to make their way from the front of house to the stage door, otherwise we would never have made it. Once, when we played the Glasgow Empire, the police had to enlist the help of the army to close off the whole of Sauchiehall Street in the city centre in order to control the crowd of teenage girls that had gathered.

In the eyes of the fans Cliff could do no wrong. He was Britain's biggest idol and the most adored man in the country.

The reaction of some of the guys, though, was very different. They detested him and everything he stood for. They were jealous, not of the singer himself, but of the effect he was having on the girls who swooned over his voice and his good looks. Sometimes they vented their anger and frustration at our concerts.

One night in Manchester the stage was pelted with eggs and tomatoes by a gang of Teddy boys when Cliff appeared. They attempted to storm the stage and attack him. It was terrifying. Fortunately the theatre staff kept control. The same thing happened in Nottingham, Birmingham and London. At the Lyceum Theatre in the Strand, we were performing on a revolving stage which just kept going round to allow us to escape from the pennies, eggs, cabbages and tomatoes that were thrown by jealous yobs. At the Trocadero at the Elephant and Castle, pennies, halfpennies and bottles were thrown down at the stage from the balcony as we attempted to storm through our act. In Romford, one November the 5th, Teddy boys attacked the tour bus just as we were about to board it after a show. Bricks, stones and large pieces of wood were thrown at the vehicle, smashing some of the windows and severely damaging the bodywork. We sprinted from the stage door and threw ourselves on to the bus, taking cover from the barrage on the floor and under the seats as the vehicle drove off, with a gang in hot pursuit. Just as we sped away a brick flew through one of the shattered windows and hit me on the head. For a few seconds I was reeling, and I saw more stars than were travelling on the tour coach with us. In the rush to get away, none of the gear had been made secure, and as the bus jolted,

Hank was floored by an amplifier which fell on top of him pinning his arms, so that he couldn't move. It all happened in a split second. He cried out for help, and in that instant a lighted firework was tossed through a window and landed inches away from his face. He couldn't move his hands to push it away no matter how hard he struggled, and had to lie there, waiting for the worst to happen. Hank closed his eyes and braced himself for the banger to explode and spew sparks and cascades of fire into his face. He waited . . . and waited . . . and nothing happened. It was a dud.

In Burnley, the police were called to stop a vicious fight that took place right in the front row of the stalls between a gang of louts, just as we started our act – and we provided the musical accompaniment as punches and kicks rained on to crumpled bodies. It was a rip-roaring rumble. The local constabulary had managed to stop it quickly when one of the young offenders decided to take the law into his own hands, punched a policeman in the face and ran off, with another copper giving chase. The boy disappeared through an exit door at the side of the theatre, only to re-emerge at the back with the constable closing fast behind. Hunter and hunted ran down the side gangway, heading for the stage. The young boy reached it first, turned smartly to his left and headed back for a door on the other side. He was nearly there when a convenient foot from someone in the front row sent him toppling. He was in full flight and the momentum of his fall carried him straight into the orchestra pit, where he was promptly arrested. It was like something out of the Keystone Cops, and while all the action was taking place out front, we just continued to play as if nothing was happening, professionals to the end.

We had a very frightening experience at the Chiswick Empire during a week of variety, when the show was stopped to prevent a disaster happening. It was a wonder that no one was killed. Two groups of rival gangland Teddy boys – one from Hackney in the East End, the other from Hammersmith in the West – had a long-standing vendetta that had seen them fighting on the streets right across London, and they arranged for a final showdown to take place at the Chiswick Empire, second house, on Friday evening, with Cliff Richard and the Drifters topping the bill. We found out later that the police had been tipped off about the incident weeks before, but no one had taken any notice until it was too late.

Before the show started, both sets of louts assembled in the upper balcony – 'the gods' – and within minutes of arriving, a scuffle broke out and developed into a full-scale battle. Eggs, coins, light bulbs and bottles were tossed down into the stalls and on to the stage from above, as the two gangs piled into each other. They were fighting in the gangways, under the seats, on top of the seats and on the floor, as innocent members of the audience rushed for safety. The commotion was unbelievable. Fists flew into faces; kicks thudded into stomachs and crotches; blood was being spilt everywhere in a mad moment of anger. Amazingly the show continued as planned, although under the greatest provocation. Kay and Kimberley, one of the support acts, staggered through their routine, and the Dallas Boys at least attempted to sing, but were pelted with eggs every time they opened their mouths. Comedian Des O'Connor thought he could handle the situation, abandoned his set routine and tried to quell the storm. He was very brave.

'And which schools do you lads come from?' he called from the stage, attempting to subdue the rioting through humour. 'Are you sure you're old enough to be out this late at night on your own?' This incited the rioting even more. Things only got worse. When one of the yobs upstairs ripped a fire extinguisher from the wall and flung it over the balcony, it was time to pull the curtain down. The heavy metal cylinder bounced off the balcony rail and down into the stalls, where it hit two women, concussing one of them. The other sustained a fractured collar bone. There was panic backstage as well, until Ray Alan, the ventriloquist, who was appearing with us on the bill, took matters into his own hands and pulled down the safety curtain to stop the show. By now fighting had broken out in the stalls and all around the theatre, but there was panic as the audience tried to get outside. Pandemonium and chaos reigned as fans tried to escape the mêlée through emergency exits. Ray had the foresight to lock the pass door which led backstage, to isolate the fighting to one area of the theatre only, so that the police could deal with it quickly. It would have been a disaster if rioters had made it on to the stage. There was far too much valuable equipment which needed protecting, plus of course, our lives.

Fortunately there were lighter moments. We were on stage at the Birmingham Hippodrome when Cliff split his trousers during one of his gyrations. He thought his zip had simply come undone, and turned his back on the audience to fix it. Instead he found a gaping rip at the front, revealing a good deal of flesh, and had to finish the number standing sideways on to the packed audience so that no one could see what had happened. He dared not move. As soon as the song was over, he nipped off stage to change while we went into an instrumental.

With so many girls around, groupies became a thriving and very pleasant distraction for some of us. And why not? We were young and single and very willing. We each had our fair share. On one visit to Bradford, no less than eight of us from the show had the same girl – not all at once I hasten to add – under the stage at the St George's Hall, because it had been rumoured she had slept with Buddy Holly during his British tour the year before. We all thought the world of Buddy and wanted to be like him in any way we could, but this was taking the hero worship a little far. In Bournemouth, a big buxom girl arrived at the stage door and announced that she was desperate to get into show business and would do anything if we would help her. She brought with her a portfolio of modelling pictures, many of which were very provocative nude shots. She was game for anything, and in the interval we took her into one of the dressing-rooms where she stripped naked and lay on top of a table. Then in turn almost every male member of the company except Cliff attempted to make love to her while the others roared on their encouragement. We were all laughing so much that none of us could get sufficiently aroused to make it.

We were on tour when we first heard the song 'Living Doll', which marked a major turning point in Cliff's career. It was one of the three numbers he had to sing in his forthcoming movie, *Serious Charge*, and had yet to record. It had been written by another old hand from the 2i's, Lionel Bart, who had composed a number of songs for Tommy Steele and was currently working on his new movie, *Tommy the Toreador*. He was rapidly emerging as one of Britain's most successful songwriters. He had written the musical *Fings Ain't Wot They Used to Be*, and penned the lyrics (to Laurie Johnson's music) for *Lock Up Your Daughters*. He was now completing a third musical project called *Oliver*, based on the Charles Dickens novel.

Before Cliff was given 'Living Doll' to record, it had been offered to one of Larry Parnes's protégés, Duffy Power, who turned it down as being uncommercial, much against the advice of his manager, who realized that the song would become a massive hit. Cliff also hated the song in its original form, and thought it was chronic. When we heard it for the first time, we were sitting in the dressing-room of the City Hall, Sheffield, and Cliff played us a demonstration record. The arrangement for the demo was terrible. It was up-tempo – played like a big band number, old fashioned and square. None of us liked that version at all, but we could see that the song had enormous potential. It was a great number. I listened to it for a while, picked up my guitar and strummed away in a slower, almost country-and-western rhythm, which gave it a much simpler style. It fitted perfectly, and a few weeks later, when Cliff and the Drifters recorded the song, this basic, uncomplicated arrangement was used. Its strength was in its utter simplicity. It was Cliff's fourth single, which he later said he recorded under extreme duress. It came out in July 1959, as a follow-up to the Ian Samwell song 'Mean Streak'.

'Living Doll' gave Cliff Richard his first No.1 single in Britain when it topped the charts in August for six weeks, and his first million-selling record. It also became his first record to make the breakthrough in America, when it reached No.30 in November, and ended the year as Britain's biggest selling single of 1959. More than that, 'Living Doll' was the record that broadened Cliff's appeal. It reached out to a different generation. He moved away from rock 'n' roll to ballads, and on to more subtle and gentler material; he moved out of the teenagers-only market and widened his scope to attract the mums and dads. The great British rock 'n' roller had joined the establishment. However, the teenagers didn't desert him.

The importance of 'Living Doll' to Cliff's career was beyond any doubt, and it also had a crucial influence on British pop music in general. Many of the lightweight, tuneful pop ballads of the next few years owed their style and success to that one record, and their domination of the charts remained until the arrival of the Beatles. There were many songs like it, including 'Cradle of Love' (Johnny Preston), 'Angela Jones' (Michael Cox), 'Why' (Anthony Newley), 'Venus in Blue Jeans' (Mark Wynter), 'My Kind of Girl' (Matt Monro) and 'Ginny Come Lately' (Brian Hyland). It wasn't a conscious decision on Cliff's part, it just evolved. Tito Burns was shrewd enough to realize as soon as he became Cliff's manager that the singer *had* to broaden his appeal.

'I didn't want Cliff to die, if rock 'n' roll died,' he admitted. 'There had to be something else. There had to be life after rock 'n' roll. He had to develop in other directions – and "Living Doll" was the first stage.'

Stage two came in December, when Cliff Richard followed Tommy Steele's footsteps into pantomime and appeared as the Sheriff's troubadour in *Babes in the Wood* at the Globe Theatre, Stockton.

It was during the run of that pantomime that the singer very nearly lost two of his backing group when Jet and Hank were involved in a serious car accident just outside the city. Jet's car swerved in wet conditions to avoid an oncoming vehicle, skidded across the road and rammed head on into a third car. The two musicians were lucky to escape with only minor injuries. Hank broke his glasses, and appeared on stage the following evening with one of the lenses blacked out and a plaster holding the frame together. When the case came to court our bass player was fined £35 15s (£35.75p) for 'dangerous driving, for failing to display "L" plates and driving unaccompanied by a qualified driver'. Hank was fined £3 for aiding and abetting. A few months earlier the Drifters had had problems of another kind when we ran into trouble in America over something as innocuous as our name. When we tried to release our single 'Jet Black' across the Atlantic, we found to our horror that there was a group in existence with exactly the same name and that they had taken out an injunction against us calling ourselves the Drifters in the USA. We'd never heard of them – they weren't at all known in Britain – but they had been working together in the States for eight years under that name and had enjoyed several hit singles in the national and rhythm 'n' blues charts. As such they had a prior claim. It meant that if we wanted to release our new single in America we had to call ourselves something different. As a result, 'Jet Black' was issued by a group called the Four Jets. It was a terrible name and no solution at all, but it sounded better than the Four Tonys, the Four Bruces, or the Four Hanks, which might have been misunderstood in America. Fortunately the single wasn't a hit. Had it taken off we might really have had serious problems. Norrie Paramor suggested we change our name permanently to avoid any kind of confusion in the future. It was easier said than done, however, and none of us could think of a suitable handle for the group, not even Cliff, until one afternoon in the summer when Jet came up with the goods.

Now that we were making a little more money, Hank, Jet and I had invested some of our earnings in Lambretta scooters. I had a 150 cc model, while the other two had purchased more powerful 175 cc machines. It was a good way of getting around London. One weekend when we weren't working, I decided to show off my latest acquisition to Aunt Sadie and my friends in Newcastle, and travelled up overnight without wearing any protective clothing. I nearly froze to death.

On this particular afternoon, Hank and Jet were out on their Lambrettas visiting Ruislip Lido, a few miles outside London, when they stopped off for a drink at the Six Bells public house – another name that should be enshrined in the annals of rock 'n' roll history. It was here that Jet solved the urgent problem of finding a new name for the band when he nonchalantly turned to Hank and asked: 'What do you think of the Shadows?' It was a wonderful name – it had instant reaction – and we all loved it immediately. Jet thought of the name because we were always performing in the shadow of Cliff Richard while he was on stage; the spotlights were trained on him while we remained in the background, in the darkness. It was our good fortune at the time that no one in Britain was aware that Bobby Vee's backing group was also called the Shadows. When we found out, much later, the American group had already split up. With a change of name we had to amend our recording contract with EMI, and a letter was drawn up by the company accordingly: 'We refer to the contract dated February 5th, 1959 and should be glad if you would kindly agree that it shall henceforth be treated as amended, in that there shall be substituted for the words "the Drifters", the words "the Shadows", the name of your new band.'

The release of our second single, 'Jet Black', which led to our problems overseas, effectively marked the end of our contract with EMI. We had honoured the terms of our agreement with Columbia Records and recorded the four sides as stipulated. When the second single failed in the wake of our first release, we were all convinced that it was the end as far as recording was concerned and that the options on our contract would not be taken up. Norrie Paramor had other ideas and renewed the agreement without hesitation. Our third single was another vocal, 'Saturday Dance', written by Hank and Pete Chester, who also picked up the writing credits on the B-side, 'Lonesome Fella'. It came out in December and was our first single to carry the name *Shadows*, even though we had appeared on Cliff's recent No.1 success, 'Travellin' Light', billed as *Cliff Richard and the Shadows*. We all felt it was the best thing we had ever done. It was certainly our most successful record to date, and it only just failed to break into the Top Thirty. Things were looking good. 'Saturday Dance' marked another milestone in our careers: it was the first record on which Hank Marvin played the guitar that was to become synonymous with him, and with the sound of the Shadows – the famous pink Fender Stratocaster. It was Cliff who bought it for him.

For quite some time Hank had been using an Antoria which he had bought in a London music store for £35, because it was a solid body instrument and had a completely different feel from any English guitar. It was a very poor relation of a Fender. In reality it was a chunk of wood with strings which gave a very interesting, if 'clacky' sound. The neck was bent, so tuning became a problem, and the action – the distance between the strings and the fingerboard – was very high, turning it into a cheese-cutter, which meant that the strings could slice through his fingers at any time. A new guitar, therefore, was a top priority.

We had been talking to Cliff about getting a better instrument for some while. We were all very influenced by the sound of Buddy Holly and of Ricky Nelson's guitarist, James Burton, on records and wanted to achieve something similar. Because he was such a great guitarist we were convinced Burton used a Fender

Stratocaster, which we knew would be an ideal instrument for Hank. Cliff agreed, and wrote to the factory in Santa Ana, California, for a brochure. When it arrived we pored over it page by page, looking at the marvellous instruments that would be available if only we lived in America. In the end the catalogue was grubby with fingermarks as we thumbed through the pages, endlessly drooling over is contents. The ban on importing American instruments into Britain still existed, but there was nothing to stop an individual bringing one in personally. So that's what we did. Eventually, after much discussion, we chose the most expensive guitar in the book at around £120, which was a fortune in 1959. It was a flamingo pink Stratocaster with a bird's-eye maple neck, tremolo arm and gold-plated hardware.

A few weeks later the guitar arrived, in a magnificent tweed flat case with a plush red velvet lining. We opened it up and gaped in amazement at such a marvellous sight. It was – and still is – one of the finest guitars ever made. I still have the guitar and use it on stage today. Much later, Hank discovered that James Burton didn't use a Stratocaster after all, he favoured a Telecaster, but it was still a Fender.

In September we made our movie début alongside Cliff in his second film, *Expresso Bongo*. Cliff played the part of a young singer who became world famous as 'Bongo Herbert', which was almost a piece of type-casting. Laurence Harvey played his unscrupulous manager, and *we* played Cliff's backing group in the night club sequence, more type-casting. It was the briefest of appearances on the silver screen, but it meant we were on call at Shepperton Studios from 8 am each morning, which necessitated us getting up at the unearthly hour of 6 am. When we weren't needed on the set, we spent most of our time rehearsing, or writing songs in our dressing-room, or just sleeping. The film was premièred to mixed reviews in November. We certainly didn't stand out.

Following the success of 'Living Doll' in the USA, we were signed to appear in America at the start of 1960 as part of a touring package show called *The Biggest Show of Stars – 1960 Winter Edition*. It was truly a dream come true for us all. America was the Mecca for rock 'n' roll – it was the home of Elvis, Buddy Holly, the Everly Brothers, and we could hardly believe we were going there ourselves . . . to play rock 'n' roll. Just two years before, I had still been bunking off school in Newcastle. It wasn't our first overseas trip, however. That had come the previous October, when we were sent on a short promotional tour to Scandinavia and Germany. It was the first time any of us had ever flown. We left Britain without Tony Meehan, who had been rushed to hospital with appendicitis. A musician we knew called Laurie Jay became an admirable deputy. He later went on to discover Billy Ocean, and became his manager.

The American tour took in thirty-eight venues across the States, playing substantial arenas to over 7,000 people each night. It was a very big bill headed by Frankie Avalon, who had recently enjoyed great success with such singles as 'Venus', 'Just Ask Your Heart', and his American chart-topping single, 'Why?', and it featured Bobby Rydell, Freddy Cannon, Clyde McPhatter, Sammy Turner, the Clovers, and Johnny and the Hurricanes. And we thought the Kalin Twins were a big deal! Wow! We were billed as 'Cliff Richard and the Shadows – An Added Attraction from Britain', and opened the second half of the programme with a fifteen-minute spot which showcased 'Forty Days', 'My Babe', 'Living Doll', 'Whole Lotta Shakin', and Cliff's current British single from *Expresso Bongo* – 'A Voice in the Wilderness'. We were unknown in America, but the audiences warmed to us and our performances were greeted with cheers and screams, though on nothing like the same scale as back home in Britain. Still, we were breaking the ice.

We travelled everywhere by Greyhound coach, with all the artistes and musicians thrown together on board. We mixed with everyone on the tour. There were no frills. Big stars we had admired from afar became buddies and genuine mates. There was no bitchiness, just a great brotherhood and tremendous empathy between us all – each one willing the other to do well. We spent most of our time together talking avidly about music, swopping stories and experiences. We were different, we were from England. Johnny and the Hurricanes used to taunt us playfully: 'Why do you British groups always try to copy the Americans' style of music?' It was guaranteed to provide a stimulating discussion which whiled away a few more hours. We talked together, argued together and sang together. There was a fantastic spirit. It was just like touring in Britain on a far greater scale, but after all, this was America. Even the tour bus was designed for comfort, with reclining seats just like an aircraft, and a built-in toilet. We were travelling vast distances each day, from venue to venue, and sometimes we would drive as much as 500 miles in one go. After finishing a show in a new town, we would drive through the night to our next destination, often spending up to twelve hours at a time on the road, sleeping and eating on the coach. Once we arrived at the next stop-off point on the schedule, we headed for our hotel rooms and went to sleep. We saw very little of the American countryside – sleeping got in the way.

The tour opened in Montreal, Canada, and wound its way across America through towns and cities we had only read about in books or magazines. Legendary places we had seen in the movies and sung about in songs. Romantic-sounding names like Philadelphia, Buffalo, Oklahoma City, San Antonio, the famous cowboy town of Fort Worth, and the motor city of Detroit. We got a tremendous kick when we played Gene Vincent's home town of Norfolk, Virginia, and travelled through Kentucky where the Everly Brothers had first started out on the road to success. But we were very apprehensive when we played in Lubbock, Texas, where Buddy Holly had come from. We idolized him that much. In Texas, when the time was available, we did all the tourist trips. We visited the Alamo, the site of the famous battle where 200 Texan volunteers held a tiny mission post for ten days against an army of over 4,000 Mexican troops before being wiped out. It was here that Davy Crockett and Jim Bowie died. The site had been turned into a museum, and the names of the heroes who died in the massacre were inscribed on plaques on the wall, including those of twenty-eight Englishmen. 'One of them must have been Irish,' said Jet. 'I've just been to the toilet and found "Kilroy was here" inscribed on the wall.'

New York was an exciting city. We were thrilled to be there. As soon as we arrived we went out and bought real cool trilby hats, and visited all the famous jazz hangouts. At Birdland, a magnet for musicians, we saw one of the world's greatest trumpeters, Maynard Ferguson, performing, and at the Metropole Jazz Club we met Cozy Cole. We found Greenwich Village, New York's equivalent of Soho, a lot quieter than back home and very disappointing.

We returned to New York later to appear on the celebrated *Ed Sullivan Show*, which was the biggest on American television at that time. This was the programme that launched the career of Elvis Presley. After one appearance on the Sunday evening show, with a viewing figure of over 60 million, he became a national name overnight. Ed Sullivan was looked on as a god in show-business parlance, he wielded so much power. But I found him totally wooden and aloof.

I have always regarded myself as the weak link musically in the Shadows. Of the four musicians I felt I was the poorest; my guitar-playing wasn't brilliant. I certainly wasn't in the same league as Hank. However, for Cliff's appearance on the *Ed Sullivan Show* we had to play live, and I was asked to take the band-call in the afternoon and run through the numbers we were performing that night. I can remember arriving in the studio and being surrounded by some absolutely fabulous New York musicians who played in the TV orchestra. I was in awe of them all. They were brilliant instrumentalists who were all names in their own right – and they looked to *me* for guidance. I was still in my teens, I couldn't read or write music and I could hardly play the guitar. But here were these great players hanging on to my every word and awaiting instructions. I slowly took out my acoustic guitar, and started to strum the chords to the song.

'Well, lads, it goes like this.'

In Minneapolis I was thrown out of a shop for being under age. A magazine headline in the window had caught my attention: 'Did the Devil send Elvis Presley?' it said. I was intrigued to read more, and went inside to buy a copy of the publication. I didn't realize that the shop also sold and displayed a fair selection of nude pin-up books and girlie magazines in full graphic detail – well, as much as they dared in 1960. By law, anyone entering the store had to be over twenty-one years of age, and when the owner found out that I was only eighteen I was unceremoniously bundled from the premises. I never did get to buy the magazine.

As we got deeper into the Southern states we came across colour prejudice and segregation for the first time. Negroes were still called 'Niggers' or 'Boy' there, and treated like third-class citizens. We hated it. In every Southern town we visited there were bars and restaurants labelled, 'Whites only' or 'For Use by

Coloreds Only'. Back in Newcastle there was a minor racial problem of sorts with the Indians and Pakistanis, but it was nothing like we encountered here. It upset me greatly that I could travel with all the black musicians and Harold, the show's compère, for many thousands of miles across the States, I could swop stories with them, sing with them, laugh with them, drink with them and enjoy their company, and yet as soon as we stopped to eat, we had to dine in separate restaurants, kept apart by the law of the state. We had to drink in different bars and use separate toilet facilities because the colour of our skin was different. It made me sick that men could treat other men that way. The coloured guys didn't argue at all, and accepted it as part of normal life.

In Kansas City, Missouri, mid-way through the tour, Cliff took a few days off and flew back to Britain to appear in front of 10,000 people at the annual *New Musical Express* poll winners' concert at Wembley *without us*. It was Tito Burns's idea for us to stay in America. I believe his plans for Cliff Richard didn't necessarily include the Shadows; after all, in his eyes we were only backing musicians. We resented the decision at the time because it would have been exciting for us to fly back to London to do the concert and then return to America again the following day. It was what *real* rock 'n' rollers did. But we were never given a chance.

Back in London for the afternoon concert, and a subsequent evening appearance on television on *Sunday Night at the London Palladium*, Cliff Richard was backed by the Parker Royal Four – not one of the truly great names of rock 'n' roll! They later changed their name to the Hunters and had a couple of instrumental hits in our wake with 'Teen Scene' and 'The Storm'. Cliff flew out the next day and rejoined the tour at Omaha.

During the time that Tito Burns was Cliff's manager, we were made to feel like an ordinary backing group at every opportunity. Nothing special, just a bunch of musicians, and dispensable. Cliff was all that mattered. On his nineteenth birthday we were appearing in Leeds, and Tito threw a surprise champagne party in his honour in one of the main theatre dressing-rooms. Cliff's parents and sisters were invited, along with some friends, his fan club secretary, and tour promoter Arthur Howes. The Shadows were conspicuous by their absence.

We returned from America to headline our own British concert tour in April, well aware of the impact and excitement black music was having in the States. The Doo Wop bands like the Coasters, the Dominoes and the Platters, who used their voices to create rhythms, were well established, while the diverse talents of Chuck Berry, Fats Domino, Jackie Wilson, Lloyd Price and Sam Cooke were becoming regulars in the *Billboard* pop chart.

We knew it would not be too long before that influence would spread across the Atlantic, and we wanted to be in at the start. So we consciously looked for black material to feature in our act – just like the Beatles did shortly afterwards – and came up with a Johnny Otis number 'Willie and the Hand Jive'. It was a great song which became a vibrant part of our stage act from then on, and served a valuable purpose for the Shadows, as it got Hank and me out of the background and into the spotlight with Cliff for the first time. We shared the same microphone to sing back-up vocals and harmonies, and worked out a very basic dance routine for the three of us, to accompany the song. On television our three faces were seen together in the frame. It looked great on camera, and gradually Hank and I became known as individual personalities within the Shadows, not just faceless members of a backing group, which made it a lot easier when we eventually made the break on our own.

Back home, the musical climate was changing and two new teen idols had emerged to challenge Cliff for the top spot. One was an old mate from our Soho days, Adam Faith. The other was a coloured singer called Emile Ford, who came originally from Nassau in the West Indies. He topped the charts at the beginning of the year with 'What Do You Want to Make Those Eyes at Me For?' and replaced Adam's 'What Do You Want?' in the No.1 position. Adam's colourful career later took him from international hit parades, through television, movies and the West End stage, into the fast-moving world of high finance.

Emile Ford, however, found the going tough after the hits had dried up (he had his last chart entry in 1963 with 'I Wonder Who's Kissing Her Now?'), and he made a living in the northern cabaret clubs on the strength of his chart success. Earlier in his career, though, he had been one of the first artistes to experiment with backing tapes on stage, and asked his group, the Checkmates, to record all the music they featured together in the stage act. Emile then turned the tapes into back-up tracks – and sacked the band. He didn't need them any more, and he went out on stage every night using two tape recorders for accompaniment. Definitely ahead of his time.

For our spring tour in 1960, we were joined on the road by a young singer-songwriter called Jerry Lordan, who had scored earlier in the year with a couple of minor hits, 'I'll Stay Single' and 'Who Could Be Bluer', which had entered the Top Thirty. Jerry utilized the time we spent on the tour bus by writing songs, using a ukelele as accompaniment and not a conventional guitar. He was a friendly guy, once you got to know him, and we spent many pleasant hours on the coach talking together when he was not otherwise occupied with his writing. We told him that we had been very disappointed when 'Saturday Dance', our third single, hadn't happened, and casually mentioned that we were always looking for new material to record.

Jerry perked up. 'I might have something you'd like to hear,' he told Hank, and proceeded to strum his ukelele while loudly humming a melody line. 'Bert Weedon recorded it about a year ago for an LP,' he added, referring to the tune he was attempting to play. 'But it hasn't been released yet, and I don't suppose Bert is going to do anything with it anyway.'

He continued playing.

Even in such a crude form we knew that Jerry's embryonic number had tremendous potential. It was another instrumental, very catchy, and somehow strangely atmospheric. It was totally different from anything else that was happening at that time. Immediately he finished humming, Hank and I fell over ourselves to ask if we could record it. It was fantastic.

'What's it called?' I asked.

Jerry looked up from his instrument, and smiled. '*Apache.*'

7

'YOU'D BETTER GET YOURSELF ANOTHER DRUMMER'

Norrie Paramor had already chosen the Shadows' next single before we played 'Apache' to him. He was very impressed by Jerry Lordan's composition and thought it was a marvellous number, but he wanted us to record an instrumental version of an old army sing-along called 'Quartermaster's Stores', which he felt was far more commercial because the melody line was so familiar. What we didn't know at the time was that Norrie's brother, Alan, had recently formed his own publishing company, Lorna Music, which published the number. It actually made sound commercial sense for us to record the song. It was so catchy. We were very young and naïve and knew nothing about copyright. We did not know that 'Quartermaster's Stores', being a traditional song, did not have any copyright restrictions, which meant that anyone could rearrange the number, add their own name to the score as 'arranger', and pick up any royalties that it generated. So Norrie's brother stood to earn a lot of money if the record became a hit. The trouble was, we didn't want 'Quartermaster's Stores' to be the A-side of our record – we were sure 'Apache' stood a far better chance because it was so different from anything else around and very unusual. 'Quartermaster's Stores', on the other hand, sounded too much like a Johnny and the Hurricanes number. Still, we never argued with Norrie; he was the boss and we trusted his judgement implicitly. He had been responsible for so many hit singles in the past, so he knew what he was doing. In return, Norrie had the wisdom to allow us to play the way we wanted to and to arrange all the music. I think he felt we had a rawness and an energy he didn't want to inhibit in any way, so he let us get on with it. He realized that as teenagers we would know best what we were trying to do, because it came naturally to us. We just wanted to rock.

On 17 June we recorded both sides at Abbey Road. Everything seemed to come together when we laid down 'Apache'. Perhaps our hearts weren't quite in harmony with 'Quartermaster's Stores'. It was the first time Hank used echo on record, and the first time I played acoustic guitar on a Shadows' session. Before then I had always used an electric guitar, and the recordings were so bad that I sounded like a 'hum' in the background. For 'Apache', which took four takes to record, I borrowed Cliff's Gibson Jumbo; it added to the overall depth of the sound and became recognized as my very own trademark, the jangling rhythm guitar. It was a fluke, but it was there. Cliff played a Chinese drum on the opening bars of the record.

As soon as we heard it on play-back we knew it was something special and told Norrie Paramor we were convinced it was the better side. We believed in it so strongly. We never expected him to change his mind; we thought he was so committed to 'Quartermaster's Stores'. Norrie did what he always did when he wasn't completely sure about a recording. He took the finished copies back home to play to his young children and tested their reactions. Fortunately for us they preferred 'Apache' too. Norrie, always the gentleman and a very shrewd operator, went along with their decision. The record was released the following month, with 'Quartermaster's Stores' making the flip-side. The EMI publicity machine had a field day. They sent out review copies of the record to all the music journalists, with an accompanying press release attached to an arrow: 'Hold on to your scalps. Here come the Shadows with their heap big hit "Apache".' The single entered the charts on 20 July at No.19. We had made it on our own at last.

The feeling of elation within the group at cracking the hit parade was overwhelming. It was marvellous to share Cliff Richard's success as a backing group, but to do it on our own as recording artistes was a different matter. It was a dream come true, and we felt so proud of Norrie Paramor because he had had faith in us, and it had paid off. I was on a winning streak, too. I couldn't lose. In the week 'Apache' was issued by Columbia, Cliff

Richard had deposed 'Good Timin'' by Jimmy Jones at the top of the charts with 'Please Don't Tease' – a number Pete Chester and I had written. So it was a great time for celebrations. 'Please Don't Tease' had been chosen as Cliff's follow-up single to the highly successful 'Fall in Love with You', in a unique way. The record company had laid on a party for eighty teenagers, drawn from youth clubs, EMI staff members and Cliff's fan club, and they were played twenty-four songs Cliff had recently recorded. They were then asked to vote for the track they would most like to see released as a single. 'Please Don't Tease' won by nearly fifty votes, ahead of 'Gee Whizz It's You', a number written by Hank Marvin and Sammy Samwell.

I received just over £1,000 in royalties for my share of the sales from 'Please Don't Tease', with which I bought my first car, a very ungroovy Rover 75, the old sit-up-and-beg type. It was black, with leather seats and polished veneer woodwork inside. I sold my Lambretta and bought the car second-hand. It was my pride and joy. On the strength of the success of the same record, Cliff Richard also bought himself a new car, a brand new Ford Thunderbird, which made my Rover look sick by comparison. The Shadows still only received a session fee for working on Cliff's records, and the money was presented to us after each recording in little brown envelopes. It was just like a wage packet.

'Apache' topped the chart for the first time on 20 August 1960, and by some strange twist of fate knocked Cliff Richard off the No.1 spot and into second place. It went on to sell over a million copies and to give the Shadows their first ever Gold Disc award. What was sickening about the affair was that someone else had the B-side. Mechanical royalties were paid on an equal basis, to the writers of the A-side and the B-side alike, on all singles. So publishing a B-side was just as lucrative as owning the rights to the A-side. There was a lot of money to be made.

During the sixties and seventies Radio Luxembourg exploited the situation to the full. The independent radio station ran and administered its own publishing company, Louvigny Music, which handled a large catalogue of songs. Luxembourg made special deals with all the major companies, to promote their singles and new releases by giving them extensive air play, in return for allowing Louvigny Music to publish the corresponding

B-sides of the records. It was an offer very few refused. Mickie Most gave them the publishing rights to many of Suzi Quatro's flip-sides, and at one time Radio Luxembourg became known in the business as 'Radio RAK' – named after Mickie Most's record company, because he had so many deals with the publishing firm. It has to be realized, however, that much of Luxembourg's programming at the time was paid for by the major record companies anyway, and that this was just another form of sponsorship and certainly wasn't illegal.

Norrie Paramor's brother made a lot of money from publishing 'Quartermaster's Stores'. That is when we all started to learn about music publishing, copyright and royalties, and vowed that in future we would try to make sure all our B-sides consisted of our own numbers.

When 'Apache' topped the hit parade we were appearing with Cliff Richard in a show called *Stars in Your Eyes* for the summer season at the London Palladium. It was presented by impresario Leslie Grade, who, with his brother Lew, was one of the biggest and most successful agents in show business, and feared by everyone. The show starred Russ Conway, Joan Regan, David Kossoff, Edmund Hockridge and Des O'Connor. Hank, Tony, Jet and I were earning £25 a week, although we had a record at No.1 in the charts and were also featured on the record currently at No.2. But the Palladium management wouldn't let us include 'Apache' in the show. We had a fifteen-minute spot and we weren't allowed to alter our act to feature the country's best-selling single. We were told it would cause all kinds of problems within the show.

Every record we made was released in America, with very little promotion, but they were favourably reviewed in the US music press. When 'Apache' was released, *Cashbox* called it 'a sure-fire winner from Britain's top teen orch. A hit throughout Europe. Surely this one must make the charts.' It did – but by someone else. The record had been an enormous success all over Europe, in Australia and New Zealand, South Africa, Rhodesia, Hong Kong and even India. And whenever Americans came to see our shows, they often wondered why we had not made it in the States. Perhaps it was only a matter of time. Part of the whole success of

Cliff Richard and the Shadows in Britain was our live performances. We created our own kind of excitement on stage, and maybe had we been able to go to America and promote our records by giving live performances, they might have become hits. Instead, a Danish guitarist called Jorgen Ingmann released 'Apache' in the USA six weeks after our version was first issued by Capitol Records. Ingmann found the number on the back of a demonstration acetate and recorded it virtually as a filler for the B-side of an instrumental called 'Echo Boogie'. Before long 'Apache' attracted more air play and the record was flipped over and went on to top the national pop charts. It sold over 2 million copies. Jorgen Ingmann was never heard of again. We were sick. Had our version reached the American charts, I am convinced we would have followed it up with a string of hits and maybe have established ourselves across the Atlantic as a major recording force. We were not consciously thinking of leaving Cliff at all, but if we had broken in the States, we would certainly have gone there on our own merit without our illustrious vocalist. But the opportunity was lost.

Shortly afterwards the Ventures struck gold with their first hit, an instrumental version of the old jazz classic 'Walk Don't Run', and cornered that whole section of the market – *our* market – while we missed out completely. The Shadows had been offered the chance to make a cover version of 'Walk Don't Run' to compete with the Ventures in Britain. But we had to get it on sale in just twenty-one days – so we turned it down. 'Apache' was beginning to break in the charts, and it would have taken away valuable sales. The John Barry Seven took up the option, recorded the number instead, and enjoyed a sizeable hit.

For the Shadows, however, America wasn't to be. The timing was somehow all wrong. British talent didn't mean anything over there. They simply didn't rate; after all, America had everything, so why import from Britain? In the past only two British artistes had topped the American charts – both singers: Vera Lynn in 1952 with 'Auf Wiedersehen Sweetheart', and fourteen-year-old Laurie London with 'He's Got the Whole World in His Hands' in 1958. Gene Pitney once told me that at the turn of the 1960s, after he had toured Britain, he took back to the States with him a terrific record by Adam Faith which he tried to get played on several local radio stations without success. None of them was interested – not because it was a bad record, but because it was by a *British* artiste. That was how our stock rated in the States until John, Paul, George and Ringo came along to rewrite the music books.

Tito Burns had been handling Cliff's career very successfully for over a year, when Norrie Paramor hinted that the Shadows should think about getting a manager of their own, to look after their interests now that 'Apache' was taking off. We needed to find the right person and were reluctant to go to anyone without a personal recommendation. We were all very wary of being taken for a ride in the music business. I think we were probably a little over-sensitive and cautious. We asked Norrie Paramor for advice and he suggested an Australian he knew called Peter Gormley.

'He's honest, very straight and trustworthy,' he said.

Peter, who came from Sydney, had been in England for just over a year looking after a singer called Frank Ifield. His background had been in journalism and the movie industry. After World War Two he became area manager for the Hoytes chain of cinemas, one of the most successful in Australia. He spoke with a broad Aussie brogue. He was forty years old. Jet and Hank went to see him in his flat in St John's Wood, near the EMI recording studios. Peter was very forthright at the meeting and outlined exactly what he felt he could do for the group.

'I'm not after a fast buck,' he said. 'I'll see what I can do for you in six months.'

Peter always told us we needed to plan for a long-term future, and convinced Hank and Jet that we could make show business our careers for a long, long time if we played it right. Shortly after, when Tony and I met him, he told us that apart from Jet, the James Dean look-alike on bass, we were very ordinary-looking guys; certainly not matinée idols from the old school, or teenage heart-throbs from the new, and we needed to diversify our talents into other areas of the business to broaden our horizons, and to look further afield than Britain and explore new markets. We liked his style immensely. Norrie Paramor had been right. Peter wasn't pretentious, and he seemed genuinely concerned for our futures. Even so, Jet suggested a year's trial period to see if we could work together. We shook hands on the agreement. There was no written contract and it remained that way for over twenty years. We all loved the man. And certainly, as far as I am concerned, Peter Gormley was like a father figure to me, the dad I never had. Within a year, Cliff Richard dispensed with Tito Burns's services and asked Peter Gormley to become his new personal manager. He could see how happy we were. Peter didn't take a percentage of Cliff's earnings for a whole year after becoming his manager, because he assumed that most of the work came from arrangements made by Tito Burns.

It was Peter Gormley who encouraged us all to develop our individual songwriting talents.

When I first started writing seriously, I signed a publishing deal with Carlin Music, who published Ian Samwell's material, including 'Move It'. They were a subsidiary of the American publishing giant Aberbach, with whom Elvis Presley was signed. I figured that if Elvis, the greatest rock 'n' roller in the world, had signed with them, it must be a good move as far as I was concerned. Franklyn Boyd, who had briefly managed Cliff's career and was a good friend, worked for the English end of the company, and I remember he had to take the contract up to Newcastle for my Aunt Sadie – as my guardian – to sign on my behalf, as I was only seventeen at the time and legally under age. It was an exciting time, and I wanted to share my news, so I wrote to my aunt telling her about it.

'I've found someone who has promised to publish my songs,' I said in my letter. 'This is it – the big time. Isn't it great?'

I genuinely believed that it was, until years later when I realized all was not what it had seemed in the contract. But then I knew nothing about publishing, and trusted everyone.

In those days the music publishing business virtually gave companies a licence to print money at someone else's expense. Horrendous tales concerning songwriters who have been manipulated out of thousands of pounds in royalties by heavily worded contracts are still commonplace in the music business. Before World War Two, publishers unscrupulously exploited composers by buying up the copyright to their songs for ridiculously small amounts of money, from which they creamed vast amounts in royalties. The writers were never told just how many times their work had been performed, or how much income it made. Sometimes they employed writers on a weekly wage to churn out a production line of new songs to order. The ties of their contracts would not allow them to sell their songs to anyone else. They were on an exclusive deal. If their songs were successful the publisher had little obligation to pay royalties in full because they were already on a salary, which they offset in lieu of the supposed royalties.

The situation changed little in the fifties and sixties, and in many cases contracts like those still existed. Publishing contracts were always weighted in favour of the company, not the individual writer. There were few advances, if any, and most deals appeared on the surface to be straightforward. A composer would receive a percentage of the money collected by the publisher from record sales and from performances of his song, based on a share of 6.25 per cent, paid for by the record company and then, for singles, distributed equally between the writer of the A-side and the writer of the B-side. It got more complicated when dealing with albums, because each of the credited writers on each of the featured tracks received exactly the same percentage. The money was then split on a 50:50 basis between the publisher and the writer. If more than one person wrote the song, the writers' royalty would be split accordingly; the publisher received 50 per cent no matter what.

This arrangement was for sales in Britain alone. It was a totally different story in international contracts. If a record was released overseas, the domestic publisher would enter into an agreement with a local company which would collect the respective royalties. They would retain 50 per cent for themselves and send the remaining 50 per cent to Britain where it was split 50:50. So the writer's share was now down to a meagre 25 per cent of the original royalty. Most publishing companies had subsidiaries all over the world, so in fact they were doing deals with themselves and picking up a royalty of 75 per cent.

It became even more complicated if a British writer was signed to a large American firm. Royalties would be collected by the local company and 50 per cent would be sent to the American end of the operation. Here 50 per cent of that total would be retained in America and the rest sent on to the British publisher, who then kept to the terms of the agreement by splitting 50:50 with the writer, who by now ended up with a derisory 12.5 per cent. It was also written into many contracts that copyrights were signed over to the publishing company for the duration of the writer's lifetime, which meant that many young rock stars would actually never own their own material. It would always belong to an outside source unless, of course, they managed to buy the publishing company themselves. It seems hard to believe, but Paul McCartney doesn't own many of his most famous compositions, written during his time with the Beatles. 'Yesterday' (the most recorded song of all time), 'She Loves You', 'Hey Jude' and 'I Want to Hold Your Hand' are just some of the songs now owned by Michael Jackson, who purchased Lennon and McCartney's music publishers Northern Songs/ATV Music in a 40-million-dollar takeover in 1985. It is one of the biggest regrets of McCartney's career.

In theory a publisher's duty was to promote the writer's material by attempting to place his songs with other artistes for recording purposes. In our case the matter hardly ever arose, and the publisher did very little for his return, because we rarely gave our songs away. Everything we composed was recorded either by Cliff Richard or by the Shadows. Nevertheless in the early days we got caught out like everyone else. We were very young and were dealing with older men whom we trusted because they were successful in their own field and thought that was its own recommendation. We never thought of getting legal advice to help us in the beginning – that would have cost us money we didn't have, and besides, we were excited by the prospect of being published writers and were looking at the world through rose-coloured glasses – horn-rimmed in Hank's case.

We weren't the only ones. There have been many outrageous publishing deals in the rock industry over the years which have only come to light when the maligned writer has taken the publisher to court. All were based on misguided composers signing away their songs without a thought for the future and without reading what they were getting involved in. It happened to Sting of the Police, and to Elton John, who managed to win more royalties from his material in a famous court case against Dick James (who was originally the Beatles publisher through Northern

Songs), and to Gilbert O'Sullivan, who successfully sued his publisher, MAM, and his manager Gordon Mills for malpractice and received around £2 million in settlement and the return of all his copyrights. Each claimed that their naïvety and lack of business know-how was exploited unfairly; each had failed to get expert legal advice before entering into their complicated agreement.

When we first got involved we knew nothing about the music publishing industry. We soon learned the hard way, and as lawyers moved in to analyse old contracts and draw up new ones, it all started to change. These days the percentage deals are very much to the advantage of writers, and no one will accept a lower split than a 60:40 deal. In many cases it works out at 70:30, and I have heard of some 90:10 agreements. Some major publishers will even sign the more successful artistes, paying them royalties of 100 per cent for the prestige and the interest in order to stimulate other, lesser-known composers to join them. Today's deals are for much shorter lengths of time, too. It is certainly not necessary now for a writer to sign away his copyrights for life. Contracts are negotiated for periods of five years or even less, after which time all copyrights revert back to the writers, who can then re-negotiate a further contract. It is a much fairer system. A lot of people got hurt before and lost a lot of money, until some of the shadier deals were brought out into the open and new guidelines were set down. Certainly the Beatles, possibly the most famous songwriters of all time, didn't receive all the money that was due to them through their publishing agreements.

With hindsight, we were all very inexperienced as writers and artistes.

When we learned more about the business, we decided to start our own publishing company for our material as soon as we could, and we formed Shadows Music. One of the first numbers we registered with our new concern was 'FBI', which Hank, Jet and I wrote one evening in our flat at East Finchley. At the time when it was released as a single in February 1961, we were having problems over the terms of our original publishing agreement. So to avoid trouble when the record came out, our manager Peter Gormley was listed as the composer. Our names never appeared on the credits. It helped us out of a situation but we still received the royalties. With Shadows Music it meant that we could now own the copyright on our own material, instead of the 50 per cent we had been used to, and we had total control of our own destiny again. We gave Aberbach/Carlin Music a 25 per cent administration fee for handling the company, and we ended up with a 75:25 split, which was better for us. We eventually placed hundreds of copyrights into the company. Even then we weren't 'fireproof'.

There was a famous publishing house called Harms Witmark, who were responsible for publishing film scores. The music for many new British film releases was handled through this company. When we made *The Young Ones* with Cliff Richard in 1961, we discovered that all the material we had written for the film had to be placed with Harms Witmark, so we lost out again. The following year, when *Summer Holiday* was made, Leslie Grade formed Elstree Music for exactly the same purpose, and all the music written for the film was channelled through this company. Like Paul McCartney, I still don't own my three biggest copyrights – 'Bachelor Boy', 'Summer Holiday' and 'Foot Tapper'. They are the property of Elstree Music, now a division of EMI Music. Yet when the Beatles made their first film, *A Hard Day's Night*, the entire musical score was published through their own company, Northern Songs. Somehow they had broken the hold of firms like Harms Witmark and Elstree Music and times were never the same again. I can remember thinking, if only we owned 100 per cent of 'Bachelor Boy' – it sold a million.

Despite all this, Hank and I got a great kick out of songwriting and found it fairly easy at the time. We often wrote together when we had spare moments, travelling to and from engagements, or in our dressing-room. Sometimes the entire group would work out brand new numbers or contribute to someone else's ideas. We didn't operate like Lennon and McCartney, who went off and wrote separately. After an initial burst, John and Paul didn't write together all the time, preferring to create their own songs individually. Ours, however, was a genuine partnership. Often we would be specifically asked for songs and write them to order to fit any situation: if Cliff needed a slow number, an up-tempo song, or something for a scene in a movie, we would write a song to measure, like a tailor making a suit. It was as easy as that. We were fledgling composers, learning our trade, writing very simple songs at first, which were full of innocence. Songs such as 'I Love You', which topped the chart for Cliff in December 1960, had very twee lyrics, and there is a classic line in 'Bachelor Boy' – 'Then I'll get married, have *a* wife and *a* child . . .' where the emphasis is placed on the wrong words. I didn't think about it when I wrote the song, I was just busking along having a good time. It has haunted me ever since. I am a member of the Society of Distinguished Songwriters (SODS), which contains some of the all-time great British composers, and often I am ribbed mercilessly for the lyrics to that song. My fellow distinguished members will never let me forget it. *A* wife and *A* child, indeed!

In our original ten-year association with Cliff Richard, we wrote a prolific amount of material for him to record on singles and albums, and composed a fair amount of numbers for ourselves as well. Lennon and McCartney were hailed as the first definitive pop writers who were creating genuine *British* material. Yet we were doing it some three years before them. I don't think people realize just how much we contributed in the songwriting stakes, as both Hank and I wrote songs on our own and with a variety of other people as well, like Pete Chester, Ian Samwell, Jet Harris, Cliff Richard, and later, Brian Bennett, John Rostill and John Farrar.

When we started writing instrumentals together, we devised a whole series of goonish titles which belied the fact that they were very good numbers: 'I Wish I Could Shimmy Like My Sister Arthur', 'Genie with the Light Brown Lamp', 'Nivram' (which is Marvin spelt backwards), 'Tales of a Raggy Tramline', 'Theme from a Filleted Plaice', 'Shadoogie' (a combinaion of Shadows and Boogie), 'I'll See You in My Drums' and 'Alice in Sunderland', which all added to our special appeal. We wanted people to sit up and take notice. We wrote '36-24-36' as a straight copy of the Champs' hit 'Tequila', and it developed from there.

'Oh What a Lovely Tune' came out of a rehearsal session when the four of us started fooling around with a silly piece of music. Brian Bennett, who had recently become our drummer, just happened to call out in a very posh accent, 'Oh, what a lovely tune', which became the title. We tidied it up considerably and gave it a Palm Court feel, and Brian provided the commentary in typical twenties flapper style. It was a subtle form of humour, which is what the Shadows are all about. Several of these numbers appeared in our début album, *The Shadows*. It came out in September 1961 and went on to top the LP chart. On 7 October we made pop history by topping three charts simultaneously, with 'Kon Tiki' at No.1 in the singles chart, *The Shadows* at No.1 in the album chart, and 'Shadows to the Fore' at No.1 in the EP chart.

Hank, Brian and I were great Goon fans – we took our humour on to the stage with us and never attempted to take ourselves too seriously. Obviously we weren't laughing through numbers like 'Apache', but the undertone was always one of humour. You can't play 'Foot Tapper' for over twenty-five years and take it too seriously. On stage we took the mickey out of ourselves in a gentle way, and the audiences loved it and laughed along with us. We made our very first stage appearance together, topping the bill in our own right as the Shadows *without* Cliff Richard, on 25 September 1960 at the Colston Hall in Bristol. Eddie Jarrett was an agent working for Leslie Grade. He could see just how successful the record had become and took a gamble on booking us on our own for a Sunday concert. It paid handsome dividends. The show was sold out. We headed a very substantial bill which included Chas McDevitt and Shirley Douglas, Frank Ifield, Michael Cox and Paul Beatty and the Beats. Shortly afterwards Eddie Jarrett became our permanent agent. He'd shown great faith in us as an act and believed in our ability as bill-toppers, so we decided to repay his loyalty. Before long he was booking us out on tours of our own.

It was during the early concerts that we developed our own special kind of stage routines when performing. I suppose it was a very basic form of choreography, and it became known as the Shadows 'walk'. It is something that is still very much part of our act today; it has been refined and refurbished over the years, but we would not be the Shadows without it. The basic idea for movement of this kind came from America.

Jerry Lee Lewis was one of our great rock 'n' roll heroes, and in May 1958 he arrived in Britain at the start of an extensive series of concert engagements up and down the country. It was to prove an ill-fated tour. Before leaving to come here, the American singer had married his second cousin, Myra Gale Brown, who accompanied her husband on the tour. As soon as he flew into the country he was greeted by a barrage of questions from waiting journalists at the airport, when it was discovered that Jerry Lee's young bride *was just thirteen years of age*, and that he had married her *before* being granted a legal divorce from his previous wife, Jane Mitcham. The resulting bad publicity had a devastating effect on the tour. Jerry Lee lasted just six days in Britain before being forced home by an outraged British public. Fortunately Hank and I managed to see the 'Killer', as Jerry Lee was nicknamed, performing his act live on stage at the Gaumont State Cinema in Kilburn. He was absolutely magnificent, and it was a crime that the press should hound him so because of his complicated private life. Jerry Lee was a great performer and should have been judged on that alone.

The band on the touring package show with him was the black vocal and instrumental outfit the Treniers, who performed a very subtle form of rhythm 'n' blues. Their act also featured some very finely honed and precise stage movements. At given moments, they would break into set routines. There was movement on the stage at all times, which looked great from the audience's point of view. Everything was perfectly worked out. The group moved together as one, despite some complicated footwork. We had never experienced anything like this before. It was new and different and seemed to be the essence of group rock 'n' roll, which we thought was fantastic. A few weeks later when we appeared on *Oh Boy* we were very taken by the five Dallas Boys, who also incorporated dance steps and choreographed routines into their own act, while they were singing. When we had a hit with 'Apache' we decided we should make our act more entertaining if we possibly could, so we worked out an arrangement of kicks and steps on stage, to give the audience something to watch while listening to the music. And that's how the 'walk' evolved. It was all very simple at first – steps to the side, steps to the back and kick. It all added to the interest. We incorporated stage movements into our act with Cliff, too, to improve the presentation after those early days on the Kalin Twins' tour of trying to get up after lying on our backs and playing at the same time. We copied the idea from the Treniers, and when we came to a guitar solo on stage, Cliff would step back into the group and join us, and all four of us – Cliff, Jet, Hank and I – would start moving around together. It was great fun and very effective.

Our major concern following the outstanding success of 'Apache', which was named record of the year by the *New Musical Express*, was how we could follow a chart-topping single that had sold over a million copies. We could go no higher. The problem was finding a suitable number to record as our next single. It was a very worrying time. After three flops in a row we had attained the ultimate. We had to keep it going. We had all seen what had happened to 'one-hit wonders' who had enjoyed success with a single record and then disappeared as quickly as they came along. It was the last thing we wanted to happen to us, although we knew we would still be able to record and perform with Cliff Richard.

It was Norrie Paramor who suggested 'Man of Mystery' to us. He was a very constructive A & R man: he was constantly searching for new songs, and was always open to suggestions. He even wrote material for the group, including 'The Savage', 'Peace Pipe', and 'The Frightened City', for the film of the same name, which we released as a single in May 1961. They were all good melodies. He was a very talented musician, besides being a brilliant producer. 'Man of Mystery' was the theme to a series of British B-movies that were based around the tales of Edgar Wallace. It was a chilling and sinister composition which was played over the opening titles to each film in the series, and it meant that in effect we were making a cover version. It was written by a Yorkshireman from Leeds called Michael Carr, who had composed such other great songs as 'Red Sails in the Sunset', 'Does Your Mother Come from Ireland?', 'Hang Out Your Washing on the Siegfried Line' and 'South of the Border', which we also recorded. Within a year Michael Carr would pick up the writing credits for our second British No.1, 'Kon Tiki'.

When we came to record 'Man of Mystery', we were still appearing at the London Palladium with Cliff, and we suggested to EMI that in order to create the right kind of atmosphere it would be a good idea if we started the recording session at midnight. It was an outrageous request. It had never been done before. Sessions at Abbey Road normally ran in three three-hour sets: from 10 am–1 pm, 2.30–5.30 pm, and from 7–10 pm. After

10 pm the studio was closed, so our suggestion was revolutionary to say the least and EMI took a lot of persuading. The powers that be couldn't quite understand why anyone should want to record so late at night. Yet within three years all-night sessions became commonplace in the business, particularly at Abbey Road. Eventually the company reluctantly agreed to our suggestion, and recording started promptly at midnight.

We finished at four in the morning. It took just twenty minutes to complete 'Man of Mystery' and create the right kind of atmosphere on the record, which included a major mistake on the lead solo when Hank's strings clanged together to give a discord at the wrong time. He kept it in, and on the final version no one noticed. Since then, every time he plays it on stage, Hank intentionally repeats the mistake and it has now become an integral part of the number. (If the truth be known, on 'Apache' the third string on the lead guitar is sharp.)

'Man of Mystery' was released in November and went on to reach No.5 in the charts, shortly after we had been named Britain's best small group on the strength of one hit record. Cliff Richard had been chosen as Britain's top male singer, and I had been told I was going to become a father. My wife Anne and I were overjoyed. Our son, Dwayne, made his début on 13 June 1961.

In anticipation of the happy event, Anne and I moved out of the flat in Long Lane, Finchley, which we shared with Hank – who by now had married his girlfriend Billie – and bought a house in North Harrow at 157 Headstone Lane. It was a detached cottage-style home set in three-quarters of an acre. I paid £6,000 for it in 1961, which was an absolute fortune then. Twenty-seven years later it was sold again for over £250,000.

Despite the trappings of success and the money it brought, it was a tough existence for our wives. It was actively encouraged by our manager and record company that our marital status be kept very quiet and almost hidden from the fans, in case it affected the popularity of the group with the girls and our record sales dropped. Male pop stars were supposed never to marry – it was bad for the image. Cliff attracted female fans by the thousand, but in our case most of the fans were guys, many of whom came along to ogle at Hank's guitar playing. Just as Buddy Holly had done before us, we gave hope to thousands of ordinary-looking lads who wanted to play guitar and emulate the Shadows, and we influenced a whole legion of kids to pick up guitars and have a go for themselves. Sometimes, during a concert, we could see guys in the audience staring mesmerized at our fingers, watching every note we played. Others would make copious notes on our stage performances, their heads buried in a book listening to the music. There were always young boys who wore horn-rimmed glasses and made it very obvious that they weren't meant for seeing through. Hank had that effect on people, and the Shadows created an audience of guys who all wanted to be in groups. I'd love to know how many teenage lads have stood in front of a bedroom mirror with a cricket bat or a tennis racket for a makeshift guitar, put 'Apache' on the record player, and imagined they were Hank Marvin.

Show-business wives weren't encouraged to accompany their husbands on tour. It was their place to remain at home and bring up the children. Sometimes our tours would take us away for up to ten weeks at a time, especially when we visited Australia or New Zealand, and there were a lot of temptations. For a wife stuck at home, usually on her own, it was a very lonely existence and had none of the glamour attached to the business. It was no wonder that so many marriages broke up. There were so many pressures. We were away a lot of the time.

In February 1960 I was on tour in America with Cliff Richard when Anne gave birth to a baby girl – our first child. We called her Karen. Almost immediately she developed problems and lived for just twenty-four hours. It was a shattering blow; a painful and traumatic experience, which Anne had to cope with on her own while I was over 5,000 miles away entertaining American audiences. It was heartbreaking.

It hit home hard. And hurt us both. I have never been particularly religious, but I couldn't understand how God – if there really is one – could let this terrible thing happen to two young people and take their baby away from them. I felt helpless and inadequate. When I was needed most, I was stuck in South Carolina and couldn't get home. I felt more angry than sad. Why should God do this to people who had done no harm? Whatever belief I might have had seemed to disappear in that one moment.

* * *

South Africa was a highly lucrative market for British recording artistes during the 1960s, and they regularly appeared on tour in the big cities of Johannesburg, Cape Town, Port Elizabeth and Durban. There was a lot of money to be made through record sales, and recording companies encouraged their artistes to go there as often as they possibly could, to promote new singles. In March 1961, after the release of our next single, 'FBI', which peaked at No.3, we embarked on our first South African tour and flew to Johannesburg, where we knew Cliff Richard was extremely popular. We have never had a reception like it anywhere in the world before or since. The airport had been invaded by fans and it was teeming with girls. Thousands upon thousands of people, screaming, cheering, crying, chanting, came out to meet us. They lined the route into the city centre, hung out of windows in tall buildings, and climbed up lamp-posts for a better view. It was an absolutely unbelievable sight. *Cliffmania.* The city was paralysed. Everything came to a complete standstill as we drove through body-lined streets accompanied by a six-strong police motor-cycle escort. Strung across the main city thoroughfare, Eloff Street, was a banner proclaiming: Welcome Cliff Richard and the Shadows. Crowd reaction became so intense that Cliff had to climb out on to a balcony in the city centre and wave to the heaving masses below. The atmosphere was charged with electricity. Two thousand people besieged our hotel chanting, 'We want Cliff. We want Cliff.' The experience was exhilarating. Unfortunately, after a few days of African sunshine, I had a less than exhilarating experience when I received second-degree burns from staying out too long in the sun.

We were billed by one South African newspaper as 'Cliff Richard and his Guitar Players'. Nevertheless our mainline tour was a sell-out, and to reinforce our popularity in the country, Cliff and the Shadows had no less than eight records between them in the South African Top Ten, including 'FBI', 'Man of Mystery' and 'Shazam' – a cover of the Duane Eddy original. We also made our first ever live recording when our concert at the Coliseum in Johannesburg was taped, which resulted in the release of a live Shadows EP, containing 'FBI', 'Guitar Boogie', 'Shazam' and the cover version of Santo and Johnny's recent US

(1a) Above left: My father, Stan Cripps, was serving in the Army with the Royal Artillery when he met my mother at the Royal Norfolk Hotel in Bognor Regis during the war. They were never married. We met for the first time when I was eight years old and he took me on holiday to Berwick-on-Tweed. I never saw him again until I was seventeen.

(1b) Above right: I never really knew my mother, Grace Welch. She died from tuberculosis when I was five years old. She was only thirty-two. When I found out I was illegitimate I changed my name from Bruce Cripps and adopted my mother's surname.

(1c) Below left: My Aunt Sadie, my mother's sister, who brought me up after Grace died. She was like a second mother to me and didn't stand in my way when I told her I wanted to leave Newcastle to become a musician. Had it not been for the money she regularly sent to me in London, Hank and I might well have starved.

(1d) Below right: Eighteen months old and already on the wagon in war-torn Bognor. I left the Sussex seaside resort when I was three and moved to Chester-le-Street in the north-east of England.

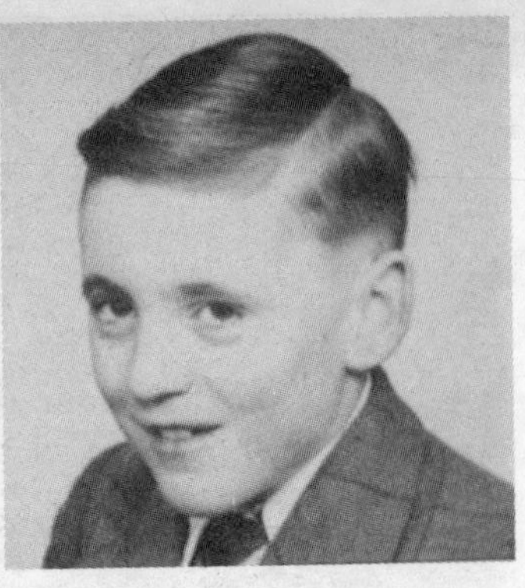

(2a) Above left: Even at the tender age of two, I was posing for the camera.
(2b) Above right: I was eight years old and dressed in my Sunday-best clothes when this picture was taken just before I set off for Newcastle Central station, where I met my father for the first time.
(2c) Below: Trying to look mean and moody in my first professional publicity photograph. I was seventeen and thought I looked like Elvis Presley. No one else did.

(3a) Above: The legendary 2i's – 'The Home of the Stars' – at 59 Old Compton Street, London. Hank and I started playing there in the spring of 1958 and soon became known as the 'Geordie Boys'. Tommy Steele, Adam Faith, Cliff Richard, Marty Wilde and the Vipers were just some of the many stars discovered in the tiny Soho coffee bar.

(3b) Below: On 21 May 1958 Jerry Lee Lewis (centre) arrived in Britain at the start of a lengthy tour. He brought with him his third wife, Myra, who was just thirteen years old. When it was discovered that Jerry Lee had married Myra before actually divorcing his second wife, Jane Mitcham, the resulting publicity destroyed the tour, and by 27 May he was forced to return home to the States. Fortunately, during the brief time Jerry Lee was in Britain, Cliff and the original Drifters managed to meet one of the true American pioneers of rock 'n' roll. The picture shows (left to right) Cliff's manager, John Foster, Cliff Richard, Jerry Lee Lewis, Terry Smart and Ian Samwell.

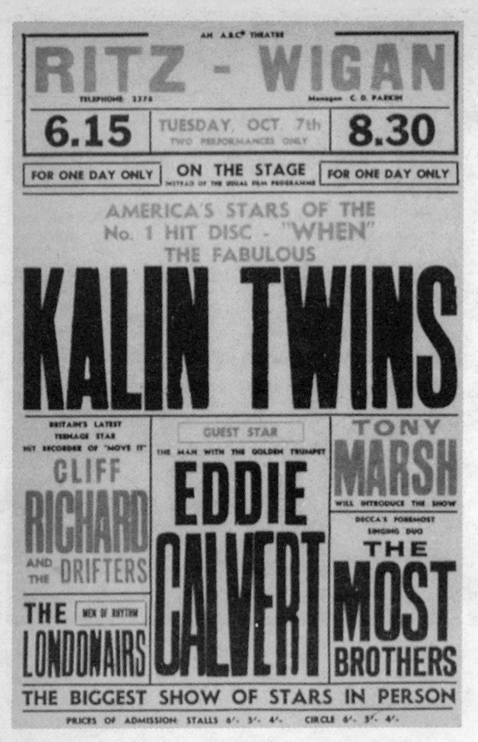

(4a) Above: The poster from our very first British tour, which started on Sunday, 5 October 1958, at the Victoria Hall, Hanley, near Stoke-on-Trent. Thirty years later we're still going strong – but whatever happened to the Kalin Twins?

(4b) Below: Cliff Richard, in the famous pink jacket, on stage at Birmingham Town Hall in 1959. It was incredible: Cliff only had to wiggle his legs and the place was in uproar – there were screams and scenes of wild hysteria.

(5a) Above: Chiswick Empire, 1959. During our second performance on the Friday evening (1 May) there was a riot in the auditorium as rival gangs of teddy boys clashed in the balcony. Light bulbs and eggs showered down on to the stage, and when a fire extinguisher came hurtling from the gods into the stalls, it was decided to call the show off. Des O'Connor was the compère, but I don't think the audience was complaining about his singing.

(5b) Below: The Shadows' luxury tour bus!

(6a) Above: A unique view of Cliff and the group entertaining on stage at the Metropolitan Theatre, Edgware Road. We used hardly any amplification.
(6b) Below: Cliff and the Shadows rehearsing at EMI's Studio 2 in Abbey Road, in North London, with the harmonica-playing Gerry Furst (centre). Gerry had been a member of the Chesternuts with Hank and me back in 1958 and was featured on our one and only record release, 'Teenage Love'. Hank and Jet, however, seem preoccupied with other things.

(7a) Above: Listening to playback in the control room at Studio 2 in the EMI studios at Abbey Road, where the Beatles recorded all of their hits and where in 1967 they created *Sergeant Pepper*. The control desk is tiny when compared with today's forty-eight-track consoles. With (left to right) Hank, Brian Bennett, Licorice Locking, producer Norrie Paramor and our original recording engineer, Malcolm Addy.

(7b) Below: The cover photograph from our first album, called simply *The Shadows*. I borrowed the white Fender Telecaster I'm holding specially for the photo session, and the price tag is still hanging from it. *The Shadows* reached Number 1 in the autumn of 1961 and stayed in the chart for an incredible fifty-seven weeks.

(8) Cliff and the Shadows and 'Willie and the Hand Jive', immaculately dressed on stage at the London Palladium in 1961. No sign of those two greasy yobs from the 2i's.

(9a) Above: Attending the première of *Wonderful Life* at the Empire Theatre, Leicester Square, on 2 July 1964 with my first wife Anne, John Rostill and Brian Bennett and their lovely ladies. Anne and I met at the 2i's coffee bar in the summer of 1958, and we were married in August 1959 at St Stephen's Church, Westminster. Cliff Richard was my best man.

(9b) Below: I met my second wife, Lynne, in March 1974 at Forest Mere Health Farm in Hampshire. We were married in August 1979.

(10a) Above: The Greeks have a word for it – *bouzoukis*! Filming *Summer Holiday* in the main square in Athens, resplendent in Greek national costume, including the skirts and the famous Shadows walk. Brian and Licorice keep time with tambourines, while Hank and I attempt to play 'Apache' on *bouzoukis*.
(10b) Below: How the Shadows won the war. A scene from *Wonderful Life*, shot on location in the Canary Islands, with Susan Hampshire as America's favourite pin-up girl, Betty Grable. John Rostill (right) had been a member of the Shadows for only a few weeks when he was whisked off to the Canaries for filming. He had yet to play a note with the group on stage.

(11a) Above: The Shadows on the set at Pinewood Studios for Cliff's sixth film, *Finders Keepers*, made in 1966. By now John Rostill (centre) was playing bass in the group.
(11b) Below: The Shadows behind the Iron Curtain. In 1968 we were invited to attend the world-famous Split Song Festival in Yugoslavia as special guest stars.

(12) Above: The Shadows *circa* 1975, with John Farrar (right), just before the Eurovision Song Contest in which we represented the United Kingdom singing 'Let Me be the One' and ended up in second place. We were beaten by a Dutch song with the typical Eurovision title of 'Ding-a-Dong'.

(13a) Opposite, top left: Peter Gormley from Sydney, Australia, was handling the career of Frank Ifield when, in the summer of 1960, we asked him to become the Shadows' personal manager. We worked together for the next twenty years and more *without* a contract. In 1961 Peter also agreed to manage Cliff and, several years later, guided the career of Olivia Newton-John.

(13b) Opposite, top right: John Rostill was a member of a Bournemouth-based group, the Interns, when we asked him to join the Shadows after the departure of Licorice Locking in November 1963. We auditioned John on stage at the London Palladium. Brian Bennett rated him as the best bass player we ever had. Tragically, ten years later he died after an accident in his studio at his Hertfordshire home. Besides being a bass player of great distinction, John was also a prolific songwriter, penning Olivia Newton-John's hit singles 'Let Me be There' and 'If You Love Me (Let Me Know)'. Together we wrote Olivia's American Number 1 success 'Please Mister Please'.

(13c) Opposite, bottom: Brian Bennett is probably one of the greatest drummers in the world – and a tremendous guy. He joined the Shadows in October 1961, replacing Tony Meehan, after spells working with Marty Wilde, Tony Sheridan, the Krew-Kats and Tommy Steele. The first number he ever recorded with the Shadows was 'Stars Fell on Stockton'. Besides his work in the group, Brian Bennett has also established his name in the music industry as a well-respected musician, composer, record producer and arranger. Several of his compositions have been used for television theme tunes, while 'Sound of Success' was chosen by ITV to accompany the television coverage of the wedding of Prince Charles and Lady Diana Spencer in July 1981.

(14a) One of the highlights of my career came when I was privileged to share the stage with one of the all-time guitar greats, and fellow Geordie, Mark Knopfler from Dire Straits. He once told us that one of his great ambitions was to play 'Wonderful Land' on stage with 'the man with the pink Stratocaster', Hank Marvin, and the Shadows. He achieved his ambition at the Dominion Theatre, Tottenham Court Road, London, in 1983. The packed audience couldn't believe their eyes or ears and gave us a standing ovation.
(14b) The 'Geordie Boys' in action again, twenty-eight years on, at the Dominion Theatre during our British tour of 1986. We were just a few hundred yards away from where we first appeared together as a singing duo in the basement of the 2i's coffee bar in Soho in 1958.

(15a) Above: The Shadows today: (left to right) Alan Jones, Cliff Hall, Hank B. Marvin, Brian Bennett and yours truly.

(15b) Below: My son Dwayne, following in father's footsteps and now making his way on the executive side of the music industry after a lengthy spell at EMI Records.

(16) Another publicity photograph, 1988, and I still don't look like Elvis!

No.1 success, 'Sleepwalk'. It was only ever released in South Africa.

The previous year we had encountered the futility of segregation in the southern states of America. Here the situation under apartheid was ten times worse. The division between whites and non-whites was vast. We could see at first-hand what was going on, with totally segregated audiences. When we were first offered the contract to go to South Africa we didn't realize that there would be these problems, and we found ourselves in an awkward position. We overcame it by purposely putting on a series of extra shows for the benefit of the coloured South Africans in the townships outside the cities. The audience reaction was tremendous. We appeared in one of the shanty towns outside Johannesburg, where the living conditions of the inhabitants were horrific. These people were living in utter squalor and deprivation, with the social diseases of hatred, bitterness and anger breeding alongside such physical diseases as diphtheria, dysentery and hunger. I was appalled that they were treated so badly by the minority running the country. It didn't make sense, and all these years later it still doesn't. It was a crazy situation, because we could see what was happening but were powerless to do anything about the political climate in the country. Today the situation does not seem any different – the terrible system of apartheid is still with us.

I have often been asked about apartheid since, and I have continued to condemn it. We live in a world with double standards, however: other countries are governed by equally obnoxious regimes, in which man's inhumanity to man is terrifying, yet no one seems to condemn or denounce those.

Nowadays very few British entertainers go to South Africa to perform. There is a United Nations blacklist in operation, on which are the names of people who have appeared there. Cliff Richard – of all people – is prominent on the list. The British Musicians' Union has banned its members from going there, although they do not have a legal right to stop any musician from going to South Africa to work. However, if we went on a concert tour, even if we played to mixed or coloureds-only audiences, we would find it extremely difficult to work again in Britain. The union would not allow any of its members to work with us again.

We would, in effect, be blacklisted into submission. It would be almost impossible for us to make records, to appear on radio and television, or to give a concert in any British theatre. We would lose our livelihood. That's how much power is wielded. Cliff Richard gets round the situation these days by taking his gospel tours to South Africa, spreading the word of Jesus.

I have always maintained throughout my career that we are entertainers, not politicians, and that as such we should have the freedom to perform wherever we like without restriction. Barring performers from South Africa does not change the situation, and we should not kid ourselves that it ever will. Double standards again.

Still on the subject of South Africa, I also believe that the Nelson Mandela concert held at Wembley in 1988 was wrong. I don't think many of the kids who paid to see the concert knew who Nelson Mandela was anyway. Some of them would not have been born when he was jailed.

The Shadows today are managed by Brian Goode, who has taken over the reins from Peter Gormley. One of the other artistes he represents is a singer-songwriter called Labi Siffre, who has enjoyed a fair amount of chart success over the years. During 1988 Labi's song, 'So Strong', which is about the struggles in South Africa, won him huge artistic acclaim, both musically and lyrically. It was a great song, with very powerful, anti-apartheid sentiments and the perfect message of hope. Yet the organizers of the concert refused to let him appear on the show, and I'm convinced it was a political decision to keep him from performing. But why? Here was a man who is black, singing about the great causes be believes in passionately, who could have performed a song he had written especially to condemn the regime in South Africa and reached a massive global audience . . . yet they turned him down without explanation. Maybe he wasn't a big enough name.

When we returned from our first trip to South Africa we started work on Cliff's next film, *The Young Ones*, which was filmed at Elstree Studios for Leslie Grade. It had an initial budget of £100,000 but went over the limit by some £130,000. It was a super, unpretentious musical that broke away from some of the earlier, dire British attempts at making pop movies like *Beat Girl*,

The Golden Disc, *What a Whopper*, and even *The Tommy Steele Story*, which were usually vehicles for current pop stars to sing their latest hits with a virtually non-existent plot and story line behind them. *The Young Ones* was different because it had a recognizable, if fairly twee, story.

Besides Cliff Richard, the movie starred Robert Morley and a young South African dancer called Carole Gray. She had been brought in as a replacement for the British actress Annette Robinson. Carole was a friend of the producer. She was not much of a singer, and another voice had to be dubbed on to the soundtrack. Sidney Furie directed the picture and later went on to make films like *Superman*. The Shadows appeared in the film playing themselves again, and we weren't acting as such, but we contributed several numbers, including 'Peace Pipe' and 'The Savage' on the soundtrack, backed Cliff on several songs, and wrote 'Got a Funny Feeling' and 'We Say Yeah'. The main title theme, 'The Young Ones', was an American song, written by Sid Tepper and Roy Bennett, who had written for Elvis Presley and enjoyed a number of big hits, including 'Twenty Tiny Fingers, Twenty Tiny Toes'. It was also suggested that Jet and Hank would be offered more substantial acting roles, and rumour had it that parts were being specially written for them. They never materialized. Instead the parts went to Melvyn Hayes and Richard O'Sullivan. By now Jet was drinking quite heavily and he believed this was the reason for his not getting the part. The producer didn't want to run the risk of being let down.

The day rehearsals started, on 15 May, Cliff's father, Rodger Webb, died from heart disease – he was fifty-seven. It was a devastating blow for Cliff, who was still only twenty and idolized his dad. I believe it was at this time that he started to question his own values. He needed something to fill his life now, and was to turn more and more towards religion.

I found filming an incredible waste of time. We were picked up at seven every morning and were on call at the studios until quite late at night, and the majority of the time was spent hanging around waiting for the next scene. If the producer got two minutes of actual film at the end of the day he was doing well. When we weren't needed for filming, we spent a lot of our time fishing for newts in a gigantic tank that had been specially constructed on one of the studio lots, for shooting such classic movies as *The Cruel Sea* and *The Guns of Navarone*.

When the film was premièred in December, it caused a sensation. One reporter called it 'the best musical Britain has ever made – and the finest teenage screen entertainment produced for a long time anywhere'. It became a massive box office success, the movie hit of the year. There was queueing at every cinema it played. Cliffmania had been transferred to the silver screen. When 'The Young Ones' was released as a single in January 1962, it had the distinction of having sold over a million copies on advance orders alone. It went straight to No.1.

Although things seemed to be going extremely well for the group from an outsider's point of view, internally there was friction.

With Peter Gormley's guidance we were now more determined than ever to make music our long-term career, just as he had suggested, whatever happened in the future. Sure, we were having success, but we all realized that it might not last long if we didn't commit ourselves totally to the Shadows to make it work, and that we also needed to have a little luck along the way. Our luck, for the time being, seemed to be holding out.

Because I believed so much in the group, I was looked upon as the regimental sergeant-major, trying to motivate everyone and often having a go if things were slacking. It wasn't personal – I only wanted the best for the Shadows. I tried to keep up standards, and I was only adopting the right professional attitude in my opinion. Cliff once said: 'Bruce is terribly reliable and he is a bit of a taskmaster in as much as he keeps the boys at it in rehearsals until everything is perfect. You see, perfection is Bruce's aim and he spares nothing to achieve his goal. His attitude has won the respect of us all.' All except Tony Meehan.

When the four of us started together, we split the money four ways. We all worked hard for it, although Tony became lazier the more success we achieved. He had a very lackadaisical attitude to work, almost as if he didn't care any more, and his time-keeping had become appalling. It was hard for him to get out of bed. Whenever we set off on an engagement together, he would never be ready and would make us wait for him for intolerable lengths of time.

One morning we had agreed to set off for Newcastle at 8.30, and a few moments before the allotted time Hank, Jet and I arrived at Tony's flat, knowing we had a long drive ahead of us. As soon as we knocked on the door of the apartment, it was a signal for Tony to get out of bed, *not* before. He was married by now, and on this occasion he invited us inside and asked us, once again, to wait for him. Instead of apologizing or attempting to get ready so that we could set off on our long journey, he asked Bridget, his wife, to make him breakfast, and then calmly sat down to eat it while we fumed.

Another time, when we were due to do a concert in Leeds, Tony left so late that he missed the train connection, caught a later one, and arrived at the theatre after the show had started. We just went on without a drummer, what else could we do? Half-way through our act, Tony nonchalantly ambled on to the stage, to thunderous applause from the audience, without even bothering to change into his stage clothes, and proceeded to join in.

Tony was a great drummer, but he wasn't pulling his weight. It seemed he had no respect for anyone, least of all his elders. One night he and Hank had a bitter argument in the dressing-room before we were due to go on stage, and Tony actually attacked Hank and bit one of his fingers. Another time, Sam Curtis, who had now become our road manager, had taken about as much of Tony's arrogance as he could stand, and he just flipped. He grabbed the drummer, turned him upside-down, pulled his trousers down and gave him a good walloping. It was just what he needed, but the message still didn't seem to have got through to him. He was still as pompous as ever. He wanted all the fame, the adulation and the money, but didn't want to do anything for it, looking upon it as his right. He always adopted a superior attitude to people.

When we toured South Africa for the first time, Tony and I shared a room together. On the day we were due to fly home to England, he overslept yet again. The rest of us had been ready for ages, and as usual we were waiting for him to appear. Time was getting tight because of our flight connection back to London. As we waited in the hotel lobby for our taxis to come, I went back upstairs to see if he was nearly ready. He was still asleep, without a care in the world. I managed to wake him, and with some urgency told him we were about to leave for home. No response. Tony seemed to be in a daze. His eyes were open, but were glazed over.

'Come on, Tony, we'll miss the plane,' I said, slapping his face to bring him round. He grunted and groaned, but didn't move. I shook him again, and still no reaction. 'Right,' I said, giving him an ultimatum. 'We are leaving in five minutes.' No response. 'I'll leave you here to get ready, and I'll be back when the taxi arrives. Come on, there's not much time.' I left him there and went back to the hotel foyer and waited with the others.

When the taxis finally turned up, there was still no sign of Tony. I was furious. I knew exactly what had happened, and sure enough when I rushed back to the bedroom I found him flat out on the bed, fast asleep. I was livid. I lost control, threw his tickets and his passport at him and stormed out of the room, slamming the door behind me.

'I'll see you in London,' I shouted. We left without him. Tony did eventually make it back home, but his days as a Shadow were coming to an end. He had brought it on himself; he was the master of his own downfall. Things reached a head a few months later, in August, when we opened for a three-month season at the Opera House, Blackpool, which proved eventful in a number of ways. Midway through the run, I was struck down by enteritis and missed two performances. Les Bennett, Lonnie Donegan's guitarist, took my place. There was more to come.

Tony's general lack of concern and commitment to the group, and his unprofessional behaviour, caused him to make another late entrance during one of our Blackpool performances. Just as we finished playing 'FBI', he sidled out on to the stage and sheepishly climbed behind the drum kit. There was no apology. By now, Hank, Jet and I had had enough.

After the show we had a terrible argument in the dressing-room. It got very heated and Tony walked out, roaring, 'If that's your attitude, you'd better get yourself another drummer.' So we took him at his word.

We needed a replacement immediately – we were not interested in bringing in a deputy for the season, we wanted someone permanently. We had a theatre season to complete as well as TV and recording commitments to fulfil. Subconsciously we all knew who we wanted to take Tony's place. We had known Brian Bennett since our days at the 2i's and, quite honestly, we would have been hard pressed to find a better drummer. It was a unanimous decision. Brian had been working as a member of Marty Wilde's Wildcats until Marty left the group and went into *Bye Bye Birdie* on the West End stage. The Wildcats briefly re-formed as the Krew-Kats and enjoyed moderate chart success with their record 'Trambone'. Most recently Brian had been working with Tommy Steele in summer season in Great Yarmouth, and he was about to take over on drums from Andy White in the pit orchestra of the Queen's Theatre in Shaftesbury Avenue, for Anthony Newley's West End show, *Stop the World I Want to Get Off*, which meant a regular income and regular hours. Fortunately, I managed to get hold of Brian's telephone number, phoned the next day and left a message with his wife, Margaret, for him to phone me back. When we eventually spoke, I simply offered him the job with the Shadows. Brian was a little hesitant. He had a lot going for him and was apprehensive about making the wrong decision.

'How much are you getting with Tommy?' I asked.

'Twenty-five pounds a week,' came the reply.

'We'll double it.'

Brian joined us the next day and has been a vital member of the group ever since. There is one slight problem, however. People will come up to him in the street and call him 'Tony', and he has always been referred to as the Shadows' 'new boy'. Tony was with the group for two-and-a-half years; Brian has already completed nearly thirty.

The first time Brian Bennett appeared with the Shadows, he mimed to our hit single, 'Kon Tiki', on a TV show called *Thank Your Lucky Stars*. It was one of the pop shows on television which allowed groups and singers to mime to their records; *Ready, Steady, Go* was another. But they had a strange rule on *Top of the Pops*.

In the early 1960s the BBC had a policy which banned artistes from miming to their own records on *Top of the Pops*. Instead they had to re-record them and *then* mime to this specially made track in the TV studios. It was a farce. When an act was booked to appear on the show, they had to go along to a recording studio for a three-hour session and re-create their sound exactly like the original record. Records that had taken many hours, even days, to record now had to be re-created in just three hours, even if it meant bringing in extra musicians and a large orchestra. A representative from the Musicians' Union was always present to protect the musicians' interests and observe that everything was above board. The BBC paid for everything, and spent thousands of pounds hiring studios and paying musicians' fees. It was a shambles, however. What really happened was that an artiste would arrive at the studio, go through the motions of re-creating the original record in the allotted time, and then, at the last moment, the tapes would be switched, and a copy of the record's original master substituted in its place, to be played on air. Everyone did it.

Tony's leaving was really traumatic for us. We were just entering our second year of success with record sales, everything was going right for us in every area, and then a quarter of the group left. We were in a fortunate position in that the public now knew us as four individuals within the Shadows – I think we were the first backing group to be known by our names as well – and it was as if the group had four distinct personalities, which we were projecting to our audiences in different ways. Our audience knew us even before 'Apache', through our work with Cliff. This was an all-important factor, and we felt that removing a quarter of the group might possibly have a bad effect on our popularity. It didn't seem to. After we topped the singles chart with 'Kon Tiki', Norrie decided to release 'The Savage', one of the featured instrumentals from *The Young Ones*, as our follow-up single, much against our wishes. We were touring Australia at the time, and Hank and I were not very happy about it being released without our being consulted, even though it got as high as No.10. Our next single reunited us with another old mate. Jerry Lordan, who had written 'Apache' for us, came up with a cracking number which we later called 'Wonderful Land'. It had a unique melody, unusual chord sequences and was different from anything we'd heard before. It was a very strong original composition. We had recorded it several months before, when Tony was still in the group, and it was put in the can as a potential single. But something was missing. It didn't excite us as much as we thought it would. It needed a lift.

We weren't happy with the end product; we didn't know what was wrong, but we knew it wasn't right.

While we were on tour, Norrie Paramor decided to over-dub an orchestra and vocal group on to our original track, highlighting French horns and violins – *the Shadows with strings*. It became a musical landmark. When he played an advance copy to us later, we were amazed. It was beautiful, and so obviously a big hit single. I don't like to think what would have happened if we hadn't liked Norrie's arrangement. EMI had paid out a lot of money in session fees, and the single would have had to have been released to recoup some of that money. The strange thing is Jerry Lordan hadn't given the number a title. It was after we heard Norrie's arrangement that we called it 'Wonderful Land'.

Norrie Paramor's contribution to the recording careers of Cliff and the Shadows must never be under-estimated. In the same way that George Martin's influence was instrumental in the enormous success of the Beatles, Norrie Paramor was important to us and, in his own way, to the development of popular music. He knew his trade. The biggest change we noticed at the time was the arrival of two-track recording, which came in around the end of 1961 and meant that at last we could over-dub and put another guitar or a vocal track on to the record. 'Wonderful Land' was one of the first British records to employ this technique, and now I was beginning to understand some of the technicalities. But I never had the confidence to ask how Buddy Holly, the Everly Brothers and Neil Sedaka could be heard singing with themselves on record. On 'Breaking Up Is Hard to Do', you could hear Sedaka's voice *three* times over, and we could never work out how this could be done.

'Wonderful Land' came out in February 1962, and went on to become our second biggest hit of all time. It sold a million copies, and stayed at the top of the chart for eight weeks from 22 March to 17 May. The B-side, 'Stars Fell on Stockton', marked Brian Bennett's recording début with the group.

Twenty-three years later, in 1985, Mark Knopfler – leader of Dire Straits – told us that it had always been one of his ambitions to play 'Wonderful Land' with the Shadows on stage.

Mark, a fellow Geordie, and a wonderful musician, had written a beautiful number called 'Going Home' for the soundtrack of the movie *Local Hero*. When I saw the film, I loved the theme so much that I got hold of the sheet music and we recorded it ourselves almost immediately. It was released as a single and featured on *The Shadows Silver Album* in 1984.

When Dire Straits toured Britain the following year they featured 'Going Home' as a very effective closing number, while the crew cleared the stage of equipment behind them. When the tour played the Odeon, Hammersmith, Mark asked if Hank and I would join them on stage to play along. It was a terrific honour for us both and we jumped at the chance. Mark was gracious in his introduction: 'When I was a kid, there was a man who played a guitar . . . who had a red Fender . . . whom we idolized and loved . . . and he's here tonight.' With that, we walked out on to the stage and started playing along with Dire Straits . . . and the audience went bananas. It was then we learnt that 'Wonderful Land' was one of Mark's favourites.

Four months later we returned the compliment when we were touring ourselves. We played the Dominion Theatre, Tottenham Court Road, and invited Mark to join us. At a given moment he came out of the audience, up on to the stage, and played 'Wonderful Land'. It was a magic moment and Mark achieved one of his ambitions.

By the time 'Wonderful Land' first topped the charts in the middle of March, Jet Harris was already out of the group.

He had been a drinker ever since we first met him at the 2i's. He loved a tipple, but in the early days he could always handle it. He certainly didn't have a problem, and it never took him over. He started drinking heavily when his marriage began to break up, which he always blamed on Cliff Richard. He later accused Cliff of having an affair with his wife, Carole, whom he had married in 1959. She was a very forceful lady – and a very attractive and sexy one at that. She was also bigger than Jet, who was only 5ft 6in tall, and tended to dominate him.

The incident with Cliff and Carole had started on an overnight sleeper taking us from London to Blackpool for an engagement. There were eight compartments in each sleeping car. Cliff had apartment number one, and for some reason Carole Harris had compartment number two; there was a communicating door.

Although they were man and wife, Jet had been given apartment number eight – it was a strange journey. We filled in somewhere in between. Cliff was vulnerable, and I believe Jet's wife probably seduced him. Jet has said that Cliff and Carole made love on several other occasions in a friend's house in London, and that Cliff only ended the relationship because his father might find out about it.

Jet couldn't handle the pressure, and turned to drink for solace and comfort. He spent much of his time propping up bars and looking at the world through the bottom of an upturned glass. The more money he made, the more he spent on drink. Jet bought his friends in the bar. He was invariably surrounded by half a dozen guys, holding court. But he couldn't even handle that, because most drinking sessions ended up in violence. Like many men of small stature, Jet seemed to have a death wish. He would always pick on someone almost twice his size and try to beat him up. With his blond, Vitapointe hair, a lot of people thought he was gay. Many times I had to drag him out of a brawl because his mouth had been working overtime. 'Go on then, call me a poof again and I'll smash your face in,' was one of Jet's favourite phrases. Sam Curtis, our road manager, saved him from a thrashing on a number of occasions as well.

I can remember playing at the Guildhall in Portsmouth when Jet went missing only minutes before we were due out on stage. He was nowhere to be found, although I had a good idea where he might be. It was inevitable. I rushed round to the public bar at the side of the theatre just in time to prevent him from being smashed into the theatre wall at the hands of a giant of a man. It was an unbelievable scene. Here we were, the top-of-the-bill act and one of the biggest attractions in the country, almost brawling in public. It had to stop, and I became obsessive about telling him to lay off the booze. I guess I picked on him a lot, but it was necessary. It got worse when Carole filed for divorce, three years after they were married.

Long before the Beatles were famous, the Shadows appeared at the Cavern Club in Liverpool. It was a hot and sweaty cellar and not quite what we had been used to playing. Jet was well gone when we went out on stage to perform, and it was a miracle he could play a correct note. He was coping well until we came to one of our famous routines. We were in the middle of a number called 'Shadoogie', when Hank and I went into our Shadows 'walk'. It looked terrific to the audience; the idea was a very simple one. As Hank and I walked forwards together and then walked back again, it was Jet's job to walk forward to complete the pattern. But as we walked back in the usual manner, Jet just continued walking forwards, straight off the stage and fell into the audience giggling. He was smashed out of his head. Fortunately it was only a small stage; if it had been any higher he would have badly injured himself. What could we do? As Hank helped him up and back on to the stage, I apologized to the audience. 'I'm very sorry, Jet's not very well,' I said.

It didn't work. Some Scouser in the audience yelled back, 'We know mate – he's pissed.'

Somebody had to tell Jet to cut down, and as usual I steamed into him in no uncertain manner. Our relationship had deteriorated. We could see that everything we had worked for could be lost through one man's stupidity. We were trying desperately to make it even bigger in the business, and he was throwing it all away. Hank and I realized we were carrying a passenger, and we hoped we could snap him out of it. But Jet didn't seem to care any more. He became more furtive with his drinking sessions, and would never drink in front of me because he knew I'd stop him. He was fast becoming an alcoholic.

When Brian Bennett joined the Shadows, Peter Gormley warned him about Jet's drinking problem and told him not to get involved. But he experienced it himself almost immediately. The first thing Jet did when they met in Blackpool was invite Brian out for a drink. When the drummer suggested a local pub he knew, Jet looked horrified. 'Oh no,' he said. 'Bruce'll see us.' He was terrified. He was becoming paranoid. He took the newcomer on a lengthy tour of the backstage area of the Opera House Theatre, continually looking over his shoulder to see if I was around. I think I had become a bogeyman to him. When the coast was clear, he ushered Brian into a toilet and produced a bottle from under his coat. 'Here, have a drink, but don't tell Bruce, he doesn't like me drinking. He goes mad if he thinks I've had too much. He hates drinking.'

Jet always blamed the break-up of his marriage for his heavy drinking. He was obviously unhappy in the group at the time; the rows in the dressing-room got worse and usually ended up with Jet in tears. He was very low for long periods of time. People who drink heavily are unhappy. As a reformed drinker, I can speak from bitter experience, and what most people don't realize is that drink is a depressant after the initial buzz wears off. It can only make things worse in the long run, and that's what happened to Jet Harris.

Hank and I didn't want to go out on stage with a drunk, so we offered him a compromise. We were prepared to stop working for three months while he sought counsel and a cure for his problem and went to a special clinic. He refused. He didn't think he had a problem. So Hank and I had one of our meetings and decided it was in the best interests of everyone if Jet left.

We were appearing at the *New Musical Express* poll winners' concert at Wembley on Sunday, 15 April 1962, when we broke the news. As usual, we found Jet propping up the bar in the artistes' enclosure backstage. He was well on the way to alcoholic oblivion. He was told that we didn't need his services any longer. It was sad, because we'd shared some great times together and had fond memories, but it was a tough business.

Jet Harris, the James Dean of rock 'n' roll, became one of its first casualties. He never really recovered. Today he lives in Gloucester, waiting for the eternal comeback and another big break. He advertises his services in the *Stage* newspaper along with the group Tangent, billed as Bristol's answer to the Shadows. It could all have been so different. It is a great tragedy, because Jet was the consummate bass player, the great technician. He was a highly respected musician who was always a much better guitarist than I shall ever be. He just couldn't handle it all; his career was ruined by alcohol. I'm sure he often reflects on what might have been. He just threw it all away.

It was Brian Bennett who came up with Jet's successor and returned to our old haunt in Old Compton Street to recruit bass man Brian 'Licorice' Locking. Licorice had played with Brian in Tony Sheridan's Trio, as a member of Marty Wilde's Wildcats, in the Krew-Kats and with Tommy Steele's group. He was well qualified. He was also a very likeable, easy-going guy, and a good friend . . . he was always laughing. He had a smile which filled a theatre. The Shadows were back in business . . . but it would never be quite the same again.

8

'IF YOU AND THE LADS TAKE CARE OF YOUR MONEY . . .'

The success of 'Wonderful Land' in the spring of 1962 coincided with the Shadows moving towards all-round family entertainment and away from our rock 'n' rolling roots. We were becoming part of the establishment. Cliff Richard had made the same move before us when he recorded 'Living Doll'. Just nine months after the success of 'Move It', he was already leaving rock 'n' roll behind. Cliff likes to think he has always been a true rock 'n' roller, but his discography belies it. He was a rocker in the true sense of the word for less than a year, before he succumbed to show business, playing summer seasons, the London Palladium, television, and pantomimes.

Like Cliff's metamorphosis, the change in the direction for the Shadows was not a conscious one. It was a gradual development of our talents. The music scene at the time dictated that we must adapt or face the consequences. Out and out rock 'n' roll had long gone, and the British artistes who were having longer careers in the business were those who had developed out of it. Tommy Steele had been the obvious example; Jim Dale and Joe Brown were others. Even though we were featuring rock 'n' roll in our stage act, we were recording much more melodic pieces of music and attracting a mature audience, as well as teenagers. Cliff was doing exactly the same. We were becoming veterans in our early twenties. We injected much more humour into our act, to give our audiences something different – variety, I guess, though at no time did we feel we were selling out or betraying the music that had inspired us in the first place, because we were doing what we enjoyed and were having fun.

We never resented Cliff's phenomenal success, in which we played our own special part. We certainly had no plans to leave him and break out on our own. And why should we? We had the best of both worlds. We were still five guys together, even though we also did our own separate things, and we still looked upon ourselves as a five-man outfit, more than a singer and his backing group. We knew that Cliff was the biggest solo singer in Britain at that time, but we worked together so closely that we felt we were a complete unit; that's the way that Cliff looked at it, too. It was always Cliff Richard and the Shadows, and there was never any animosity about being billed second to him. We continued to tour as bill-toppers in our own right when Cliff was committed elsewhere.

In our own way, the Shadows had become pioneers of the British rock and pop industry in the early sixties for others to follow, and we were acclaimed by the press as 'the world's first pop group'. In Italy, one newspaper said: 'There would have been no pop group industry without the Shadows.' Sure, there had been groups before us, but they were usually vocal groups and sang with big bands or orchestras. We were the first to become known individually, and set the pace for all the others who came immediately afterwards, like Shane Fenton and the Fentones and Johnny Kidd and the Pirates, who, without doubt, were one of the finest British rock 'n' roll bands of all time. 'Shakin' All Over' is a classic record which, like 'Move It', has weathered the test of time magnificently well. Early in their career, the group that later became the Beatles changed their name to Johnny and the Moondogs because it had the same ring to it as Cliff Richard and the Shadows. Many other contemporaries on Merseyside modelled themselves in similar ways, including Rory Storm and the Hurricanes, Gerry and the Pacemakers, Billy J. Kramer and the Dakotas, Les Curtis and the All Stars. As yet they were all unknown outside the boundaries of Liverpool. We also set the standard style for most modern groups, and were the first to popularize what became the conventional line-up for many bands – lead guitar, rhythm guitar, bass guitar and drums.

Through our own recording success, and certainly that of Duane Eddy, guitar instrumental records became extremely popular in the early 1960s, and we found ourselves stimulating and influencing a lot of groups who tried to copy our style. I'm sure it was through our success that hundreds of groups sprang up all over the country and that sales of guitars increased, too. Record executives from all the major companies had seen the impact we were having, and were falling over themselves to join the bandwagon and sign up instrumental outfits with similar sounds to our own. Over a very short period of time, dozens of British groups emerged from virtual obscurity long before the Merseybeat boom heralded the arrival of vocal groups in the charts. Many of them enjoyed a brief flirtation with success before disappearing back where they came from, like the Cougars (whom Norrie Paramor produced), Nero and the Gladiators, the original Eagles (from Bristol), Brian Bennett's own group the Krew-Kats, Group X, the Hunters, the Planets and many more. Their staying power and careers were minimal, though some individual musicians survived. They couldn't create a sufficiently new and distinctive sound that could last.

It must be said that, despite our success, the level of our own musicianship at that time was pretty poor, compared with today's standards. We improved as we went along. Hank admits that he wasn't as good as he would have liked to have been. We were working so much that it was very difficult to practise for any length of time, which would have helped to improve us. He has always been a much better guitarist than me. I can't play single-string melodies, at which he excels. I can't play 'Apache', yet I have always had a feel for rhythm. My life has been dedicated to playing rhythms for other people, so when kids came up to me and asked me how I managed to play so fast on something like 'The Savage', I was very touched by their interest – it made it all worth while.

These days, the degree of musicianship among youngsters is very high. If we were just starting out now, playing as we did then, we would really struggle. What kids have today wasn't available to us, because rock music was so new. They can go into record shops and pick up thirty years of experience, listen to three decades of great singers, marvellous guitarists, superb keyboard players, hear all the various forms of music that have developed over that period and learn from it, taking a bit from here, a bit from there, and copy anything they like until they evolve a technique and style of their own. Everybody copies from somebody else in the beginning, everybody borrows other people's styles. We learnt from Elvis, Buddy Holly, Gene Vincent and the Everly Brothers, but what we lacked was that thirty years to choose from, and that's the difference. The equipment today is far more advanced and sophisticated than anything we used at first, and obviously the better the gear, the better the musician. You don't even have to be too talented to play some of today's sophisticated keyboards, for instance. The strides technology has taken in the development of musical instruments since the 1950s have been phenomenal.

One of the most successful instrumentals of the early sixties was by the Tornados, who were formerly Billy Fury's backing group. They topped the British hit parade in the summer of 1962 with 'Telstar', and managed to achieve something that had eluded us when they took the record to No.1 in America. Twenty years later we recorded 'Telstar' and released it as a single. At the time, we saw most accomplished instrumental outfits like the Tornados as a threat to our careers. However, it was a great record, with a distinctive sound of its own and a plaintive melody line that was created, surprisingly, not by a guitar but by a wailing organ. Despite its unbelievable success around the world, the group received no royalties for their achievements. When they made the record, they were paid the standard Musicians' Union session fee.

'Telstar' was written by Joe Meek, who was one of the leading pioneers among British record producers. He started his career as an engineer at the IBC studios in London, where he worked with, among others, Frankie Vaughan, Tommy Steele and Chris Barber before moving on to Lansdowne Studios where he recorded Lonnie Donegan. In 1960 he formed his own independent record label and built a studio in his North London flat above a shop in Holloway, where Michael Cox recorded his big hit single 'Angela Jones'. It became the first and only hit on an independent label in ten years. After he ran into financial problems, Joe was forced to close down the label and concentrate solely on recording. He leased his productions to the major companies – and in the early days Brian Bennett and Licorice Locking played on many Joe Meek sessions. The guy was a genius; over the next few years he emerged as one of the first and most successful independent producers in Britain, and made some historic records. Besides the Tornados he produced John Leyton, including his chart-topping 'Johnny Remember Me' (which, rumour has it, was recorded in Joe's bathroom to get that authentic echo effect), followed by Mike Berry, Heinz, the Honeycombs, and several others.

Despite his success, Joe was not a happy man, and his life ended tragically when he shot himself and his landlady, Violet Shenton, on the morning of the anniversary of Buddy Holly's death in 1967. I think he had a morbid fascination for Holly.

The instrumental boom was not confined to Britain. It swept across America at the same time, courtesy of the Ventures, Duane Eddy, and Johnny and the Hurricanes, though not with the same kind of impact and intensity as back home. It was fuelled by groups like the Fireballs, String-a-longs, Chantays and Safaris. The boom also crossed the world: Sweden had the Spotniks, France had Les Fingers, Holland had Wout Steenhuis. What made instrumentals so important in the history and development of rock 'n' roll was that they pioneered a new and accepted style for local rock bands, who maybe couldn't find a singer to front the group but wanted to make music of their own anyway. Contrary to the belief that rock 'n' roll died when it was cleaned up and handed over to the likes of Pat Boone and Frankie Avalon, the 'squeaky clean stars', and absorbed into another facet of show business, it took a new lease of life in other directions, and the link between the establishment of rock 'n' roll in the mid-1950s and the emergence of the beat group boom of the early 1960s was, in the main, supplied by instrumental groups.

For our follow-up single to 'Wonderful Land' we attempted something different – and for the first time since we established ourselves we brought the full wrath of the music press down around our ears. 'Guitar Tango', which had been sent to us in the post by two French composers, was the first Shadows single to break away from the electric guitar sound and echo chamber we had instigated, and we recorded the number acoustically. Hank bought a flamenco guitar especially for that session. In actual fact we laid down two different versions of the song. After we initially recorded it with Jet Harris we found that the arrangement didn't sound quite right, so we went back into the studios and tried again. By this time Jet had left the group and Licorice Locking sat in with us, and we recorded a far more commercial track which was released as a single in 1962. It came out to a barrage of criticism from the media. One paper called it 'the worst record they've ever made'. Another added, 'a shameful example of their work'. David Jacobs on *Juke Box Jury* commented: 'I simply don't know what it's all about.'

We were furious. The press were saying we had blown it because we were trying something new, and instead of being applauded for our versatility we were condemned for deserting our successful formula. In truth, they were worried that the record didn't sound like the 'safe' Shadows, which was exactly what we were trying to break away from. Despite what the press thought, the public liked it sufficiently to send it to No.4 in the chart. Looking back, it was a bit of a gamble to take, but it paid off. Norrie Paramor, bless him, stuck by us and told the *New Musical Express*: 'I think it has tremendous individuality and freshness, and shows the boys to be considerably more versatile than many realized.'

The record came out in Britain while we were in Greece making Cliff's next film, *Summer Holiday*, which very nearly proved to be *my* last. We had been staying at Glyfada beach, outside Athens, where, during breaks in shooting, we were thankful to relieve the monotony and boredom of filming and spent most of our time swimming and sunbathing. There was a raft moored a few hundred yards out from the shore, and one day we all decided to swim out to it and continue our sunbathing on board. It seemed like a good idea at the time, and the raft looked a lot closer to the beach than it was in reality. So I gave it a go. I wasn't used to swimming such long distances, and sixty yards from safety I started to flounder. I was gulping for air as I tried to tread water. I panicked. I was going under fast and thought I was going to drown. Luckily Herb Ross, the film's choreographer, dived in and managed to drag me out of the water before I went down again.

Summer Holiday was a lot of fun to make, because instead of being stuck in a studio, bored out of our minds with the tedium of it all, we were sent out on location, and away from Britain. A change of scenery did us all good. We were also featured more extensively than in *The Young Ones*, and we seemed to spend our time getting in and out of various outfits, which included dressing up in the Greek national costume – skirts and all – for a film sequence in Athens city centre. However, we were musicians, and we didn't expect to do a lot of acting. Cliff was on call for the full eight weeks of shooting, but we were only required for twenty-one days, which was a great relief. The film reunited several of the stars from *The Young Ones*, including Una Stubbs and Melvyn Hayes, while Cliff's leading lady was played by another unknown actress, Laurie Peters, who had recently married an equally unknown American actor called Jon Voight. Barbra Streisand had originally been proposed for the role by Herb Ross, who had recently choreographed her first Broadway show and thought her an ideal choice. The producers, in their wisdom, turned her down.

The Shadows were more involved with the musical side of the film. We wrote three instrumentals – 'Les Girls', 'Round and Round' and 'Foot Tapper', which had originally been destined for another movie. The previous March we had been introduced to that wonderful French actor and director, Jacques Tati. He had seen our show and invited us to write the theme tune to his next movie. We were very eager to write more film music, having recently contributed to the soundtrack of the picture *The Boys*, starring Jess Conrad, and we were honoured to be paid such a compliment by so distinguished a figure. The result was 'Foot Tapper', written especially for 'M. Hulot'. Shortly afterwards the film project fell apart, and we put the number in *Summer Holiday* instead. It gave us our fifth and final No.1. I wrote the main title theme to Cliff's movie with Brian Bennett in exactly twenty minutes, after reading through the provisional script. It became one of my most successful copyrights, along with 'Bachelor Boy', and both topped the British charts and sold a million copies each. 'Bachelor Boy' was written to order, several weeks after the movie had been completed and the crew and cast disbanded. The film was being edited at Elstree Studios at the time, when the producer discovered, to his dismay, that it was too short and under-ran by several minutes. The easiest solution to the problem – and the cheapest – was to include another song on the soundtrack, and Norrie Paramor was contacted. Fortunately, Cliff and I were sitting in his office when a frantic call came through from the producer. We started work immediately and the song was completed in less than two hours. Then we had to troop back to

Elstree to film an extra sequence on the studio lot that doubled up as Greece. 'Bachelor Boy' and 'The Next Time' were the biggest hits in the film, along with 'Foot Tapper' and 'Dancing Shoes'. The film came out in January 1963 and became the biggest grossing film of the year. For the second year running, Cliff Richard was voted the most popular film star in Britain. Where was rock 'n' roll now?

When Cliff's previous movie, *The Young Ones*, was released in America at the beginning of October, its name was changed to *It's Wonderful to be Young* for reasons known only to the US distributors, and we flew to the States on an extensive promotional tour to plug it. It was one of the biggest campaigns ever mounted to launch an unknown British singer to American audiences, despite the fact that we had toured the country before. Quite honestly, our return visit to America was an unmitigated disaster.

The formula for the tour could have proved very successful. The movie was shown in selected cinemas across the States, and immediately it was over we came bounding out on stage and gave an hour-long live performance. It was a great idea for promotion, but audience attendance was abysmal. Theatres that would normally have held 2,000 people or more were only half full, which was something we hadn't experienced back home. We picked the wrong time to make our second assault on the most lucrative record market in the world. America was jittery. She was bang in the middle of the Cuban crisis, and President Kennedy and the Russian Premier Nikita Khrushchev were on the verge of taking us all into World War Three and oblivion. So the last thing Americans wanted to see was *us* having fun. It was little wonder that the film flopped, and that we failed to make much of an impact after we had had such high hopes of a breakthrough. It was a terrible disappointment, and a golden opportunity missed. It proved to be the last time Cliff Richard and the Shadows ever toured America together.

The schedule took in an appearance in Memphis, Tennessee – one of the legendary rock 'n' roll cities, along with St Louis and New Orleans – where we were introduced backstage to Vernon Presley, Elvis's father. He told us his son was away, filming in Hollywood, but he knew all about Cliff Richard and the great success he was having in Britain, and he hoped to tour there one day and met him in person.

'If Elvis had been here,' said Vernon, in a wonderful, slow Tennessee drawl, 'he would have invited you all over to the house. But as he is out of town I would like to extend the invitation myself instead.'

It was an opportunity not to be missed. Elvis was our great idol, and we were honoured that his father had gone to the trouble to look us up. After the show that night, Vernon Presley escorted us to Graceland and treated us all to some good downhome Southern comfort. It was a mind-boggling experience.

Graceland was a huge, imposing building, set in its own grounds and totally outrageous. It was a colonial house – a southern mansion straight off the *Gone with the Wind* film lot – with large white Grecian-style columns at the front. There was a six-car garage, housing a Cadillac for every day of the week, each one colour-coded. I can vividly remember walking through the front door and sinking into the pure white carpet, with a pile over two inches thick. On Vernon's guided tour we were shown into the music room, which contained a solitary white grand piano with the initials E.P. carved in gold. Elvis's initials were everywhere, even on the wrought iron gates at the entrance to the drive. There was a study that doubled as a pool hall, where more gold records and awards than I had ever seen hung from the walls. There were six gold discs for 'Don't Be Cruel' alone. It was the stuff of which dreams are made. Elvis's father even allowed us to venture into his son's bedroom, which contained a giant round bed with a single photograph of Priscilla Beaulieu, the girl who was to become his wife in 1967, by its side. One apartment that we weren't allowed to visit belonged to Gladys Presley, Elvis's mother. The rooms had been locked ever since she had passed away in 1958.

I had to keep reassuring myself it was for real, and that I wasn't dreaming. It was like being in a huge box of chocolates. It was only four years before that I had left Newcastle for London, inspired by the music of Elvis Presley, and here I was, standing in Elvis's home in Memphis, Tennessee, being entertained by his own father. I couldn't believe it.

Sadly, I never met Elvis Presley. Sampling the hospitality of his home was the nearest I ever came to it, but I did manage to catch him performing in Las Vegas only a few weeks before he died. I had seen him only in the movies and on television before, and he always had such magnetism and presence on screen. I was horrified by what I saw in Las Vegas. Instead of the great-looking guy from the movies, it was almost like someone impersonating him; a caricature, a cartoon of a former existence. He looked terrible, overweight and bloated, and he spent most of the time on stage kissing girls from the audience and handing out chiffon scarves, which he took from round his neck and gave as special souvenirs, replicas of which could be obtained from the foyer after the show for a handful of dollars . . . and presumably a percentage to the Elvis Presley Organization. He was on stage for no more than fifty-five minutes and performed as if working on autopilot. This was my great musical hero, my inspiration, the 'King of rock 'n' roll'. It was a pitiful sight.

During my trip to Vegas I had become quite friendly with a couple of musicians who played in Elvis's band and they told me some horrendous stories about him. He needed an injection to get him high enough to get out on stage and perform each night, and another one to calm him down afterwards. He needed pills to help him sleep, and pills to keep him awake. What a way to go.

When we arrived home from America, I can remember hearing the Beatles for the first time. Their début single, 'Love Me Do', had been released only a few days before and EMI had high hopes for its success. It eventually peaked in the chart at No.17. I just thought, how could anyone have a bloody stupid name like that for a group? How wrong can you be? I didn't get a shiver down my spine listening to that single, and obviously didn't think very much of this new group from Liverpool. Syd Gillingham, who was head of press at EMI, told me that his department had received a directive to promote the Beatles' single extensively, not because it was a good record, or because the group had a promising future, but simply because their manager, Brian Epstein, was also a very important record dealer on Merseyside. They didn't want to upset him in case he cancelled his orders with the company.

Epstein once brought the boys to see us at the Liverpool Empire, to show them how an established group conducted themselves on stage. We were in tuxedoes by then. After that he put the Beatles into suits.

The arrival of the Beatles as the major musical force was inevitable. It had to happen. Had it not been John, Paul, George and Ringo, somebody else would have filled the huge void that had existed since Elvis Presley. The music industry was meandering; it was safe. It needed a kick on the backside to save it from stagnating altogether, and the Beatles provided just that. Rock 'n' roll had such a short life-span, for something so influential.

After its popularity waned, the business stood still and looked inwards, instead of outwards to new horizons. We entered a phase, particularly in Britain, that saw new trends coming in and going out virtually every week as we all searched for something more permanent. To be honest, we had all, including Cliff Richard and the Shadows, gone on to sweeter things; the guts and aggression of rock 'n' roll had been tamed. It had become acceptable and part of the establishment. Now we had nice melodies with a beat – everything was getting far too smooth. Dance crazes like the twist, the bossa nova and the Madison emerged to titillate the public's fancy for a while, followed by a series of spin-off records as we clamoured for a new direction. There was a brief boom of traditional jazz, which saw the likes of Acker Bilk, Kenny Ball and the Temperance Seven enjoying chart success, while comedy records still continued to be popular. The British Top Ten was the most diverse chart in the world at that time – and still is – Benny Hill, Ken Dodd and Mike Sarne could all rub shoulders with Elvis Presley, Cliff Richard and the Shadows, and Adam Faith – and it was difficult to predict what might happen in the future. There was a fine range of solo singers in the shape of Craig Douglas, Helen Shapiro, Eden Kane, Mark Wynter, Danny Williams and our old chum Frank Ifield, who all had hit records, but none of these were musical innovators. They didn't lead from the front, they simply followed. The only constants in the chart were Elvis Presley, the Everly Brothers, Cliff Richard and the Shadows.

Then the Beatles came along and changed it all. They breathed fresh air into the music industry; they were what everyone had been waiting for. Like Elvis and Cliff before them, the Beatles had a new kind of energy and vitality which they injected into their music. They gave it back to the kids. They were young and very eager and had sparkling personalities to back up all their brashness. They had the same musical influences that Hank and I had grown up with – Elvis Presley, Buddy Holly, the Everly Brothers – and something we lacked, the inspiration and drive of black American rhythm 'n' blues, which had been introduced first-hand into Liverpool by British merchant seamen who worked the steam liners across the Atlantic and brought back black American records to their home port to fuel the fire of a rock revolution. I had never heard of people like Arthur Alexander or Barrett Strong before the Merseyside groups played their music.

On their first album, *Please, Please Me*, the Beatles covered several songs by black American groups. These encouraged British audiences to discover black music, and through the Beatles' endorsement certainly helped establish the Tamla Motown sound and groups like the Miracles, Martha and the Vandellas, the Supremes, and the Marvelettes on a worldwide scale.

The Beatles, without doubt, were the greatest thing to happen to pop music, not only in Britain but all over the world, and their influence was far-reaching. They established themselves so firmly because they were performing wonderful songs, which, of course, they wrote themselves.

John and Paul's songs were simple yet so effective. Like Buddy Holly before them, they wrote superb teen lyrics that conjured up simple images, memorable phrases that said so much in just a handful of words. Funnily enough, many of their songs revolved around three or four basic chords, but it was the way they put them together which made them special. Musically they were always experimenting in their songwriting, anticipating future tastes, which is what kept them so fresh and original – and one jump ahead of the rest of us. They started to put things like sixth chords into numbers which any of us could have played years before they arrived on the scene, but nobody had had the foresight to do so. The chord at the end of 'She Loves You' is a classic; the introduction to 'A Hard Day's Night' is breathtaking. I knew the group would be really big after I heard *Please, Please Me*, which was so inventive. After that there could be no going back.

In the spring of 1963, after we had returned from our second tour of South Africa and completed a very successful series of engagements in Britain, I held a party at my home in Harrow to which I invited John, Paul, George and Ringo and some other friends from the music business. I wasn't a great drinker then, and at one point in the evening I went into the kitchen to make some tea. Shortly afterwards I was joined there by Cliff and the three other Shadows, and a few minutes later in came the Beatles. We started talking about records, particularly the Beatles' new single which was due out shortly, and we were all eager to hear it. Lennon was flattered, and disappeared into the hall to re-emerge with a guitar. A moment later, John and Paul opened up with an on-the-spot version of 'From Me to You'. Even in the confined space of my kitchen it sounded magnificent, and it was so obviously a hit. When they had finished the song, Hank and I got our guitars and treated them to a version of our new single, 'Atlantis', played acoustically, before we were joined by Cliff in a mickey-taking version of the Beatles' 'Please, Please Me'. Not to be outdone, the four Liverpool lads replied with an hilarious (and out of tune) imitation of the Shadows, complete with the famous Shadows 'walk', which they grossly exaggerated. And so it went on. We spent most of the evening singing together – impromptu versions of 'Shout', 'He's So Fine' and some of the great rock 'n' roll favourites like 'Blue Suede Shoes', 'Heartbreak Hotel' and 'Twist and Shout'. The jam session went on for several hours; the rest of the party was forgotten. It was a fantastic evening.

I had recently bought a brand new E-Type Jaguar, which was parked proudly in the driveway outside my house. As Paul McCartney was leaving, for some reason our conversation turned to money and I took him to one side.

'Paul,' I said, 'if you and the lads take care of your money, and don't fritter it away, you, too, can have a lovely home and an E-Type Jaguar like me.' Perhaps Paul took my advice after all! He hasn't done too badly for himself since.

We met again socially in June, when Paul invited us to his twenty-first birthday party. We were appearing in Blackpool for the summer season, and we drove down to Liverpool for the night. We arranged to meet Paul and his girlfriend, Jane Asher, in the darkened stage doorway of the Empire Theatre in Lime Street, and then follow them both back to the house where the party was taking place. It was at Paul's Aunty Jin's home in Dinas Lane, Huyton, where a marquee had been specially erected in the garden. Unfortunately the evening was soured when John Lennon – much the worse for drink – got into a heated argument with Liverpool disc jockey Bob Wooler; the atmosphere turned nasty, and Lennon began punching him in the face. Bob, who was a very close friend of the Beatles and had introduced them many times on stage at the Cavern Club, ended up in hospital.

The argument had started when Wooler and Lennon were discussing John's recent holiday trip to Spain with Brian Epstein. The Beatle took exception to something that was said, and started talking with his fists instead. The famous Spanish holiday had taken place in March, while we had actually been out in Sitges, near Barcelona, rehearsing what became our *When in Spain* album, and John and Brian had turned up unannounced to meet us.

Paul McCartney and I became quite good friends. I had recently bought a villa on the Portuguese Algarve in Albufeira, which was the perfect place to get away from it all and escape the pressures of the music business. It was unspoilt, undiscovered by tourists, and an ideal spot to relax. The village was a five-hour drive from Lisbon airport. Paul and I were talking one day when he casually mentioned that he was having great difficulty getting away for a holiday. Everywhere he went he was mobbed by screaming fans and his peace was disturbed, and he and Jane could go nowhere without causing a riot. So I told him about my Portuguese villa and how quiet and private it was, and invited him to stay there. Shortly afterwards he accepted the invitation.

Paul had written a new song for which he was having great difficulty finding suitable words, and he had carried the unfinished version around in his head for weeks, desperate to complete it. For the sake of a title, Paul provisionally called it 'Scrambled Eggs'. He was working on the song on his holiday flight to Portugal and during the lengthy car journey from Lisbon to Albufeira. When he arrived at the villa, I greeted him at the door and Paul almost fell out of the car with excitement. 'Have you got a guitar handy?' he asked. 'I've written a song. I want to see if it works.' I nodded, and Paul hurried inside the house, picked up my guitar, and proceeded to sing the new words he had just completed for his 'old' song. It was 'Yesterday'.

Another McCartney melody, 'Here, There and Everywhere', was featured on the *Revolver* album – yet originally Paul offered it to Hank for the Shadows to record as an instrumental. They met at Abbey Road studios, and Paul played the melody to Hank on the piano. Naturally our guitarist was very taken with the song, as he knew that with the right arrangement, it could be a monster hit. Paul was flattered, and told Hank he would send a cassette immediately so that we could start work. We waited for it to arrive for several days, but it never did. Paul had a change of heart, wrote a suitable lyric and used the number himself.

Many years later I was in Studio Two at Abbey Road, mixing some live concert tapes, when I was interrupted by one of the staff, telling me that Paul McCartney had rung and wanted to use the studio immediately, and would I object to moving out? Of course I objected. I was working very hard to meet a tight deadline, and refused to budge. McCartney would have to wait. Apparently Paul was so annoyed at being turned down that he went off and made plans to build a replica of the studio in the basement of his London office in Soho. He built an exact copy of Studio Two, right down to the smallest detail, including the same acoustic ceiling tiles.

The Beatles went on to revolutionize pop music. They were the first of many groups from Merseyside who began to attack the hit parade with amazing regularity – groups like Gerry and the Pacemakers, Billy J. Kramer and the Dakotas, the Merseybeats, the Fourmost and the Searchers. For the first time ever, artistes were establishing themselves and making the breakthrough to success not from a London base, as in the past, but from a provincial city. We had come to London in 1958 because we believed it was the only way to crack the music industry. Within four years all that had gone, as the world swiftly focused its attention on Liverpool. In true music-business fashion, A & R men rushed to Merseyside to sign up every rock 'n' roller they could find, and for a brief moment Liverpool became the new home of the rock industry. The Beatles also made it possible for acts to make it from other cities as well – they lifted the restrictions – and before long groups and artistes emerged from Manchester (Freddie and the Dreamers, Wayne Fontana and the Mindbenders, and the Hollies, with their magnificent harmonies) and from

Birmingham (the Move, Idle Race, Rockin' Berries and the Moody Blues). Unlike Hank and me, the Animals actually made it from Newcastle upon Tyne.

Unfortunately the vast majority of Mersey groups, who had made it riding on the Beatles' success, didn't have sufficient talent to sustain any kind of long-term musical career, and within two or three years they disappeared completely.

One of the other groups to challenge the domination of the Beatles and the Mersey sound in the early sixties did come from London. The Dave Clark Five were formed in Tottenham in 1960, and started playing together at the local Locarno ballroom. When they failed to secure a recording contract after many attempts, Dave Clark and the group invested their money – and borrowed a lot as well – in making records of their own. They hired a studio and produced 'Do You Love Me' themselves. Dave then hawked it around the major companies, ending up with a deal at Columbia, where he leased the record for the company to release, while still retaining ownership of the master tapes and copyright. He made a lot of money from the venture, and pioneered a whole new business practice for artistes in this country. In effect, they became the first group to own their tapes themselves, long before it became fashionable. Dave Clark has always been a very shrewd businessman. Recently he bought up the tapes of *Ready, Steady Go* from Rediffusion Television, and has 'a nice little earner' from marketing them. In 1985 he wrote and produced *Time*, the show which gave Cliff Richard his first starring role in a major West End musical.

Yet the advent of the Beatles sadly brought about the demise of many other artistes, some of them household names, who simply couldn't adapt and embrace modern tastes. The days of the solo singer were numbered for a while. The Beatles were indirectly responsible for ending the careers of global artistes like Bobby Vee, Del Shannon, and Bryan Hyland, who had all contributed much to the charts around the world. America doesn't treat its pioneers very well. You can have two hits in Britain and work for ten years. In America you end up in the dumps and dives or in the car wash. I think Buddy Holly would have lasted, though, had he lived. Sadly, the Larry Parnes stable of stars came to an abrupt end at the same time, and for some reason Larry refused to involve himself in groups when the boom started. I would have thought that his extraordinary talents would have been well used. He could actually have played a major part in the career of the Beatles themselves.

Towards the end of 1962 Brian Epstein was trying to book a series of Sunday concerts for the boys, and he approached Larry Parnes, who was already presenting pop shows at the Britannia Pier in Great Yarmouth. Larry wanted to book them for eleven consecutive dates, but failed to reach an agreement with Epstein over a suitable fee. Brian's value of the Beatles far exceeded Larry's opinion of their true worth, so a deal was never struck. Epstein went elsewhere. At the time, however, the Liverpool impresario was tentatively feeling his way in the music industry, and was looking for someone with experience with whom to go into partnership and co-manage his protégés. Larry Parnes would have been perfect.

Without the Beatles, British artistes would have waited a lot longer to make it in America than they did. It was directly through them that British music started to dominate the world. They broke down the barriers. However, in America their success didn't happen overnight. Their first four US singles failed miserably, and it looked as if the Beatles would go the same way as Cliff Richard and the Shadows. 'I Want to Hold Your Hand' was the record that made the breakthrough, helped by a brief promotional tour and very effective publicity. The scenes of unrivalled Beatlemania and uncontrollable screaming, which greeted the group's arrival at Kennedy Airport in New York on their first visit, were hyped by their American marketing representative. Capitol Records ploughed 50,000 dollars into a 'crash' campaign, and every fifteen minutes, on the New York radio stations WMCA and WINS, an announcement proclaimed that anyone who met the Beatles at Kennedy Airport would receive a T-shirt and a dollar bill. It worked, and 5,000 people turned up to greet them. After that and the resulting media coverage it generated, the Beatles were on their way.

Their talent went a lot further – before they arrived on the scene, the musical world was divided by the barrier of language. Each record-selling territory was treated separately, on a purely parochial basis, and many British and American artistes had to re-record their English-speaking hit singles in other languages in order to tap into the markets in Italy, Germany, Spain and France. Indeed, Cliff recorded several singles in Italian, French and Spanish. One of the reasons the Shadows were so successful abroad was that we were purely an instrumental group: our music needed no language. There was a lot of money to be made from overseas sales. When the Beatles emerged, their songs were so good that English suddenly became the universal musical language. They crossed over the borders and opened up vast new markets around the world for themselves and everyone else who followed.

With all that acclaim, it is worth remembering that the Beatles gave their last live public performance together in Candlestick Park, San Francisco, in 1966, *only three years* after their breakthrough to success. But in that time they also helped to pioneer an event that has become commonplace in the rock industry for the super groups of the eighties – the stadium concert. The Beatles were the first. They were appearing in stadium shows in Australia and America as early as 1964 to satisfy the overwhelming demand of people who wanted to see them play. They had some spectacular successes, notably at the Philadelphia Stadium and at Shea Stadium in New York, but the truth is that the Beatles soon tired of touring. What had once been an exciting adventure together on the road had now become a monster that had taken over their lives, and one they could well live without. They were tired and bored, and they didn't like being manipulated by promoters. And what was the use of performing to 56,000 a night, if – through the screams and mass hysteria they created – they couldn't even hear themselves play anyway?

Instead of touring, they retreated to the security of the studio and broke all the rules again. They began calling the tune at Abbey Road as they became more and more successful, and virtually ended up running it. They were responsible for so much change. They wrote many of their songs in the studio, which was unheard of, and they worked all through the night, which was something that had never been done before. Nothing seemed to matter because they were so creative.

Sgt Pepper's Lonely Hearts Club Band was their ultimate masterpiece, and it is incredible to realize that it was recorded only on four-track tape machines. This meant that four separate tracks of music could be recorded on to one piece of tape and played back simultaneously but separately. The volume balance and tone of each track could be individually controlled. But the Beatles experimented. When four tracks were full, producer George Martin carried out a series of intermediate mixes and recorded the four completed tracks on to one or two tracks on another four-track machine, leaving two or three tracks open to take new recordings – and so it went on until they had created the sound they wanted. It took nine months to make. When I first heard it I thought it was mind-blowing, as did everybody. I listened to it with a feeling of hopelessness. How could these people be so far ahead of anyone else? It was their finest hour.

There was a postscript to this album. The Beatles told the world that they had recorded it under the influence of LSD, which I think was the wrong thing to do. It gave ideas to impressionable kids, who would try to copy the group by experimenting with drugs, and in this way, I guess, the album had a very negative influence. After *Sgt Pepper* it was inevitable that the group would split up, but it was a sad day when it happened, and they were very brave to allow their break-up to be so graphically detailed and filmed for the movie *Let It Be*, when they were going through their 'warts and all' period. It was tragic to see that sort of talent tearing itself apart; you could almost feel the tension in that film. They had gone as far as they could go. What else was there to achieve? They were four very talented people who were finding it increasingly difficult to work in a single unit.

Not surprisingly, neither John Lennon's nor Paul McCartney's solo achievements matched those of the Beatles as a group; neither had the same impact as songwriters after the break-up, which is strange when you realize that Lennon and McCartney had been writing many of their songs separately since 'She Loves You'. It was a partnership in name only. But as songwriters, John Lennon and Paul McCartney peaked together. They were never quite the same again, and the quality of their later material, good as it was, suffered. While they were together they spurred each other on to write, to try new chord sequences, new melody lines and arrangements, and to experiment with their music . . . and most importantly, I think, they bounced ideas off each other and constructively criticized each other's work.

George Harrison never shared the limelight as a songwriter to the same degree as his colleagues, but he did write 'Something', a great song that Frank Sinatra and Barbra Streisand sing. 'My Sweet Lord' was also a good song, but unfortunately someone had written it before him. He was accused of taking the melody line from the Chiffons' hit, 'He's So Fine', and using it for the basis of 'My Sweet Lord'. The publishers of 'He's So Fine', Bright Tunes Publishing, took him to court over alleged copyright infringement. He was found guilty of 'unconscious plagiarism', and the composition royalties from the number, which had topped the British and American charts, had to be made over to Bright Tunes. To be fair to George, it is something we have all done in the past. It is easy to write a song and not realize that it is very close to something else. There are only a certain number of notes in the scale, after all, so there are bound to be duplications. It is not a conscious thing, but the law states that a composer is only allowed to 'borrow' four bars of someone else's material before having to pay royalties to the original writer.

Strangely enough, even though the Beatles changed the musical world and everyone sang their songs and they pioneered new recording techniques, very few people copied their style in the same way they had done with Elvis, Chuck Berry, Buddy Holly and, particularly, the Everly Brothers. The exceptions were the Bee Gees and the Electric Light Orchestra, and it's ironic that ELO's Jeff Lynne has become such a driving force behind George Harrison's musical revival in the late eighties.

At the height of Beatlemania in 1963, and in the face of such strong opposition, Cliff Richard and the Shadows had an incredible year, and we spent much of the time at the very top of the charts. We reached the No.1 spot on two occasions in our own right, with 'Dance On' in January and 'Foot Tapper' in March, and we enjoyed an incredible run of hits – 'Atlantis' reached No.2 in June, 'Shindig' was No.6 in September and we ended the year with 'Geronimo' at No.11. With Cliff we also reached No.1 with 'The Next Time', and 'Bachelor Boy', followed immediately by 'Summer Holiday', and we consolidated that success by scoring with 'Lucky Lips' (No.4), 'It's All in the Game' (No.2) and 'Don't Talk to Him' (No.2). At the same time our two former colleagues, Jet Harris and Tony Meehan, joined forces to make their own assault on the chart, and during the next twelve months they reached No.1 in January with 'Diamonds', No.2 in April with 'Scarlett O'Hara', and No.4 in September with 'Applejack'. We were among friends. It was a spectacular year all round. It was also the year I learnt about our first accountants' methods of dealing with the Inland Revenue.

Every twelve months we were summoned to our accountants' office and shown into the boardroom to meet these men in suits and ties of whom we were very much in awe, which was stupid really, because *we* were paying their fees. We were all represented by a large firm of accountants called Maw, Ellis & Warne, which we nicknamed 'More or Less'. In 1963 I earned £50,000 from my music and songwriting, which was an incredible amount in those days. I spent £17,000 in expenses; had to pay £22,000 in income tax and ended up with a profit of £11,000. I was just twenty-two years old. The following year I ordered the ultimate status symbol – a Rolls-Royce Silver Cloud, with black leather upholstery. It cost £5,000. We were appearing in Chesterfield when I took delivery of the car at the theatre. The others thought I was mad, but I was dying to drive it. We all got in to give it a spin, and I gingerly drove off in the direction of Sheffield. Sting was to say years later that he once saw me driving the Rolls-Royce through Newcastle. He was standing in a queue outside the Stoll cinema in Westgate Road when I drifted past in my Silver Cloud, looking very superior, and he vowed to himself then and there that *this* was the business he would get into.

When Licorice Locking joined the Shadows, we didn't appreciate that he was a Jehovah's Witness. Religious convictions were not a qualification needed for playing in the group. To be quite honest, we didn't care. He was a good, steady bass guitarist without being flashy, and great fun to be around. He had an infectious personality and a great sense of humour. Brian Bennett had also been of the same religious persuasion for a short time, which might have explained why they got on so well together. Brian's wife, Margaret, has remained a faithful follower.

It was Licorice who started to fire Cliff Richard's interest. After Cliff's father died, he was lonely and his life seemed empty. He had everything going for him professionally – fame, success, money – and yet something was missing. Coming off stage each night was something of an anti-climax. Back in his hotel room after a show, he would sit all alone and ask himself 'Now what?' He had been very close to his father and felt drawn to contact him at a seance by means of a spiritualist, until Licorice discovered his plan and told him in the strongest terms, *not* to get involved in such a stupid idea. Instead he talked to Cliff about his life and his own spiritual guidance through the Bible, and then pulled a copy out of his pocket and proceeded to read relevant chapters out loud.

Cliff warmed to his conviction and his faith, and the two talked passionately together on many occasions, discussing a wide variety of subjects. Later, Cliff accompanied Licorice to Jehovah's Witness meetings in London to savour the atmosphere. They were soon joined by Brian and Hank, to whom Licorice had been talking quite seriously. (I think he realized by now that I was a lost soul, at least to their beliefs.)

When Cliff discovered religion, he was emotionally involved with a young dancer called Jackie Irving, and you could see that they were very fond of each other. They first met when we were starring at the London Palladium, and started going out together shortly afterwards. I think at one stage they may have been considering marriage, though to my knowledge they didn't sleep together. Cliff was in a position to have almost any woman in the world at this time . . . but he didn't, because he had started studying the Bible and living by the Ten Commandments. When people asked him why he never married, he always defended his decision by saying he had never met the right girl. Maybe Jackie Irving could have been the right girl for him, but his religion intervened and she later married Adam Faith.

When we opened our summer season at the ABC Theatre, Blackpool, at the end of May, all four of them (Cliff, Licorice, Brian and Hank) would meet regularly to take part in what seemed like intense and complex discussions in the dressing-room or back at the hotel after the show, in which they would talk and study the Bible together.

Since then, it seems, Cliff and Hank have devoted almost all of their lives to their own individual religions, each one believing the other is wrong in his convictions. In fact, in Cliff's own autobiography, *Which One's Cliff?*, he goes on record as saying that he can't be close to Hank Marvin because he is a Jehovah's Witness and adds: 'I can't be at one with anyone who doesn't share my faith.' To me it seems silly that these two men, who for so many years helped create each other's success, cannot now sustain the closeness they always had before because of their different opinions. And yet to my mind, surely, they are worshipping the same God. They simply refuse to believe each other's interpretations of the Christian faith. I don't judge anyone by his religion, but on what kind of person he is, and if two learned religious fanatics like Hank and Cliff can't agree, what chance have I got?

Cliff spent two years exploring the Jehovah's Witness faith with a close circle of friends, and persuaded his mother and sisters to convert. In the end, however, other friends helped him change his mind in favour of a more open Anglican persuasion, and in 1966 he made world headlines when he walked forward at Earl's Court, at a Billy Graham rally, and in front of 5,000 people pledged his life to God. He reaffirmed his own commitment by singing, 'It's No Secret What God Can Do'.

One of the people who helped him more than most in the early days of his conversion was Bill Latham, who was head of religious education at Cliff's sister Joan's school in Essex. It was through Bill's help and teaching that Cliff's faith started to take over his life. They have been the greatest of friends for over twenty years, sharing a mutual interest in Christianity and charity work, each one spiritually guiding the other. Today, Bill Latham organizes every aspect of Cliff's gospel tours and promotion. In 1966, when Cliff decided to give up show business because he believed he was setting himself up on a pedestal as an idol for kids to worship, against the wishes of the Lord, it was Bill who talked him out of that decision to quit. Bill reasoned with Cliff that it was perfectly acceptable, and that he could do far better work for the Lord by talking about his beliefs from the stage as Cliff Richard. So Cliff – who had originally intended to become a teacher of religious instruction – carried on.

The more Hank found out about the Jehovah's Witnesses, the stronger his belief became. In 1973, after much counselling, he was baptized, along with his second wife, Carole, and appears completely fulfilled. Today, like Cliff Richard, he puts his religion before anything else in his life, which has on occasions affected the Shadows' own career. At one time he even refused to work with the group on Tuesdays, Thursdays and Sundays, because of his meetings on those days. Of course this caused the occasional argument. I couldn't see how anyone could plan their career around Mondays, Wednesdays, Fridays and Saturdays. It didn't make sense; to my mind it wasn't acceptable because we were trying to run our careers, and we had to explain to Hank that it was unfair to make such demands. But the divide between us became greater.

It is ironic that today Cliff and Hank are far more contented with their lives than I will ever be. It seems they have found their nirvana; I'm still searching for mine. The two schoolboys who came down to London together, to seek their fortune and share a spectacular success, can't ever be as close as they once were. There seems to be a screen between us. He's my partner, and we work on stage together, but there is a gulf between me and the Jehovah's Witness doctrine, and Hank knows my feelings well. I have asked him on occasions what would happen if a member of his family needed a blood transfusion. What would he do? The Jehovah's Witness attitude takes an uncompromising position on blood transfusions, and teaches that they are forbidden, no matter what the circumstances. Hank has always given me the same answer: he will face the problem if it ever arises. Of course this is the old 'chestnut' question.

I have always found it difficult to commit myself to any kind of religion, when each faith seems to deny the right of the others to exist. Each religion believes *it* is the chosen one, and supplies all the right answers. All others are wrong. I don't go to church and I rarely pray to my God, and I don't try to convert people to my way of thinking, yet I live my life by a set of rules, standards if you like, and that is basically what the Bible is teaching.

I really admire Cliff. He is a tremendous Christian, and a great example to all. Yet I do not think that he is really qualified to preach from the stage during his concert tours on subjects like divorce, children, sex, AIDS, and how we live in this modern age. Quite simply, most of the things he speaks about he hasn't experienced. I know he means well, but I think he is a little misguided.

For my part, I'm sure religion is not the answer to my particular problem. I would be a hypocrite if I said it was. I don't believe in this 'born-again' business either. It is too shallow and too convenient. If you are born a Christian, you will always be a Christian, no matter what. You might slip from the fold occasionally – we are only human after all – it's as simple as that. A born-again Christian believes that when he has reaffirmed his faith, everything he has done before in his life – all the sins and temptations – will be wiped away, so that he can start again with a clean slate. The Jehovah's Witnesses believe the same thing. I think it's naïve to suggest that any of us who have broken any of the Commandments in the past can wake up one morning and say: 'Lord, I have sinned. Here I am, a born-again Christian.' And that makes it all right.

Despite all this, I am not an atheist. One has to believe that something, or somebody, created all life and the human form, because it is so stunning. The human body fascinates me, the machinery is wonderful. The creation of life and the world in which we live is magnificent – but I cannot in all honesty spend every day of my life thanking someone for it. And when you see the terrible disasters – plagues, floods, famine, and earthquakes – happening around the world, it seems to me that God is out a lot of the time. Where was He when they needed Him?

While Cliff and the boys were indulging in their private theological discussions, I was having problems of my own, and my life had reached crisis point. For some time now I had been having trouble tuning my guitar. I don't know how it happened, but it developed into a phobia. It came to a head in Blackpool in 1963, where I was becoming paranoid – I couldn't handle the situation and was rapidly heading for a nervous breakdown.

We were playing two shows each night, and we were due on stage for our opening spot at 6.15 pm. I used to go into the theatre at 3 pm to start tuning my guitar. Three hours later, it was still out of tune – or I thought it was. It was an obsession. My problem almost caused us to come to blows in the dressing-room – I couldn't take the pressure, and screamed at the rest of the lads to be quiet as I was tuning up. I was so easily distracted, the slightest thing put me off.

I was worrying far too much about every tiny detail – was my suit pressed correctly, were my shoes clean, would my amplifier work, was the microphone switched on? Instead of enjoying my life and the success I was having, I was hypercritical and tormenting myself. I couldn't relax, I felt constantly wound up and tense, I was anxious about everything; it was part of my need for perfection.

Licorice's behaviour didn't help my condition, either. I was a stickler for punctuality – it was the sergeant-major syndrome that had upset Jet and Tony, and now I was giving Licorice an equally hard time when he turned up late. One evening he missed the start of the show completely, and I told him in no uncertain terms to buck his ideas up and get to grips with himself. That was good coming from me, in my state!

Being totally dedicated to his religious calling as a Jehovah's Witness, Licorice put his free time to good use and spent it walking the streets of Blackpool, knocking on doors and preaching the word of Jesus Christ, with a copy of the Bible in one hand and the Jehovah's Witness magazine, *Watch Tower*, in the other. It was a one-man crusade which Licorice seemed to thrive on. On the day he missed his call on the stage at the ABC Theatre, he had been canvassing for converts in Preston, some twenty miles away, and was so involved in his work that he didn't notice how late it was. By the time he got back to the theatre, we were already on stage. I was furious at his attitude and wouldn't take any excuse. I felt it was unprofessional, and reminded him again that the show *had* to come first in his life. It was paying his wages.

When I eventually sought help from a psychiatrist, he told me that I would certainly have a nervous breakdown if I didn't slow up, and that meant leaving the group. It seemed my only salvation. My health had to come first. I spent several days agonizing over the decision and finally realized that it was the only way. I had to do it, for my own sanity. Reluctantly, I told Cliff and Hank of my intention to leave the Shadows in October, after we had completed tours of France and Israel. Then I had every intention of starting a new career for myself, possibly with our own music publishing company. I also wanted to continue writing songs, and I was looking forward to a less hectic lifestyle. I had been a musician for five years and had rarely seen my wife and son Dwayne for any length of time because we were always touring. In the three years since I had bought my house in North

Harrow I had spent exactly twelve weeks there. Now it was time for a rest. The thought of leaving the group, however, was a terrible wrench.

At the same time that I decided to throw in the towel, Licorice Locking was also agonizing over his career. Shortly afterwards he, too, made the decision to stand down. He was a super guy, and you could not wish to meet a nicer man. His dedication to the work of God through the Jehovah's Witness faith meant far more to him than his work with the Shadows. His religion was taking over his life. He had been a Shadow for just eighteen months when he turned his back on stardom and success and walked away from an outstanding career . . . for the sake of his beliefs. I admired and respected him tremendously for what he did; it certainly couldn't have been easy. Nowadays Licorice plays in pubs and clubs to keep his hand in . . . and he's still smiling.

In the middle of our most successful year, the group was falling apart.

9

'THERE'S A FRIEND OF YOURS IN TOWN . . .'

The Shadows' tour of Israel gave me a chance to relax and unwind a little and helped sort out my problems. By the time we came back to Britain I was feeling in much better shape, good enough to have second thoughts about leaving. Once the French excursion was completed I definitely didn't want to go, and sought medical advice once more. This time I was given a clean bill of health, a little medication, and permission to carry on. I was back, although I hadn't really been away. It was a great relief to me; I wasn't really looking forward to a life without playing music. I still had to solve the problem of tuning my guitar, though, which had started the fiasco in the first place.

With Licorice's impending departure we had to find a replacement quickly. And we originally attempted to recruit John Paul Jones, who was playing with Jet Harris and Tony Meehan's backing group on tour. He was a superb bass guitarist, very expressive, but somehow, with his cigarette holder, he didn't fit the image of the Shadows, so we looked elsewhere. In 1968 he joined Jimmy Page, Robert Plant and John Bonham in Led Zeppelin.

Instead we turned to a young bass guitarist we had first encountered during a Sunday concert engagement at the Queen's Theatre in Blackpool a year or so before. His name was John Rostill. He was an immensely talented bass player, and was playing with a group called the Terry Young Six when we first noticed him. It was John, and not the drummer, who laid down the beat in that band. He was also a very good-looking guy and smartly dressed, and reminded me of Don Everly. He was perfect for the Shadows. We found out that he had left Terry Young some time before, had formed a group called the Interns, and was presently working in Bournemouth. We sent our tour manager, David Bryce, to see him and ask him to audition. He jumped at the chance, and drove from Bournemouth that night to meet us at the London Palladium the following morning.

'Can you play "Dance On" in A?' we asked him. He could – and that was it. Brian Bennett rated him the best bass player we had ever had, because he was so steady and allowed him the freedom to experiment with his drumming instead of having to keep a rigid line. John did things which other bass players would not attempt at the time. He was playing chords on the bass and would slap the strings as he played, and in order to improve even more he was taking lessons in sight-reading and musical theory – a truly dedicated musician. His impact on the group's songwriting was outstanding, and he became a prolific composer. John was equally at home writing on his own, or with one of us. He and I struck up an immediate friendship. While the others concentrated mainly on their religion, we wrote songs together and indulged ourselves in music and other delights. We became close mates over the years; he played an important role in my life behind the scenes, and gave me back my confidence. John Rostill was such a good musician that we came to a special arrangement. For £10 a week, he agreed to tune my guitars for me before each performance. He tuned using harmonics instead of the more conventional way, which was something I hadn't come across before. I trusted him totally, and never questioned his tuning the way I questioned my own. John was my salvation, and the agreement was to last for five years. He always arrived at engagements an hour or so before everyone else, in order to organize guitar tuning.

John Rostill joined the Shadows at Christmas 1963, and the first performance he ever made with the group was in the movie *Wonderful Life* with Cliff Richard. It was shot on location in the Canary Islands, and I'm sure no one knew what the film was about. We certainly didn't. It was all very confusing, and it appeared that the film was being written as it went along. It was to have been a Western, set in Mexico, and ended up as a film-within-a-film. We spent three weeks on location with the rest of the cast, which included Susan Hampshire, Walter Slezak, Derek

Bond, Richard O'Sullivan and Una Stubbs, and none of us knew what the hell was going on from one minute to the next. Most of the filming took place on the sand dunes. We dressed up in a lot of costumes and that was about it. There was a ten-minute sequence in the middle of the film on the history of the movies, which was excellent – the rest of the film stank. It took twelve weeks in all of complete and utter boredom, although for John it was a never-to-be-forgotten experience. But he had yet to play a note on stage with us.

Despite a poor script, we wrote some good songs for the movie, including 'On the Beach', which I wrote with Cliff, 'A Matter of Moments', and 'Theme for Young Lovers'. The first single John played on was 'The Rise and Fall of Flingel Bunt', which we wrote together in the studio. I suppose we were all taking a leaf out of the Beatles' book now. It was written around an opening guitar riff with bags of fuzz. Hank suggested we make a twelve-bar instrumental out of it, because at that time rhythm 'n' blues was starting to take a stranglehold on the British market and people were attracted to the heavier type of twelve-bar blues. Norrie Paramor thought it had potential as a single. The title came about courtesy of Richard O'Sullivan, with whom we had worked on *The Young Ones* and *Wonderful Life*. It was the name of a character he had invented – it was perfect. We had recently seen a movie called *The Rise and Fall of Legs Diamond*, and we liked the title so much, we borrowed it. The record was released in May 1964 and was hailed by the music press as 'the Shadows' new sound'. It put us back in the Top Five and was voted instrumental of the year.

By now a harder edge was creeping into pop and rock music, with the emergence of bands like the Rolling Stones, the Animals, Them, the Yardbirds, the Pretty Things and Manfred Mann, followed by the Who, John Mayall's Blues Breakers, and, of course, Eric Clapton and Cream, whose influence had come from authentic American blues men like Muddy Waters, John Lee Hooker, Otis Spann, B. B. King, Howlin' Wolf, T-Bone Walker, Lonnie Johnson, Robert Johnson and Sonny Boy Williamson. The music was tough, rough and ready, and these groups adopted the same kind of attitude in their approach to the business: they snarled at the clean-cut, suited image of Cliff Richard and the

Shadows, and of the Beatles, for that matter, and dressed as casually as they could. A group uniform was certainly not part of the act. They dumped show business for street credibility and adopted a much more aggressive and defiant spirit. Image meant nothing, they rose and fell by the music they played. They re-created the old ideals first pioneered by rock 'n' roll of challenging the authority of the establishment; and they aimed their music specifically at the young. It was too raucous and too obscure to appeal to the middle ground. It was hard-driving and dirty. Their acceptance as recording artistes brought about some major changes to the structure of the British music industry, and saw the emergence, in particular, of the independent music labels and independent producers like Shel Talmy, Kit Lambert, Andrew Loog Oldham, Tony Visconti, Giorgio Gomelsky, Simon Napier-Bell, Larry Page and our old pal, Mickie Most. As early as 1963, rhythm 'n' blues was gaining a considerable airing in Britain through a remarkable network of small clubs that sprang up originally in London, just like the coffee bars had some five years before. There were the Marquee and the Flamingo, in Soho, where a much more jazz-orientated style of rhythm 'n' blues was on display, peddled by such bands as Georgie Fame and the Blue Flames, Cliff Bennett and the Rebel Rousers, Zoot Money's Big Roll Band, and Chris Farlowe and the Thunderbirds. Before long clubs were opening up all over the south of England and beyond. There was the Crawdaddy Club in Richmond, the Cellar in Kingston and the Ricky-Tick, which started in Windsor and later gave its name to a chain of small venues throughout the southern counties. Slowly r'n'b began to spread all over the country, with venues opening up in all major cities, including our home town of Newcastle where the famous Club A-Go Go became the launching pad for the Animals.

This rhythm 'n' blues revolution was orchestrated by the Rolling Stones, from Dartford, whose name came from an old Muddy Waters song. They became the bad boys of British pop, in direct contrast to the happy-go-lucky good-guy image the media perpetrated around the Beatles, who were now looked upon by these street-wise bands as part of the establishment. The Stones were different, and refused to conform to any musical conventions from the outset. They wore day clothes on stage and looked particularly scruffy. We weren't admirers of their sartorial elegance. We heard stories of how they went on stage in their street clothes and at the time we were horrified. I think they set out deliberately from the start to shock the public, and then spent the rest of their careers trying to live up to the image. They were sullen, they didn't smile on stage and they went against the entire show-business ethic, which they carried on into their everyday life. They lived the rock 'n' roll lifestyle to the full – sex and drugs and rock 'n' roll – and courted outrageous publicity, which seemed to make them even bigger stars. Nothing seemed to affect them. They manipulated the media into featuring articles headlined: 'Would you let your daughter marry a Rolling Stone?' In 1964, when they were arrested for insulting behaviour after urinating against the wall of a London garage in Romford Road, Forest Gate, they just happened to have a photographer on hand to take pictures. When the case subsequently came to court, Brian Jones, Bill Wyman and Mick Jagger were fined £5 and they even appealed against the sentence. The kids loved them because they totally lived up to what they thought a rock 'n' roll lifestyle should be, and you could see the influence they were having everywhere. They were as far removed from the Shadows as they could possibly be. We were sedate, staid and safe – the Stones were menacing.

Nevertheless they were an exciting band on stage, and their records captured perfectly the expectant atmosphere of live performance. Their music was dynamic, and Mick Jagger was probably the best front man for a group in rock 'n' roll history, but he wasn't in the Cliff mould. They came out of the Crawdaddy Club in Richmond and brought with them a large following. They were very much musical innovators, and for the next few years led a remarkable new wave of performers and groups in Britain: Pete Green's Fleetwood Mac, the Spencer Davis Group, Ten Years After, Rory Gallagher and Taste, Love Sculpture, Jethro Tull, the Climax Blues Band, Chicken Shack and Rod Stewart. The Stones started their recording career by covering obscure rhythm 'n' blues songs like 'Little Red Rooster', but once they realized their own potential as songwriters there was no stopping them, and they made a major contribution to British music. Mick Jagger and Keith Richard were inspired to write songs together by John Lennon and Paul McCartney, who had written 'I Wanna Be Your

Man' especially for the Stones to record, after hearing them playing at the Crawdaddy Club. Lennon and McCartney actually wrote the song to order, from a table in the corner of the dimly lit Richmond venue. Mick Jagger and Keith Richard were impressed by their ability, but as Jagger said later: 'If they can write songs so bloody easily, why shouldn't we try?'

They did, and produced some of the most powerful rock songs of the sixties. 'Satisfaction' was a classic. So, too, were 'Honky Tonk Woman', 'The Last Time', 'Jumpin' Jack Flash' and 'Brown Sugar'. They wrote 'Blue Turns to Grey' for Cliff Richard.

Once Mick Jagger had established himself as the leader of the group, Brian Jones, who had put the group together in the first place, became paranoid about the popularity of the front man. Whenever they appeared on television Brian would write notes afterwards, jotting down the number of times the camera was focused on Mick, Keith, Charlie or Bill and how many times he had been in the frame. He read the daily newspapers and all the teenage magazines to see if Jagger's name was mentioned more times in articles than his own, and counted how many photographs of the group were printed. It was a big hang-up with him, and he could see that Mick Jagger and Keith Richard were taking over what essentially was his group. In the end it was inevitable that he would quit the band. Jagger certainly wasn't going to move over.

The Stones were followed by two bands led by two of the greatest writers in British pop – Ray Davies of the Kinks and Pete Townshend of the Who, both of whom moved on in their writing from adolescent, teen-dream lyrics to become great social commentators of their time. Their songs echoed urban society in Britain in the sixties: the Kinks with 'Waterloo Sunset', 'Dead End Street', 'Sunny Afternoon' and 'Dedicated Follower of Fashion'; and the more aggressive Who with 'My Generation', 'Pictures of Lily', 'Tattoo' and 'Substitute', which would later lead Townshend to writing the rock opera *Tommy*. Both groups had their roots in rhythm 'n' blues.

Our own reaction to the emergence of the growing popularity of rhythm 'n' blues was to send it up in a gentle sort of way, using our own goonish humour. We were the establishment, the elder statesmen of the music business, untouchable, and cushioned by the entertainment industry. We were playing all the major prestige engagements, but were losing sight of our original ideals and were out of touch with modern trends. We couldn't compete on equal terms with bands like the Stones, being essentially an instrumental group. We had never heard of the Crawdaddy Club, or Ricky-Tick for that matter. Some of us didn't even know where Richmond was. So we wrote an instrumental and called it 'Rhythm 'n' Greens'. Actually, the song wrote itself. Nothing was planned when we went into Abbey Road studios to record the number, apart from a basic outline – we wanted to have some fun. We set up our gear and just busked along to see what might happen, adding a few raucous r'n'b shouts like 'Yeah baby', and 'Ooh yeah' along the way. It was a total improvisation from start to finish; we recorded it in one take, and still managed to capture what we thought was the spirit and atmosphere of rhythm 'n' blues. It was a total piss-take. We all thought it would stand a chance of making the charts on the success that rhythm 'n' blues was enjoying in Britain, and we released it as a single. It was a bit of a disappointment and only reached No.22. Perhaps we under-estimated our audience. No one else got the joke.

'Rhythm 'n' Greens' became the title theme to a half-hour comedy movie we were asked to make, which traced the history of life on the beaches of Britain and featured several musical interludes. We filmed it on our own, although Cliff made a supporting appearance playing King Canute, during our summer season at Great Yarmouth. The film was nothing more than a series of cameos from the caveman to the spaceman, and all points in between, linked together with a narrative by Robert Morley. It gave us a good excuse to dress up and act the fool – and the chance to write more movie material, contributing 'Rank a Chank', 'The Lute Number', 'The Main Theme', and 'The Drum Number'.

The film, which was originally (and some say aptly) called *A Load of Old Rubbish*, came out on general release with the X-rated *King and Country*, thus limiting our audience considerably.

Over the next few years we worked steadily – the pattern was very similar. We were cocooned in show business, as far away from rock 'n' roll as you could get, but we didn't miss it. We'd grown up this way, writing, recording, touring, appearing on television . . . it was a way of life. We had become family entertainers without even trying.

At the end of 1964 we appeared at the London Palladium opposite Arthur Askey and Una Stubbs, in the pantomime *Aladdin*, for which we had written the entire score. Out of that show, Cliff enjoyed chart success with 'I Could Easily Fall (In Love with You)' at the beginning of 1965, while we also contributed 'Genie with the Light Brown Lamp'. It was a marvellous experience working with show-business doyen and music-hall legend Arthur Askey, but after a while the run began to get us all down. It was too long. We started our season on 22 December and played twice-daily performances for three-and-a-half months, finishing in April. The first show went on at 2.45 pm, and the final curtain fell on the second house at 11 pm. We were at the Palladium for ten hours a day, six days a week, so any recording had to be slotted in during the mornings. It was so inhibiting, and it became too much like a proper job. The following year we wrote a score for another Palladium pantomime, *Babes in the Wood*, which starred our old friend and colleague Frank Ifield, and by 1966 we were asked to go back for more. *Cinderella* was the subject with Cliff playing Buttons; Hugh Lloyd and Terry Scott played the Ugly Sisters while the Shadows doubled up as the Brokers' Men. Another lengthy run. Once again we were responsible for writing all the music, including the hit single, 'In the Country'.

1966 was an eventful year for Cliff and the Shadows. In May we started shooting *Finders Keepers* at Pinewood Studios in Buckinghamshire, with a cast that included Robert Morley, Peggy Mount and Viviane Ventura.

The Shadows were featured more in this film than in any of Cliff's previous movies, and when it was released the following January it was billed as starring '*Cliff Richard and the Shadows*'.

At first Cliff commuted daily to the studios from his home in Nazeing in Essex, which meant a journey of ninety minutes each way. His friendship with Bill Latham was flourishing, and they regularly attended Crusader meetings and adventure camps together and worshipped at the same church. Bill lived with Mamie, his mother, in North London, which was on the route to the studio. To save Cliff travelling time, Bill suggested that he should stay with them at their home during the six-week schedule.

Cliff readily accepted the offer, and moved in with the teacher and his mother. It set the seal on a long-lasting friendship, which survives today. Much later, the three set up home together in Weybridge, Surrey. In his autobiography, *Which One's Cliff?*, published in 1977, Cliff dedicated the book 'To Mamie, "Mum" Number Two'. His real mother also made news in her own right when on 18 June she married Derek Bodkin, Cliff's former chauffeur, who at twenty-four was a year younger than her own son. Dorothy, Cliff's mother, was forty-five. Although he said very little at the time, I'm convinced the marriage upset Cliff. He had lost his father only five years before, and now he was effectively losing his mother. I feel it was another blow in his life which turned him more towards his religious calling, and he found comfort in the Bible.

It was during the filming of *Finders Keepers* that Hank met Carole Naylor, one of the dancers in the film, who was later to become his second wife and join him as a Jehovah's Witness.

The hit song from the picture was 'Time Drags By', which Hank, Brian, John and I wrote together and for which we received an Ivor Novello Award. When we recorded it, former Yardbird Jimmy Page played harmonica on the session.

The following September we were appearing in Bournemouth as part of a British tour schedule when I met Olivia Newton-John. She was seventeen years old and over in Britain from her home in Australia with her singing partner Pat Carroll. I was twenty-four. The girls worked as a singing duo and were part of our supporting bill that week.

Olivia wasn't a great singer at the time, but people liked her. She was a stunning blonde – very good-looking – with a bright and bouncy personality. The two girls had won a talent contest in Australia, the prize for which was a trip to Britain, but were set to return home shortly. Olivia had been born in Cambridge and had gone to live in Australia with her parents when she was five years old. She had grown up in Melbourne, and now considered herself Australian. She had started singing when she was very young, and by the age of fourteen she was working on local radio and television.

I was very taken with her, to say the least, and we went out together on a number of occasions. I used to take her to Danny La Rue's club in Hanover Square, which was a late-night haunt for many people in show business. I wasn't a member, but they always let me in. The more I got to know Olivia the more I was convinced she would make a superb Cinderella in our forthcoming Palladium pantomime – and I wanted her to audition for the part. Unfortunately she was committed to return to Melbourne at the end of the year, and turned the offer down.

Olivia and Pat were a good act of their kind, covering songs by Dionne Warwick and the Beatles. They were both good-lookers and sang in tune, so there was never any shortage of work. I used to see them in the Celebrity Club in London, which was owned by Paul Raymond. He paid them £25 a week. When Pat's work permit and visa ran out in December and the two girls returned home, I thought that was the end of a very pleasant relationship. However, just as our Palladium season was coming to an end in April 1967, John Ashby, a friend of mine who was the Seekers' road manager, dropped into the theatre one night with a message for me. 'There's a friend of yours in town who would appreciate a call,' he said. Olivia was back.

It was great news. I was so excited, and we started going out together again. I was married at the time, and it wasn't long before Anne found out that Olivia was on the scene again. She had known about our brief liaison before.

Olivia's effect on me was devastating. Looking back, I think I fell in love with her immediately, despite the fact that I had a wife and family. I needed to be with her – and towards the end of that year, after much heartache, I decided to leave home and we started living together. We rented an apartment in St John's Wood, on the ninth floor of a block overlooking Lord's Cricket Ground.

I wasn't proud of what I did, walking out on my wife and family. There were many painful moments, but I was infatuated by Olivia. My wife tried to talk me out of leaving, but my mind was not for changing. I was bowled over by my new love. Maybe it was because Olivia and I were both involved in music that there was a bond between us, I don't know. I just fell in love, and it was sad and unfortunate that two other people should get hurt – my wife Anne and my son, Dwayne, who was only six. Looking back, I realize I was selfish. I wanted to be with Olivia all the time, no matter what happened. Everything I had promised myself in the past, to keep my family together, was destroyed. I broke up the family I had always wanted and ruined two people's lives. I had been determined to have a family of my own and to cherish it. Now it was all falling apart.

Anne had had a pretty unglamorous lifestyle since our wedding. I was hardly ever at home. I was always away on tour, or recording, which put a terrific strain on our marriage. Obviously being away from home can lead to affairs happening. It certainly led to a messy divorce, and my adultery was cited as the cause. Olivia was named as the 'other woman'. We even had to organize a private detective to observe us together so that the divorce would proceed smoothly. Looking back, it was very seedy.

The previous summer, on our way to Australia for a tour, we had broken our journey to appear in Israel at the Ramat Gan football stadium in Tel Aviv, with Nana Mouskouri and Peter Seeger. We arrived in the country on one of the anniversaries of the founding of the State of Israel, and found the security at the airport a little over-zealous. The officials decided to take our AC30 amplifiers to pieces to see what was inside. They even tore the skins off Brian's drum kit. The atmosphere was extremely tense as we completed the concert; we had the only amps that worked, following their close inspection at customs – the other musicians weren't so lucky – and we flew on to Australia. Quite honestly, it was a relief to get out. When we arrived in Sydney we were told that hostilities had broken out in Israel the previous day; the Six Day War had started with a vengeance. We were very nearly part of it.

By 1968, relationships within the group were becoming extremely strained. It amazes me that people expect four guys to work together, play together and virtually live in each other's pockets – and still be the best of pals all the time, and behave like brothers. We had been working together now almost non-stop for nearly ten years, touring the world without let-up. We were on a treadmill of tours, recording sessions, live engagements, TV work . . . and so it went on, year after year. Although we were established as an international act, the domestic hits slowly came to an end. We hadn't had a Top Ten success since 'Don't Make

My Baby Blue', one of our rare vocal records, in August 1965. We were so well established that we didn't need to rely on hits. I suppose it was inevitable in a way that things should come to an end between us all. We were four headstrong individuals and needed a change.

At the beginning of the year we broke new ground again by becoming the first group to headline at the Talk of the Town in London – then one of the most prestigious venues in Europe. It was an incredible season for us, because we had no less than *three* different line-ups during the three-week engagement.

John Rostill was having a particularly bad time, following the break-up of his relationship with his girlfriend, Lyn Walker. He suffered a nervous breakdown, and collapsed from nervous and mental exhaustion midway through our run. Instead of pulling out of the contract, we called in a replacement for our remaining two weeks. It was none other than Licorice Locking, who came to our rescue, smiling as always. For the first time in five years, the group that recorded 'Foot Tapper' and 'Atlantis' was back in business. That reunion was short-lived, too. Brian Bennett was rushed to hospital with suspected appendicitis. This time Tony Meehan answered our call and stepped in. It was good working with him again. It was fortunate that we only had a week to go, because we had the distinct feeling that we were jinxed, and each night we wondered who would be the next to succumb to illness.

The following spring we toured Australia once more and I grabbed the opportunity of taking Olivia with me, which gave her the chance to visit her family. During our time in Melbourne, we met a guy who was to play an important part not only in our career but in Olivia's as well. John Farrar was a brilliant young guitarist in a local band called the Strangers, who supported us on a couple of occasions. He was a great fan of ours, and in turn we were very impressed with his musical prowess. He certainly was the star of the group he was playing with, and quite an exceptional vocalist. At that time John was going steady with Olivia's former singing partner, Pat Carroll, so we struck up a long-lasting friendship. Back home in June my divorce finally came through, and Olivia and I planned our future together. We had every intention of marrying, although not immediately. We wanted to wait and spend some time together just enjoying each other's company. She was still only eighteen, and was rather young for such a commitment.

My private life was now blissfully happy, but events within the group reached crisis point and came to a head a few weeks later when we were appearing in cabaret at the Talk of the North in Eccles near Manchester.

John Rostill and Hank had been carrying on a private feud for some months now. They didn't appear to be getting on at all well together, and the atmosphere in the group was becoming rather tense. Still, it didn't affect my relationship with them; we remained the best of friends. When we were out on the road we had a set routine which we stuck to rigidly. John would arrive at the venue at least an hour before we were due on stage, in order to tune up. He was responsible for tuning the guitar I used on stage, a spare – in case of accidents – and his own bass. Hank was always the next to arrive, half an hour later, and would take care of his own guitar. Then, with John's assistance, he would complete the tuning-up process by making sure all three guitars were in tune with each other. Brian and I would roll up ten minutes or so later, to change for the performance. We were so laid back by then.

It was the last night of our season in Manchester, and when Brian, Olivia and I arrived at the night club fifteen minutes before we were due to go on stage, we found John Rostill fuming. He was shaking with rage. He had been waiting for over an hour for Hank to arrive and there was still no sign of him. He shouted at us, demanding to know what had happened to Hank. I hadn't seen Hank for hours, and had assumed he was already at the venue.

I'd never seen John in such a state before – he was livid, and acting like a madman. It was so out of character. I was generally the one to complain about time-keeping, as Tony and Licorice had found out to their cost. Five minutes before the show started, Hank breezed into the dressing-room laughing and joking with his girlfriend Carole as if nothing had happened.

'Hi, fellas,' he said, picking up his guitar and turning to John for assistance. 'Right. Let's get tuned then.' Hank smiled, oblivious to the atmosphere that was brewing.

John exploded and flew at him, demanding to know why he

was late. I thought they would come to blows. John refused to co-operate, he was so distressed by Hank's attitude. By now, of course, Hank realized he was in the wrong, and he tried to extricate himself from the situation, but he knew he had let everyone down. It was so late now; no one was interested in his excuses. When Hank saw that everyone was ganging up on him and that no one would help him tune his guitar, he burst into tears. I'd known him for a good many years, and it was the first time I had ever seen him cry.

The mood of the room was awful, and I decided I'd had enough. I wanted to go home. The tension had reached breaking point, and now I was jumpy and on edge myself. I stormed out of the night club and into my Rolls-Royce which was parked outside, hastily followed by Olivia, who was trying to calm me down and act as peacemaker.

'You can't go . . . you've got a show to do. Think of the audience . . . they've paid good money to see you . . . you can't let them down over a petty squabble.' She was right, of course.

For once, personal feelings were getting an upper hand over our professionalism. We had to go on, but no one dared agree with her. It was the worst scene I'd experienced in the group's ten years. We were all so highly strung, so wound up with tension I suppose, that when we snapped we turned on each other. Hank was in the wrong, but the situation had got out of hand. After a few moments, he went outside to get some fresh air and to come to his senses. When we had all calmed down sufficiently to make a temporary peace, we went on stage half an hour later than expected and gave a mediocre, lack-lustre performance. The tension on stage was unbearable, with each of us watching the other.

It was the beginning of the end for the Shadows. I could stand it no longer. Now was the time to get out. We were due to headline a long season at the London Palladium in the autumn, and I decided that at the end of that show, in December, I would leave the group. This time I meant it.

On Saturday, 14 December 1968 I made my final appearance on stage with the Shadows. It was an emotional farewell – and as we took our final curtain call together on stage at the Palladium,

Hank presented me with an engraved clock in appreciation of my services.

I didn't perform on stage again for nearly two years. Instead I took the job I had intended to take five years before, looking after our own publishing company, Shadows Music, and travelled each working day to the London office in Savile Row. Olivia and I bought Jerry Lordon's old house at Hadley Common, near Totteridge, and set about turning it into our home. I turned my hand to decorating – something I had never done before – and became a real homebird. I wanted to spend as much time with Olivia as I possibly could. I had seen what long absences away from home had done to relationships in the past; they had ruined my marriage, and I didn't want it to happen again. I was contented, and easily slipped into a new way of life. I was happy with my lot and in love with Olivia.

I did very little during 1969 other than set up home and get to know Livvy. The Shadows, meanwhile, recruited Alan Hawkshaw on keyboards and accompanied Cliff Richard on a tour of the Far East. In Tokyo they recorded a live album at Sankei Hall, which was released shortly afterwards as *Live in Japan*. Hank thought it was awful, and I could only agree.

Peter Gormley had been interested for some time in making records with Olivia. She had a pleasant voice and looked good, and we both decided that with the right material we could certainly do something for her. So I set about searching for songs. It's funny how the best-laid plans get swept away.

Don Kirshner, the American producer who had created the Monkees for NBC Television in 1965, had decided that the time was right to repeat what was a decidedly successful operation and 'manufacture' another group along similar lines for a forthcoming project. The group he created was called Toomorrow, and, as with the Monkees, he picked four different personalities to appeal to different audiences. After lengthy auditions, he had signed up three guys – Vic Cooper, Karl Chambers, and a young American actor/singer called Ben Thomas. Kirshner was now looking for a girl singer to complete the line-up, and was toying with the idea of using Ben Thomas's girlfriend, Susan George, when, for some reason, he heard about Olivia Newton-John. Before the final decision was made, he rang the Gormley office and asked if Olivia would like to go and meet the movie's producer, Harry Saltzman, who had been responsible for the James Bond movies, in his Mayfair office.

It was a pleasant meeting, and I could see that Olivia had captivated both Saltzman and Kirshner with her good looks and charm. It was obvious, too, from their attitude, that they had found the girl they were looking for. Before we left the office, Olivia was offered the part. It was a very exciting project. Instead of starring in a TV series, like the Monkees, the group were being launched through a major musical feature film. It was set for worldwide release the following year. An album would be issued by RCA Records, and that, they said, was only the start. If the movie and the music took off, there was no end to the possibilities.

It was a strange situation that I found myself in. I had recently retired from the Shadows to spend more time with Olivia, and now she was the one with the opportunity to make records, be in a movie, and be whisked off to America – and probable stardom. I couldn't stand in her way, despite all the things we had planned together and promised each other. I'd known Don Kirshner long before he created the Monkees, through his work with Carole King and Neil Sedaka. He was a very famous publisher and I thought it was a wonderful idea, knowing his track record in the business. I firmly believed the idea would work. Olivia agreed to become part of Toomorrow and appear in the movie. She was put on an immediate retainer of £10,000 a year.

Over the next few months, while the movie was being completed, we spent our time commuting backwards and forwards to America. I had no ties as such, and it was all very exciting for me as I watched Olivia work. We travelled first class to New York and stayed in the best hotels, all paid for by the film company, who were ploughing millions of dollars into the project. Olivia's only worry at that time was that she didn't want anything to get in the way of our relationship. She was very concerned for our future.

When the movie was finished, we flew to New York for a spectacular launch. We were expecting great things, considering how much had been spent. But it was such an anti-climax and a big disappointment. The film was a disgrace. It was reminiscent of so many of the low-budget pop pictures that were made during the early sixties, and the biggest let-down of all was the music. It was all so lightweight. There were no hit songs – the numbers were naïve and instantly forgettable.

I could remember when the Monkees first appeared on television – the music was so good. Kirshner had hand-picked some of the greatest songwriting talent in the world to produce original material for Peter Tork, Mickey Dolenz, Davy Jones and Mike Nesmith to perform during their TV show, including Harry Nilsson, Neil Diamond, Neil Sedaka, Gerry Goffin, Carole King, Bobby Hart and Tommy Boyce, and the songs produced a very definite backbone on which the show was built; well-constructed and catchy tunes like 'Daydream Believer', 'Last Train to Clarksville', 'I'm a Believer', 'Pleasant Valley Sunday', 'A Little Bit Me, a Little Bit You' – good pop tunes which helped to establish the group among the élite. So I was expecting something similar with *Toomorrow*, but it just didn't happen. Instead of going for the best songwriters available, Kirshner had simply handed the job to some unknown writers he had signed to his publishing company and, of course, it couldn't possibly work.

It was a great blow to me. In an effort to save the movie and inject some new life into it, which was all it needed to make it work, I arranged a private screening for some of my songwriting colleagues, hoping we might get together to write a decent score. I contacted the cream of British composers – Roger Cook, Roger Greenaway, Les Reed, Mitch Murray and Tony Hiller – who had all enjoyed major chart success with some classic songs in the sixties. But it was an impossible task. It would have meant reshooting some of the major scenes, and adding thousands to the budget. In the end the film came out in Britain and proved a disaster for everyone concerned. Toomorrow, the group, made one album, which was the movie soundtrack, and released two singles . . . and then the whole thing fell apart.

For Olivia, fortunately, nothing was lost, and it proved a great experience despite the failure of the film. She came out of the whole fiasco with a lot of money and a career on which to build. We announced our engagement on her twenty-first birthday in 1970.

Having seen Olivia working, I began to get restless myself. I wanted to work – so I phoned Hank and suggested we write some songs together again. After the Shadows split, Hank had released two solo singles of his own – 'Goodnight Dick' and 'Sasha' – with little success in Britain, and he had also made a solo album. He had been working with Cliff Richard on a number of projects in the past few months, including his own BBC television series, on which he was featured as special guest-star with Una Stubbs and appeared not only as a musician but as a comedian as well. He took part in sketches and knockabout routines – hardly the image for one of the world's greatest guitar heroes. Cliff and Hank had also recorded together, putting out two singles, 'Throw Down a Line' and 'The Joy of Living', which had been very successful. At the same time, Hank was also offered a position to play lead guitar in the chart-topping group, the Move. He was flattered by their approach, but turned the job down because he didn't particularly want to go rushing off around the world again on tour.

Hank and I had always written well together, but not for a long time. We thought that if we could create enough material for an album, we might be able to record it. He was all for the idea. He and Carole were living together now in Barnet, only a few minutes away from Hadley Common. So I went over to his house. We sat in the garden and engrossed ourselves completely in our writing. It was a wonderful summer, and I think it inspired us to write some exceptionally good material. The break had done us both good.

We wanted to write songs that were far more meaningful than instrumentals and to get away from the typical Shadows sound: we wanted to break the stereotype. Music had been changing quite considerably. Dylan was the biggest influence to come out of America during the sixties. He made me cringe because his guitar and harmonica were never in tune with each other, but he made us all think about the music we were listening to because the lyrics were so good, so thought-provoking. He led that whole protest movement against America's involvement in Vietnam, which brought to the attention of the world singers like Joan Baez, the Byrds and Joni Mitchell. They were going to change the world, too. It was the era of the anti-hero, and of songs making social and political comment, more thought-provoking than mere puppy love. The protest revolution spawned the whole hippy generation of peace and love and San Francisco, a few years later. It was a sublime reaction to the war in Vietnam, and out of its shadows emerged a group of musicians whose music was much softer and more melodic, based around beautiful harmonies: Crosby, Stills and Nash, James Taylor, Simon and Garfunkel were perfect examples. Its roots were in folk and country rock.

It was the kind of material Hank and I had written, very much in the mould of Crosby, Stills and Nash. The original intention was to write and perform the songs as a duo – back to the good old days of the Geordie Boys – but I felt that to get the maximum potential from the material we should bring in a third voice, which would create more interesting harmonies. However, we couldn't think of anyone with a good enough voice for harmony whom we could ask to join us. It was Olivia who suggested John Farrar, the guy we had first met in Australia two years before. It was a great idea. He was a perfect choice, because I knew he had a great voice and was particularly good at falsetto. We phoned him in Australia and invited him to England. By now he had married Pat Carroll, so the invitation was extended to them both to come and stay with us at Hadley Common. John arrived in August and the three of us took off to Portugal to rehearse and finish our writing. Hank and I had already written ten songs for our proposed album, and we completed a further two in the Algarve with John. When it came to recording and arranging the material, John Farrar came into his own. He had a great talent for harmonies which suited our voices perfectly, and he gave our overall sound another dimension. He was such a great musician; he knew exactly what he wanted to do, and how to get the maximum impact from voices and instruments. Our first album, called, appropriately, *Marvin, Welch and Farrar* – which we produced ourselves, another innovation – came at the beginning of 1971, following a short European tour. It was a serious attempt to do something different, but we had a hard job convincing people we weren't the Shadows any more. No matter how hard we tried, we couldn't shake off the image of 'Apache' and 'Wonderful Land'. We were caught in the wrong environment. The songs had credibility, but we were playing them in the wrong places. At Batley Variety Club, one of the country's most celebrated night clubs, we walked off stage on the first night of our engagement to the sound of our own footsteps. All the audience wanted from us was 'FBI' and 'Man of Mystery'. Almost every night some joker would call out from the audience, 'When are you going to give us "Apache", Hank?' Of course we never did, but the audience expected it, and they couldn't quite understand what we were trying to do.

Our début album charted in its first week of release in April, and took everyone at EMI by surprise. They hadn't printed enough copies and it fell out of the hit parade shortly afterwards. By the time more copies were pressed it was too late, the impetus was lost. Our second effort, *Second Opinion*, failed to capture the imagination of the public sufficiently to put it in the charts at all. The poor public reaction to our project was very disappointing, because we felt the material on these albums was very good. It was well recorded and well produced. We had a little success in Australia and New Zealand and on the Continent, where they weren't so conscious of our former image, but the British would not accept that we were trying to do something different.

Peter Gormley was involved in a record company called Festival, an Australian label run by an old colleague of his, Mike Sloman. Dahlia Lavi and John Rowles were just two of the artistes signed to the company. Peter acted as consultant, but Sloman ran the day-to-day operations. It was Mike who played us 'If Not for You', which had been written by Bob Dylan and was featured on George Harrison's first album away from the Beatles, *All Things Must Pass*. It was a great song for Olivia, and we recorded it at the beginning of 1971. Both John Farrar and I produced it. We worked well together; John arranged the song and handled the musical side, while I produced Olivia's vocal performance. I was becoming very interested in recording, and the thought of creating something in the studio really appealed to me.

The record was released in March and reached No.7 in the British chart. By July it had made No.25 in America. On the strength of that success, Olivia appeared extensively on television and became a regular on Cliff's own TV series, after recording 'Don't Move Away' with him, which was issued on the B-side of his 'Sunny Honey Girl' single.

For Olivia's follow-up single, John and I re-wrote a traditional song, 'Banks of the Ohio', which made the Top Ten in October and peaked at No.6. Our relationship was still going strong. We both appeared with Cliff for a season at the Palladium before embarking on a series of concerts around the country – and a short European tour. Olivia became the new resident star of Cliff's second TV series, which was screened at the beginning of 1972, and she later went out to work on her own and was booked to appear on a short British variety tour for Leslie Grade in the early part of the year. If the show proved to be successful in the provinces, it was earmarked to go into the Prince of Wales Theatre, in London's West End, in the spring. It was a great opportunity for her.

It was becoming a good year. I was very happy and content; I had Olivia, who was now having hit records on her own and appearing on television. Marvin, Welch and Farrar were slowly building their name, while John and I were establishing ourselves as record producers, particularly now, as Olivia's third single – a version of George Harrison's 'What is Life' – had entered the charts. Life was good. Then it all came crashing down around me.

Towards the end of March 1972, when everything seemed to be going so well for us both, Olivia arrived back home really late after a concert appearance. It was well after midnight when she walked in and calmly announced that she was ending our relationship and breaking off our engagement. It was like a blow from a sledgehammer, and came completely out of the blue. Here was I, planning for a future together, and she was telling me that there was none. I couldn't believe what I was hearing. I didn't want to believe it. I was dumbfounded. Shattered. I thought it was a dream and that at any moment she would come along and wake me up and tell me nothing had really happened. But it was true.

I tried pleading and reasoning with her. I begged for an explanation.

'Why? What's happened? What's gone wrong? What have I done?' I kept blaming myself – maybe it was my fault. Olivia would not tell me at first, and shrugged it off, but she was insistent that the relationship was over. The more I pressed her, the more secretive she became. I knew there had to be something deeper.

I was in an impossible situation. The following morning I walked out of the house and moved into a flat in Soho I had bought some time before. I never went back to Hadley Common. I desperately needed someone to help me, someone to turn to, but there was no one. It was at this time that I needed the strength and support of a family around me, but I had none. Anne had met someone else and was living with him and Dwayne in Majorca. Even if she had still been in Britain, why should she help me after the way I had treated her? I went to see Sadie in Newcastle a couple of times, but it hurt her to see the state I was in. So instead, like many before me, I found my comfort in a bottle of brandy. Maybe Jet had been right after all.

The show Olivia was appearing in had by now transferred to the West End, and I used to go and see it at the Prince of Wales Theatre just to be near her. It was stupid and only made matters worse. At home I started to play her records over and over again. I was tormenting myself, and I drank even more. I was going through almost two bottles of brandy a day, and wine as well. The more I drank the worse I became. I was a wreck physically and mentally. I would wake in the morning and start drinking to numb my senses and get me through the day. Invariably the drink sent me to sleep – and when I was sleeping I was not conscious of my problems until I awoke. I certainly couldn't work. Prior to our break-up I was due to start work on a new Marvin, Welch and Farrar album, followed by a tour. But it was impossible, there was no way I could perform in front of an audience now. Hank and John were furious with me and had every reason. I had let them down badly, but I couldn't help it.

Our house at Hadley Common was sold and I sat in my Soho flat drinking myself stupid. I cried a lot, too. Some of my friends and colleagues were very kind to me, and were concerned for my well-being; people would ring me up to see how I was – but after a while there is nothing worse than a crying drunk. Two people, in particular, helped me immensely. Peter Gormley was more than a friend when I needed him, and I also had a lady friend called Petra, who worked at Aquascutum in Regent Street. She would come into the flat to check that I was all right and cook meals for me. However, I was going downhill rapidly.

In May, two months later, I discovered the main reason Olivia had called off our relationship. She was having an affair, and I was unlucky enough to catch them together at her flat. I felt utterly dejected when I realized the truth.

I was still producing Olivia's records with John Farrar at the time, and we were mid-way through an album when the break-up came, but after this second blow it was an even harder situation to handle in my state. There was no way I could cope with that, so I had to let it go. I handed the production over to John and backed down. Shortly afterwards, they made 'Take Me Home Country Roads', which became another big hit.

When you are depressed, the worst thing to do is drink. The more I drank, the more depressed I became, and I felt like death. In July, I'd had enough, I couldn't take any more. I was tired of life.

10

'LET'S GET TOGETHER AND WRITE SOME SONGS'

I thought I had planned it so well. I thought I had covered every eventuality.

I had told my friends that I was going away for the weekend and couldn't be contacted at home. The flat would be empty. There was no point in worrying about me – I would be all right and I would be back first thing Monday morning.

I had cancelled the milk and the newspapers. I didn't want there to be any tell-tale signs to draw attention to what I was about to do.

I convinced myself that I had thought of everything.

I can remember that it was a Sunday when I took a last look out of the window across the London skyline, before casually swallowing a handful of Portuguese barbiturates I had picked up on my last trip to my villa in the Algarve . . . and drank as much brandy as I could, until my senses were numbed into submission once more.

Then I waited, not really knowing what would happen. I didn't care. The last thing I remember was the red sky at night.

I had forgotten about the window-cleaner as I made my final preparations. He came to the apartment once a month and was due on Monday afternoon. I didn't give him a second thought. Punctual as always, the man arrived at my flat and was let in by the caretaker with a pass-key. They found me lying on the floor, motionless, but still breathing. I was in a coma. They called an ambulance immediately and I was rushed to the Middlesex Hospital. It was a very close thing. The tablets were very strong, but I hadn't taken enough of them.

I came round on the Tuesday to find Peter Gormley and my friend Petra waiting at my bedside. The first thing I felt was not remorse for my actions, or relief at being alive – but pain. Terrible pain. My skin was blistered and burned. The barbiturates had started to burn through my skin from inside. And my left leg hurt like hell. I couldn't move it. When I had finally slumped to the floor unconscious, I had fallen awkwardly and brought the full weight of my body down on to my left leg, severely restricting the blood supply. I lay there for many hours, and as a result I had badly damaged the nerve endings.

The press had a field day when they found out what had happened, and sensational stories of my attempted suicide were wired across the world to make the morning newspapers: 'Ex-Shadow in Drugs Overdose'.

I was in hospital for two months, during which time Olivia visited me twice.

The condition of my leg was quite serious, and for a while I had to walk with the aid of a stick. When I came out of the Middlesex Hospital I was sent to the RAF Rehabilitation Centre at Hadley Court for physiotherapy. I was still very depressed. It was at Hadley Court, however, that I started to realize that there was more to life than feeling sorry for myself. I was surrounded by service personnel, many of whom were recovering from terrifying injuries: there were casualties from Northern Ireland; bomb blast victims; people without arms or legs; stroke victims . . . and *me*, a failed suicide. I felt very humble in their presence, when I saw the guts and determination of these people. They were all desperately trying to get themselves well and fit again. I realized that I had no right to be so self-centred. My problems were self-inflicted and small by comparison – and that spurred me on. Their attitude to life was so infectious, and they pulled me through my crisis point. It was sobering to attend fitness classes in the early morning, surrounded by people without limbs.

I was discharged in October, and moved to a new house I had purchased in Hampstead High Street, with the intention of making a new start in my life. It was a delightful area. The condition of my leg had improved tremendously, but the condition of my mind was still very confused. I started drinking again. Six months had passed since Livvy and I had split up; now it wasn't bitterness I felt, I just looked forward to the day when Olivia's affair would end and she might come back to me. I hung on to that faint hope. I hadn't worked for a year, but fortunately the royalties from our previous success sustained me.

Olivia and I would often talk together on the telephone, and I spent a lot of my time asking her friends how she was, and what she was doing, just trying to glean as much information as I possibly could. I was still very much in love with her. Occasionally we would bump into each other in Peter Gormley's office. Olivia invited me to spend Christmas with her and the family, but it didn't lead to a reconciliation as I hoped. Still, by now we were slowly piecing our friendship back together again.

Almost a year after we had parted, Olivia asked if we could get back together again. We were in a tea-shop in Hampstead at the time, and when she told me, I almost fell on the floor. It was like winning the jackpot. Suddenly everything I had dreamed about for a year was becoming reality. I almost floated out of the shop, I was so happy. I didn't ask her for details of what had happened to her former relationship, I didn't think it was my place to do so. But the affair was obviously over. For that I was thankful. Olivia's lover was a married man, and I believe that she had always hoped he might leave his wife and be with her one day. When it didn't happen, she decided to end the affair, a little wiser in the ways of the world.

Our reconciliation had come at a good time for me, for I was slowly pulling myself together and regaining control of my life. It was just the extra tonic I needed – a ray of sunshine. In April, Livvy moved into my house in Hampstead and we set about starting life together again. I was determined to forget about the past and get on with my life. We lasted about eight weeks together, and in the end I asked her to leave. After everything that had happened, it was ironic that I should be the one who ended it this time.

Every time we made love, all I could focus on was Olivia in the arms of her lover – no matter how hard I tried, I still kept seeing the two of them together. When I told Olivia about it, we both broke down and cried together. There was nothing I could do about it. I never thought at that time of seeking expert advice from a doctor, or counselling.

Two months later Olivia went on holiday to the South of France with a mutual girlfriend of ours. I joined her for a few days, just on the offchance that we might rekindle the fire again, but it was over. When I flew back home she went on to Monte Carlo, where she met Lee Kramer, who subsequently became her manager in 1976.

Since the Shadows' break-up in 1968, EMI Records had been trying to get the group together again to record. The company realized that there was still a large market for the type of music we had played before, and wanted to exploit it. In the past we had all resisted any attempts, but now things had changed and we decided we had nothing to lose. It was a great opportunity for me because it gave me something positive to do with my life again, to occupy my time, and it was good therapy. Hank, Brian and I formed the basis of the re-formed line-up, which included John Farrar and a session bass player called Dave Richmond. The result was an album, *Rocking with Curly Leads*, which was released at the end of the year. It didn't exactly set the chart on fire for us, but nevertheless it put our name back in the frame.

I had also been helped out of the anguish I was going through over Olivia by another old friend. In 1969 John Rostill, our bass player, had become part of Tom Jones's backing group along with Big Jim Sullivan, and he had spent most of the last four years in America touring extensively with the Welsh singing star and backing him in cabaret in Las Vegas. He had been married since 1970 and had set up home in Radlett, Hertfordshire, where he lived with his wife, Margaret, and his young son, Paul. John was a real electronics wizard, and had converted one of the rooms in his house into a multi-purpose eight-track recording studio, rigging up banks of Revox tape recorders. The studio was called 'Radlett Notown', in tribute to Tamla Motown. The demos he made were almost good enough to release as masters. Both Hank Marvin and Brian Bennett were to move out to Hertfordshire shortly afterwards and follow John's lead by setting up their own home recording studios. John had also spent a lot of his spare time writing songs, and had a certain amount of success behind him. Engelbert Humperdinck, Elvis Presley and Family Dogg were just some of the artistes who recorded his material.

We met socially again in September 1973, after he had returned to England following a hectic tour of the USA with Tom Jones. He seemed in good spirits at times, but I later learnt that he was having problems himself, which made him very depressed. When he found out what I had been going through over the last few months, he forgot about his own troubles and tried to help me.

'You need motivating, Bruce, and what you need to do is work,' he said, and put his arm around my shoulder and hugged me. It was a spontaneous act of friendship. 'Let's get together and write some songs.'

We had been good mates in the Shadows and got on very well together, so it seemed like a natural progression. It gave me something to look forward to and fired my own creativity. I went out to his house in Hertfordshire and attempted to write. It wasn't easy. At first the songs we came up with weren't good enough, but we persevered and after a while we managed to write a few good lines. One of the songs we collaborated on together was called 'Please Mister Please', which was inspired by my break-up with Olivia. So many good songs have been created out of anguish, as if the composer has to exorcize himself by pouring out the pain he feels inside. John had written several songs of his own, which he played to me, asking for my honest opinion. Since going to work in America he had absorbed many musical influences he had heard around him, and it had improved his writing no end. Two numbers stood out from the rest for their commercial value. 'Let Me Be There' and 'If You Love Me Let Me Know' were well-crafted country pop songs with great potential. I was very excited when I heard them, and knew they would be ideal for Olivia to record.

He made a demonstration tape immediately, and I took the finished product to Peter Gormley at his home in Sunbury and played the songs to him. As soon as he heard them he agreed they were perfect for Olivia, and suggested that John Farrar and I produce them. So I was back in the studio, and back working with Livvy.

'Let Me Be There' came out shortly afterwards and flopped badly, selling no more than 8,000 copies in Britain, and that was that. Olivia went back to her boyfriend, Lee Kramer, and I went back to my writing with John. We'd been working well together now and were pushing ourselves hard on new material for Olivia to record. John was also preparing for Tom Jones's forthcoming season at the London Palladium, so he was under pressure.

On Sunday, 25 November, we had been writing as usual in John's studio and he seemed in a very contented mood as I left him and returned to Hampstead. He helped me back my car out of his drive, and we arranged to meet the following morning to continue our writing. It was going well. John had been working extremely hard over the last few months. Besides the writing, he had also been carrying out a lot of improvements to his Radlett home, which included completely rewiring the property, and changing and rearranging the studio. He had also set his wife up in a small business of her own, and often helped out with the accounts. What I didn't know was that he was thinking about emigrating to America.

John had always had difficulty in sleeping, and sometimes took tablets as a remedy. On most nights when he couldn't sleep, he would stay in his studio and work on new material, and it wasn't unusual for him to work right through.

Next morning I arrived at his house at about 10.30 as arranged, and I was met at the door by Margaret, who ushered me into the kitchen for a cup of tea and a chat before starting work.

'Where's the old man?' I asked. Margaret smiled.

'We had an argument last night,' she replied. 'He's locked himself in the studio. He's been up there working since 2 am.' There was nothing unusual in this, and we weren't unduly concerned. After a few minutes, I was eager to get working.

'I'll go up now, then,' I said, and called from downstairs, 'John, it's me. It's Bruce. I'm coming up.' There was no reply. At the top of the stairs I banged on the studio door and tried the handle but it wouldn't open.

'Come on John, it's Bruce.' I thought maybe he had fallen asleep. I banged on the door even harder, but still there was no sign of him. Now I was getting worried.

I went back downstairs to Margaret. 'I can't get an answer,' I said anxiously. 'Do you think he's all right?'

Margaret looked scared. We went outside and looked up at the studio window. The curtains were drawn, but we could see that the lights inside were on. It was very strange. I went into the garage and found some ladders, leaned them against the side of the house and up under the studio window, and climbed up. My heart was pounding. I knew something was seriously wrong. Although the curtains were closed, I could just see through a tiny chink if I cupped my hands together, and made out the familiar shape of a piano that seemed to be pushed against the door, barring entry from the outside. I could see nothing else apart from various cables strewn across the floor. I climbed down again and told Margaret what I had seen.

The family employed a young nanny to look after their baby, so I enlisted her help and we both went back upstairs to try to open the studio door. With her assistance we pushed hard against the closed door, which actually *wasn't* locked but was being held shut by the piano. After a great struggle we managed to move it aside sufficiently for me to squeeze through a tiny gap and into the room.

I found John in the middle of the floor, slumped at a strange angle, lying with his bass guitar strapped around his neck. His hands were touching the strings as if he were still playing the instrument. He was surrounded by a tangled mass of high-voltage wires and cables. His body was stiff. He was obviously dead and had apparently been electrocuted. It was an awful sight. I went numb with cold. I was shaking with shock; Margaret broke down. We called the police, and a doctor arrived to certify the time of death as 3 am. I had to stay at the house all day to answer questions. The undertaker came shortly afterwards, and John's body was zipped up in a black plastic bag and taken away. It was all very undignified and degrading.

I had never lost anyone like this – he was the guy who was helping me through my troubles and now he had gone. I was desolate.

The press got hold of the story and sensationalized it. 'Riddle of Ex-Shadow's Death', was one of the headlines. Others talked of a bizarre suicide and cited his bouts of depression as the cause, but at the time of the tragedy he had everything to live for.

It left a gaping hole in my life. I was so close to the man.

Tragically, John never lived to see his most spectacular success, or to reap the benefit financially and artistically. 'Let Me Be There' was released in America the same month, and at the end of the year went on to reach the national Top Ten and to pick up several prestigious awards from the American music industry in the process. The record also launched Olivia Newton-John's career in the States. 'If You Love Me Let Me Know' came out shortly afterwards and became an even bigger success. A year later, the song we had written together, 'Please Mister Please', went on to top the US national chart. The three records each sold in excess of a million copies. The American public just took Olivia to their hearts; over here she was still looked upon as the little girl from 'The Cliff Richard Show', with no credibility, despite having four hit singles. America gave her that recognition. In 1974 she represented Britain in the Eurovision Song Contest, singing 'Long Live Love', but was beaten into second place by a group from Sweden called Abba and their song, 'Waterloo'. A year later, Livvy decided her future lay away from Britain and set up home in Los Angeles.

After we co-produced 'Let Me Be There', I handed over the production of all Olivia's songs once again to John Farrar. He followed her to the States, and continued to write and produce for her until 1988. Together they had some spectacular success. John wrote her No.1 hit, 'Have You Ever Been Mellow', and he was responsible for her most outstanding success of all time, 'You're the One That I Want', featured in the hit movie *Grease*. I had taken Livvy to see the London stage production of *Grease*, which starred an unknown actor called Richard Gere. Four years later she was starring in the movie herself.

By the spring of 1974 I was slowly getting organized again. I hadn't stopped drinking completely, but I was taking things easier. Ever since I was a teenager, however, I had had a weight problem. It used to fluctuate and I sought many remedies to control it.

Several years before I'd read about a treatment called 'colonic irrigation', which in fact was nothing more than a sophisticated form of enema, if an enema could ever be called sophisticated. I was game to try anything to lose weight, and duly enrolled at a clinic in London's Seymour Place. The treatment required me to strip off, lie on a table and tuck my legs up under my chin, with my backside exposed in a very undignified position. A long tube was then inserted into my backside and a high-powered jet of liquid was released internally. Then nature took its course. It was absolutely awful, but despite the discomfort and the fact that it didn't seem to be doing me any good, I persevered and kept up my regular visits.

One afternoon, I was lying there awaiting my fate when a very attractive nurse came into the room to administer the treatment. Just as she was about to shove the tube up my backside, she smiled at me.

'I think you're great,' she said. 'I love your records, I've got them all. "Wonderful Land" is my favourite.'

I never went back. Whenever I listen to that song now, it conjures up a whole new image to me.

By March I felt decidedly fat, and my weight had increased considerably through my drinking, so I decided to visit a health farm to try to do something about my rapidly expanding waistline. I chose Forest Mere Health Farm in Hampshire. I had never been to one before and was pleasantly surprised. During a quiet and interesting week I was finally losing weight, when I met Lynne, the woman who was to become my second wife. I knew the moment I met her that she was special. We had an instant rapport and got on very well together. She was married at the time to racing driver Jackie Oliver, with a young son, Jason. She was at the health farm to help her get over an horrendous illness.

Lynne had recently returned from South Africa, where she had eaten a raw meat dish and ended up with tapeworm. She had had to be treated at the Hospital for Tropical Diseases. When she described what had happened to her, I cringed. The worm itself was fifteen feet long and had attached itself by its hooks to the inside of her throat, then curled round her intestines. To remove it, the doctors had to put tubes inside her and poison it out of her system. Fortunately the treatment worked, and she was at the health farm to recuperate. It was while we were sitting having afternoon tea, swopping stories, that this beautiful woman told me her horrific tale.

What Lynne did without knowing it was give me back my self-respect – and she made me realize that there were other women in the world besides Olivia Newton-John. I was very taken with her, but I really couldn't see a future in a relationship because of her domestic situation – she had a husband and a son. We started meeting on the odd occason, though, and romance just blossomed.

I think she was happily married, but her husband was away racing most of the time. He was the Can-Am racing champion, so he was always away. In the end things reached a head, and she left him in 1976. She was divorced a year later and I was cited as the co-respondent, although unnamed. We were married at the Marylebone Register office in August 1979, and went to live in a house I had bought two years earlier in Walton-on-Thames. I had stopped drinking completely by then, and even on my wedding day I stuck rigidly to tea. I haven't touched a drop of alcohol since.

Towards the end of 1974, Cliff Richard and the Shadows played together at a special benefit concert for the widow of BBC producer Colin Charman. The group re-formed specially for that one performance. In the audience that night was Bill Cotton, head of light entertainment for BBC Television, who was very taken with us. After the show he asked if we might consider representing the United Kingdom in the 1975 Eurovision Song Contest. Olivia had competed in it the year before, and Cliff had sung for Britain on two separate occasions – in 1968 with 'Congratulations', and five years later with 'Power to All My Friends'. Both times he came second in the contest, but ended up with bigger hits throughout Europe with his 'losing' songs than the acts that won. 'Congratulations' topped hit parades all over Europe. The Shadows didn't really exist at that time as a group, but with the addition of John Farrar, and Alan Tarney on bass, we gave it a go and sang the six songs from which the viewers would choose a winner to represent the country, on Lulu's TV show. We later recorded all six songs with six further instrumentals, and packaged them on an album called *Specs Appeal*.

The song the British viewers chose as our entry was called 'Let Me Be the One', written by Paul Curtis, which we were due to perform live to an audience of several millions on Eurovision in Stockholm the following April. So we decided to do a handful of concerts to get the feel of playing together to an audience. When we hit the road, the six concerts were a complete sell-out. We were billed as the Shadows for the first time in six years, and when we came out on stage on the opening night at the Fairfield Hall, Croydon, the audience stood up and applauded for five minutes. We hadn't played a note. People were so pleased to see us back together again. It was a heart-warming reception. The ovation was repeated at the other five venues. There was so much warmth and love in the audiences, it was marvellous to be back.

I thoroughly enjoyed our Eurovision appearance, although we could have taken a pasting. There were twenty acts competing against us in the show, and we might well have come twentieth in the contest, with no points to our credit, which would have been a great embarrassment. We had worked out a special routine to accompany the song, and it looked very good on television, so we were confident we stood a chance. It was a very nerve-racking experience. It was the first contest Hank and I had competed in since the one that started it all off for us at the Granada Cinema, Edmonton, all those years ago. We had come a long way since then. Fortunately, Malaysia wasn't in Europe, so there was no chance of being beaten by a Malaysian opera singer this time.

It was a live show. Everything was planned to a very strict time schedule. As each act finished its number, the next one came out on stage and prepared to sing. When it was our turn, and while we were being announced to the TV audiences off-camera, the Swedish stage-hands rushed on stage and set up our three microphones in front of us. As the curtain came up on cue, it hit my mike and knocked it to the floor. I froze. What could I do? This was *live* television, in front of millions of viewers. There was nothing for it – I calmly bent down and picked up the microphone just as I was due to go into the opening line of the song. I panicked and forgot the words completely, which was a terrific start. As it was, we had to be content with second place in the competition, which was really no disgrace. The Dutch group, Teach In – singing 'Ding-a-Dong' – came first. Our entry eventually made No.12 in the British charts and put us back among the best-sellers after an absence of eight years. It also proved to be a big success on the Continent, and started us off again on a second career, but it had never been a serious attempt at a reunion. We had formed solely to appear on Eurovision and that was all. Public demand, however, deemed otherwise. We followed our Eurovision success by appearing in Paris at the Olympia Theatre, where we made a live album. We took Tony Clarke from Abbey Road studios with us, and the RAK mobile studio, and captured the whole concert on tape. France had always been one of our most successful markets, and we were actually more popular than Cliff Richard. I was very pleased with the album; the singing and playing were very good indeed, and for once everything worked. It was released at the end of the year as *Live at the Paris Olympia*. It was intended to be our last public performance together before splitting up yet again.

Earlier in the year, when the *New Musical Express* had printed their annual chart survey for the previous twelve months, Cliff Richard had been placed at 129th, his lowest-ever showing. In fact in 1974 he had reached the charts with only two numbers, 'Take Me High' and '(You Keep Me) Hanging On'. The table was headed by the Bay City Rollers and Alvin Stardust.

I don't think Cliff was too worried. He was too involved in his religious projects for most of the year, and had other things to occupy him that were far more important than hit singles. But the situation was worrying Peter Gormley. Cliff had been going through a lean time as far as records were concerned. All the material he had been recording was bland and uninteresting. It was a barren time as far as chart success went.

I had actually found a great song in America called 'Honky Tonk Angel', which Hank, John and I produced for Cliff in September 1975 and which was later released as a single. It was a simple country-and-western song. It would have been a very big hit and would have put him back in the charts, had it not been for one of his religious friends asking him bluntly how he could sing a song about prostitutes. Shortly afterwards, a national newspaper picked up the story and posed the same question in print. Cliff had no idea that in America 'Honky Tonk Angel' was a slang term for 'hooker'. He rang up the American Embassy for confirmation, and when he found out it was true he was horrified and refused to promote the single. He was quoted in the newspapers, telling his fans not to buy it, and apologized for making the record in the first place. His religious commitments got the better of him. In the face of such a strong attitude, EMI had no other option than to withdraw the single. Yet the following year Cliff had no objection whatsoever to the release of 'Devil Woman', which was a song virtually about the same thing. There is a line in it about 'neighbourhood strays', which refers to prostitutes and not *cats*. Cliff put his own interpretaton on that number. He couldn't see anything wrong in the lyrics.

We were meeting in Peter Gormley's office one day and the conversation turned towards Cliff's recording career. Peter expressed his concern, but something he said made me think hard – that whoever came up with the right songs could have the chance to produce Cliff. After all my experience in the studio recently, producing Olivia Newton-John, I was very eager to get back to production and this seemed an ideal way. I took the bait, accepted the challenge, and set about looking for new material.

I asked publishers to send me their new songs, and contacted my songwriting friends in the business to see if they had anything that might be suitable for Cliff. Then I went to America, where I was introduced to Lionel Conway, head of Island Music in Los Angeles. He played me two songs by writers he represented, but I wasn't very happy with either of them. However, I agreed to take them back to London with me and listen to them again at some length. When I got back home I put the songs on the tape machine and had a long hard listen to them both, but I still wasn't impressed with the quality. They weren't right for Cliff. I flipped the cassette over to see if there was anything on the back, and I came across 'Miss You Nights' for the first time. It was amazing! I was stopped in my tracks. I couldn't believe it. Here was this wonderful song and the publisher had not even bothered to tell me about it. It was such a great contemporary ballad, with a magnificent lyric.

By now I had managed to get together a package of half-a-dozen songs I thought would be ideal for Cliff's voice, and I whittled them down to a final choice of three. Then I went down to Cliff's house in Weybridge and played him the selection. When he heard 'Miss You Nights' he very nearly fell on the floor; the hairs stood up on his arms. He then told me he had some other songs he had not done anything with. One of them was 'Devil Woman' by Terry Britten, which he had been sitting on for over eighteen months.

'Miss You Nights' was the first single we recorded, in September 1975, and it came out the following month. But we had terrible problems getting it played on radio, even though it was such a beautiful record and the superb vocal arrangements by

Tony Rivers were really stunning. We were told it was far too slow. It finally took off and reached No.12, and Cliff was back in the charts.

My relationship with Lynne was getting stronger all the time, and I dedicated 'Miss You Nights' to her and had it engraved into the vinyl of every record pressed.

Producing is a creative thing, and having the chance to work with Cliff as his producer was an exciting challenge. Peter Gormley was thrilled by the outcome and the success of that record, and decided to take the whole thing further and make an album, which became *I'm Nearly Famous* and revitalized Cliff's recording career. It was a water-shed in his life.

Cliff's recording career had become too safe. He had been drifting for a while, becoming a middle-of-the-road artiste. He was in a rut, he needed to break out and try new things. I needed to help him regain his credibility, but he had to work hard at it himself. I pointed out to him that he came into the business as a record star, but had sadly ignored that part of his career for far too long, in favour of involving himself in television appearances and his religious activities. The fire and the passion for making records had deserted him. I'm sure he was even bored by it all. The man who made 'Move It' had to recapture, and return to, his rock 'n' roll roots. He had become almost blasé in the studio, and was so adept at recording that he could arrive for a three-hour session at 7 pm and leave by 8.30. He would have put down his three vocal tracks in that time and gone home. He wasn't really interested in anything else. I told him that if he wanted to be successful in the mid-1970s, he would have a lot of hard work in front of him. I didn't want him in the studio for only three hours to do just the voice-overs. I needed him involved in everything we were doing, from beginning to end. I wanted him there when we laid down the backing tracks. Cliff had to become a part of every single process. He agreed to give it a go, and got very interested in the project. I think it excited him. As soon as we got into the album he was totally involved, and was in the studio all the time. He also realized that recording techniques had changed tremendously over the years, and he was eager to learn all about them. It was one of the most satisfying things I have ever done.

I abandoned the idea of using all-girl backing vocals as well. The idea was far too old-fashioned. Instead I put together an all-male vocal group which was led by Tony Rivers and featured John Perry and Stuart Culver. Tony Rivers did all the vocal arrangements. They were superb. The material we were recording was fresh and totally different from anything Cliff had been used to. He handled it very well, and midway through the sessions he realized that his interpretation of the songs was changing. They were far more ambitious and uninhibited. On 'I Can't Ask for Anything More Than You' he sang half the number in falsetto, something he had never attempted before. But it worked.

Prior to recording the album, I had discovered a young songwriting team, Michael Allison and Peter Sills, who signed to my publishing company, Bruce Welch Music. I rated them very highly. They contributed four tracks to the album, including the title song which was such a great rocking number. When the album was released in May 1976 we had special merchandise made, with T-shirts proclaiming 'I'm Nearly Famous' across the front. They were very collectable. Elizabeth Taylor and Elton John wore them.

The album went on to reach No.5 in the chart. A month before, 'Devil Woman' was released as a single, and peaked at No.9. Suddenly, after two years of mediocrity, people started to sit up and take notice of Cliff Richard again. The music papers hailed it as 'the renaissance of Cliff Richard'.

On the strength of the success of *I'm Nearly Famous*, I went back on tour with Cliff, playing rhythm guitar. Apart from myself, his backing group was made up entirely of the musicians featured on the album, including Terry Britten on guitar, Alan Tarney on bass and Tony Rivers and the guys on vocals.

We were on stage in Japan one evening in August when I noticed one of our tour managers in the wings waving his hands frantically, trying to attract our attention. I went across to see what was happening.

'"Devil Woman" has just got into the American hit parade,' he shouted over the noise of the music. I went over to Cliff, and in a suitable break told him the news. He was absolutely exhilarated, as we all were. We had worked so hard and so much as a team on that album. The song was put out on Elton John's Rocket label in the States, and when Cliff flew out for a short promotional tour, it soared to No.5 in the chart and sold more than a million copies.

The worldwide reaction to *I'm Nearly Famous* was phenomenal. It was, quite simply, the best thing Cliff Richard had done, and he was back, stronger than ever. Besides re-establishing his credibility as a recording artiste, it gave my career as a producer a tremendous lift. We were all excited about the success; we had a hit album for the first time in many years, and Cliff and Peter Gormley asked me to carry on the good work. I went out on another expedition looking for songs.

I produced Cliff's next two albums, *Every Face Tells a Story* (which included one of my songs, 'Hey Mr Dream Maker') and *Green Light*.

After the third album was released, I had a meeting with Peter and Cliff at my home to discuss what we should do next. I can remember that when the discussion turned towards albums for the American market, I told Peter and Cliff that we were dealing with a totally different situation. I added that American albums tended to have a feel of their own, an atmosphere created within a general framework, which was often achieved by having only one, or maybe two, writers instead of various ones. There could be no continuity if each track had been penned by a different composer. I had told them that instead of gleaning songs from as wide a range of sources as possible, we should concentrate on one or two people writing specifically for the album to sustain continuity.

I thought no more about it, and over the next few months I went about my job of collecting new songs as usual, assuming that I was producing Cliff's next album. I had no reason to doubt that I would be. I was at the Abbey Road studios one day, working with Tony Clarke, one of the engineers. We had been great mates for a long time and had worked together on many records for Olivia Newton-John and the Shadows. After I had finished what I was doing I was leaving for home.

'I'll see you in Paris next week then, Bruce,' Tony said.

'Paris?' I asked. 'Why, what's happening?'

Then, to my amazement, Tony explained that Cliff was recording a new album in the French capital – and when he realized I knew nothing about it, he went red with embarrassment. *It was a great way to find out I had been fired.* Here was I, carefully selecting new material for Cliff's next album, and no one had the decency to tell me to stop. No producer expects to work with an artiste for ever, and I certainly did not expect to be Cliff's producer for life. It is quite normal for artistes to want to change producers after two or three albums, to give them fresh ideas and a new approach. I wasn't upset that I had lost the job – that was an occupational hazard; it was the way I found out that hurt, considering that Peter Gormley was my manager as well as Cliff's. So whose interest was he representing?

To this day, neither Cliff Richard nor Peter Gormley has ever offered me an explanation as to why they didn't tell me I was no longer needed. What annoyed me even more was that they had taken the ideas I had discussed with them only a few weeks before for keeping continuity on the album, and they had employed my mate Terry Britten to write the bulk of the featured material. Terry and Cliff were also going to produce the album themselves.

I rang Peter, who tried to take the heat out of the argument by saying that I couldn't expect to be Cliff Richard's producer for ever.

'But I can expect to be told,' I said. I went on to accuse him of wearing two hats as a manager. I couldn't see how he could represent my best interests as a producer when he was also looking after the artiste in question. I felt cheated. I had produced three successful albums and a number of singles. I had given Cliff Richard back his credibility and revived his recording career. People respected him again . . . and they didn't have the guts to tell me to my face that I was no longer needed. The whole episode soured my relationship with both Peter and Cliff. This is a wonderful example of Christianity, I thought, going behind my back without telling me. And we were supposed to be friends.

Shortly afterwards, in 1980, Peter called the Shadows together for a meeting at Hank's house at Radlett and broke the news that he had decided to step down as the group's manager. He added that he intended to run down all his business over the next few months and retire, and suggested his assistant, Brian Goode, take over. Brian has been our guiding light ever since.

However, Peter finally gave up managing Cliff's career in 1988 *– eight years later*.

11

'THERE'S NOTHING QUITE LIKE IT IN THE WORLD'

After our success in the Eurovision Song Contest in 1975, we were very anxious to keep the group together. However, when John Farrar decided to quit Britain and set up home in Los Angeles and renew his working partnership with Olivia Newton-John, our plans had to be shelved, for the time being at least.

We had become great friends with John over the past five years. We worked together so well, and we dearly wanted him to become an integral part of the group. When it didn't happen, we drifted into other things. Brian Bennett was probably the busiest. He was emerging as a prolific composer. He turned his hand to writing virtually anything – penning songs, musical scores, TV themes and library music. He was particularly good at writing for television, and several pieces of his incidental background music had been used in such series as *Dallas* and *Knots Landing*. He was also responsible for writing a number called 'Chaseside Shoot Up', the theme music for BBC TV's golf programmes. In 1981 his composition 'Sound of Success' was chosen by ITV as the music to accompany their live coverage of the wedding of HRH Prince Charles and Lady Diana Spencer.

Brian involved himself in virtually all aspects of the music industry, and had recently made a name for himself as a producer for his work with Dennis Waterman. He was still very much in demand for session work, too, and for live performances, and it was in this capacity that he became Cliff Richard's musical director for a tour of Russia. Brian, who had written and recorded several solo albums in the past, had followed the late John Rostill and moved out to live in Hertfordshire. He too had installed an eight-track recording studio in his house, in which he became totally engrossed, and he was soon known to his friends as the 'Radlett Recluse'. At that time he was working so hard that there was very little room on his schedule to fit in the Shadows.

Hank Marvin, meanwhile, had been baptized into the Jehovah's Witness faith and was very much involved in his religion. He had also started work on a solo album project, with guitarists Kevin Peek and Vic Flick. I was getting my act together as Cliff Richard's producer, as well as working as a music publisher, having formed my own company, Bruce Welch Music, in 1974. Quite simply, none of us had time for the Shadows.

During 1976 EMI Records enjoyed considerable album chart success with a series of compilation albums, which they put out under the title of *Twenty Golden Greats*. Indeed, the Beach Boys had topped the album chart with their own *Twenty Golden Greats* in July, followed by Glen Campbell in November. EMI had carried out extensive market research and had come to the conclusion that an album in the series by the Shadows would be very well received. We were surprised by their decision, but they convinced us it would be a chart-topping album when they approached us with the proposal – which included a large amount of money being spent on promoting the project, including television advertising. It was the first time in our career that the company had ever advertised one of our records on television.

As the Shadows' *Twenty Golden Greats* was a compilation album taken from our old master tapes, there was no need to re-record anything. After the tracks had been chosen, I attempted to clean them up and modernize the sound by putting on 'mock' stereo. I tried to stretch the stereo image wider. They had originally been recorded in mono.

The album came out at the beginning of 1977, and with extensive plugging and promotion, it climbed to No.1 in the charts, where it remained for eight weeks. EMI had been proved right. In fact the album charted just forty-eight hours after its release, and went on to sell 1.25 million copies – our biggest-selling record of all time. With the release of the LP, we made Brian an equal partner in the group. The phenomenal success of the album made us consider the possibility of re-forming once again. The following May a series of engagements was arranged under the obvious title of 'Twenty Golden Dates', and we hit the road again. Everywhere we appeared was sold out.

For that tour the Shadows line-up included two new recruits. Bass player Alan Jones was a well-respected session musician with whom we had worked before – and coincidentally was another of the guys who was inspired by the Shadows to start playing guitar and making music. At school he was in a group that won a Cliff Richard and the Shadows look-alike contest, and he later worked with George Harrison, Olivia Newton-John and Gilbert O'Sullivan. Much later he replaced John Rostill in Tom Jones's backing group, the Squires.

We also felt we needed to enrich our sound on stage and make it nearer to the original records, by the use of keyboards and synthesizers, which could simulate a whole orchestra. Francis Monkman, who quite simply was a musical genius, agreed to sit in with us. He later went on to form Sky with John Williams and Kevin Peek.

Francis was such a brilliant keyboard player that he had no difficulty mastering any of the numbers we were planning to feature on tour, and could have played them standing on his head. After our opening night he was bored out of his skull with the music, and phoned Hank the following day to ask if he could be released from his contract and leave the tour. Could we find someone else? Hank refused – he had a contract, and after all it was only for twenty days. Francis persevered. One night, just as Hank and I were about to go into one of our numbers, I turned round and glanced towards the back of the stage, and there was Francis Monkman, sitting at his keyboards, fast asleep.

That tour was fantastic. It reaffirmed our popularity and convinced us all we should keep going. The following year we were reunited with Cliff Richard to celebrate our twentieth anniversary in show business, with a special series of concerts at the London Palladium in February and March which resulted in another live album, aptly titled *Thank You Very Much*. It went on to reach No.5 in the chart. We toured Britain again in the autumn, and for the first time, Cliff Hall – another session musician who had worked with Cliff Richard for a number of years – joined us on keyboards. Before long he became a permanent member of the line-up, and both he and Alan Jones started to record with us. It was during that tour that we featured an instrumental version of the Andrew Lloyd Webber/Tim Rice number, 'Don't Cry for Me, Argentina', in the act, and each night it played to a quite outstanding reaction from our audiences. The song, taken from the hit musical *Evita*, had been a big hit for Julie Covington two years before, so it was well known. We actually had no intention of recording it ourselves – it was purely for our stage show – until public opinion changed our minds. Then after we recorded it, Brian Bennett took the master tape along to the EMI studios, where he mixed in some spontaneous applause taken from our *Thank You Very Much* album. It was just what was needed and recaptured, essentially, what we did on stage. It was released as a single just before Christmas, and entered the charts at No.43 in the first week of January. By the middle of February it had reached No.5, and gave us our first hit single since our Eurovision song, 'Let Me Be the One', back in 1975. 'Cavatina' – the theme from the movie *The Deer Hunter* – which was another beautiful piece of music and a show-stopper on the road, followed it into the charts in April, and peaked at No.9. Both numbers were featured on our 1979 album, *String of Hits*, which came out in September and topped the charts at the beginning of the following year. It stayed among the best sellers for forty-one weeks and gave us the distinction of having two consecutive chart-topping albums. It was the first time we had been in such a privileged position since 1962, when *Out of the Shadows* had followed our début album, *The Shadows*, to the coveted No.1 spot. Our career was turning full circle and we were back in the old routine. We had a third hit single from the *String of Hits* album shortly afterwards – a version of the old Ramrods hit, 'Riders in the Sky', which reached No.12.

My own standing in the record industry had shot up following my involvement with Cliff Richard on *I'm Nearly Famous* and his two subsequent albums, and I suddenly became very much in demand as a producer. I was approached by a diverse collection of artistes all wanting me to produce records for them. I turned most of them down. I had some strange requests from a few managers, and artistes who had disappeared years ago came out of the woodwork to see me because they thought I could revive their careers. I was looked upon as a resurrection specialist. One artiste I did work with, however, was a young British girl singer called Charlie Dore. Because of my commitments to the Shadows, I also involved Alan Tarney – who had played bass with us in the Eurovision Song Contest, and was featured as one of the musicians on the production of *I'm Nearly Famous*. Together we produced an album from which we had a Top Twenty hit in America, in the spring of 1980, with 'Pilot of the Airwaves', which was incredible for an unknown artiste, and my stock as a producer went even higher.

It was while we were recording material for this album that Alan Tarney came into the studio one morning with a new song he had written, which he wanted me to hear. He was a very talented writer and Cliff had recorded several of his numbers. I listened to his song in a break during the session . . . and couldn't believe what I was hearing. It was called 'We Don't Talk Anymore', and I knew instantly that it would be a smash hit. Despite everything, there was only one person who could record it – Cliff Richard. I phoned Peter Gormley and told him I had a marvellous song in my possession which would be ideal for Cliff, and I added that I wanted to produce it myself. Peter loved the song, and when I played it to Cliff his reaction was immediate: he was very excited, and we all realized its potential. It sounded like a hit record, and a big one.

We recorded it in June and it was released the following month; incredibly, it was Cliff Richard's seventy-fifth single. It took a lot of people by surprise when they heard it. Was this really Cliff Richard singing in falsetto? It's impact was tremendous. On 25 September it climbed into the No.1 position, where it remained for a further four weeks. It was Cliff's first chart-topper since 'Congratulations', eleven years before.

'We Don't Talk Anymore' became Cliff Richard's biggest-selling single of all time, with sales around the world in excess of 5 million. In America it became only his fourth hit, and reached No.7 in the national chart.

By now Cliff and Terry Britten had completed their new album, which was provisionally called *Rock 'n' Roll Juvenile*. It was ready for release, but heated discussions developed between the singer and his record company. EMI insisted that he include 'We Don't Talk Anymore' on the new album because it would guarantee bigger record sales. Cliff was having none of it. This was his album and he wanted to release it as it was. But the record company was loath to put the album out without the hit number on it, and in the end Cliff climbed down. It came on to the market in the autumn and reached No.3 in the charts. It was a good album, featuring some impressive songs, including 'Carrie', which, when released as a single, reached No.4. To be honest, 'We Don't Talk Anymore' stole the show and sold it. Not surprisingly, Alan Tarney was later asked to take over as Cliff's producer. Both Terry Britten and Alan Tarney went on to establish themselves as two of the most successful writer-producers of the eighties, and I have nothing but respect for them both. Besides working with Cliff Richard, Alan produced a number of groups including the Norwegian band A-ha. Terry's work with Tina Turner earned him a Grammy award for his song 'What's Love Got to Do with It' in 1984.

The role of the record producer has changed quite considerably over the years, and the influence and power they command today is enormous. Yet it was only as recently as the 1960s that producers were first given any kind of credit for their involvement with hit records. George Martin, who along with Phil Spector and, to a lesser extent, Norrie Paramor, was possibly the most influential and successful producer of the sixties, was never credited on any of the Beatles singles until 'All You Need Is Love'. Being a staff-man at EMI he was on a fixed salary, and although he was making multi-million-selling singles and albums, he never received a penny in royalties from their sales until he left in 1965 and set up his own independent company, AIR (Associated Independent Recording), taking the cream of EMI's recording talent with him, including John Burgess, Ron Richards and Peter Sullivan. Later Norrie followed George's lead and set up on his own with his assistant, Tim Rice.

In the early days of recording, A & R producers were all-powerful, choosing the material for their artistes to record, undertaking the arrangements, and organizing the instrumentation. They also had the final say in which records were released. Most were musicians who could read music and could score arrangements, yet because they were employees, they were called upon to diversify their particular talents across a wide range of artistes and musical styles, and could often find themselves working with a rock 'n' roll band in the morning, a brass band in the afternoon, and a comedian in the evening, each one requiring a different specialist talent. It all started to change in the mid-sixties with the emergence of the independent producers, who demanded not only recognition of their own, but – like the artistes they were producing – a percentage of the record sales in royalties. Mickie Most, Shel Talmy, Larry Page and Kit Lambert would all have taken royalties from the records they produced. The change occurred because gradually the employee role of producers by the big companies was being broken. The 1970s producers had become artistes in their own right, to rank alongside the groups and musicians they were working with. The big companies still employed their own staff-men, but they were very rarely credited. The popularity and standing of the independent producers allowed them the freedom to choose their work, and in the main the artistes approached them. It also meant that artistes themselves could pick and choose the producers they felt might enhance their sound and talents. The balance of power in the studio was changing.

The start of the seventies also saw more and more artistes producing themselves, and it became just an extension of being a musician. They possessed the technical know-how, knew their way round a studio and were not over-awed by it all. It was still necessary to employ engineers, however, and it was from this source that the next wave of new producers emerged, including Glyn Jones (who has recorded among others Joan Armatrading, Eric Clapton, and the Eagles), Gus Dudgeon (Elton John), and Steve Lillywhite (Peter Gabriel, Siouxsie and the Banshees, and XTC). Some artistes, however, took production to its logical conclusion by building their own studios, capable of producing finished master tapes, like 10CC, Mike Oldfield and Abba.

The eighties saw the establishment of the 'superstar' producers who emerged as personalities in their own right but could still deliver the goods in the studio, like Trevor Horn. He first rose to prominence with the studio-created group, the Buggles, who had a No.1 hit in 1979 with 'Video Killed the Radio Star'. Trevor later turned his attention to Dollar, before creating Frankie Goes to Hollywood. The production of their first three singles 'Relax',

'Two Tribes' and 'The Power of Love', and the album *Welcome to the Pleasure Dome*, is outstanding. Colin Thurston brought Duran Duran to the attention of the public, while Daniel Miller did the same for Depeche Mode, and there were also the multi-talented Mike Batt and Dave Stewart. Most recently, Stock, Aitken and Waterman have managed to produce records that explode with energy and excitement. They seem to have a magic touch, and have used their enormous expertise to create remarkable new stars out of unknown artistes. Rick Astley came out of a northern working men's club and has become an international star in less than two years. A comparison can be drawn between their approach to the recording business and that of Holland, Dozier and Holland, creators of the Tamla Motown sound, who wrote the songs and produced the records.

I admire tremendously what Stock, Aitken and Waterman have done, but I don't necessarily admire every single record they have made. Like Mickie Most in the seventies, they have produced a series of well-made, well-produced records that appeal across the board and have developed their own stable of stars, their own label and their own publishing company. Their success has been phenomenal.

It's a sign of the times. The 1950s saw the emergence of Elvis Presley as a world-beater, and yet, after he left Sam Phillips at Sun Records, no one ever knew the name of his record producer, and no one cared. Apart from Norman Petty with Buddy Holly, Chet Atkins with the Everly Brothers, and Milt Gabler with Bill Haley, we weren't interested in record producers, only in the artistes themselves. Producers weren't really considered that important.

These days the producer holds the reins, and the essential quality of a good one, apart from being able to pick material of great potential, is an ability – whether conspicuous or discreet – to bring out the very best of any artiste, no matter who. A good production, despite the technology, will stand the test of time.

In 1980 our contract with EMI records came up for renewal, and we looked long and hard at the contents of the agreement. EMI had been very good to us in the past, but we felt we needed a change. Since 1959 we had always been signed directly to the company, which meant that they paid for all our recording sessions, but the records we had made over the years were owned by EMI themselves and they had the power to release and re-package them whenever they wanted to. Obviously they wanted to negotiate the contract on basically the same terms, because we were having success. But we wouldn't agree. After all these years, Hank, Brian and I had decided that we wanted to sign a lease-tape deal with them instead, which would give us our independence. We wanted to make and finance the records ourselves, and then lease them to EMI to be released in the same way as before. It meant that we retained the rights to our own material at all times, and after a period of five years it reverted back to us. Then, if over that period of time we had enjoyed a great deal of success and the record company wanted to release a series of compilation sets, or a *Greatest Hits* album, they would have to pay us a royalty for the privilege. We felt that by this point in our career we should own our own tapes. It was our pension. We negotiated with EMI on that basis. It was a simple idea, and one that was becoming commonplace in the music industry. However, it also made sense to sign with EMI because they controlled all our back catalogue.

We negotiated for five months but couldn't come to terms. EMI were only looking for direct-signed artistes and said it was not their policy at that time to enter into lease-tape agreements. The fact that they already had a similar deal with Queen was ignored. There was another problem. EMI wanted to sign us to a world-wide agreement, which again was not acceptable from our point of view.

We formed our own company, Roll Over Records, and eventually arrived at a very favourable agreement with Polydor, who paid us an advance royalty of several hundred thousand pounds for a three-year, three-album deal. After twenty-two years of devoted and loyal service to EMI, they in effect slammed the door in our faces. They must have made a vast amount of money from sales of 'Apache' over the years, considering how many times it has been featured on compilation albums. It took twenty minutes to make and cost the company a negligible amount of money.

The following September our first album for the new label was released to coincide with our extensive European concert tour. It was called, appropriately, *Change of Address*. It reached the Top Twenty and went gold. Ironically, EMI issued an album of their own, called *Another String of Hits*, which also made the album chart at the same time, and on one occasion we were sharing consecutive places in the Top Twenty. Two years earlier, following the success of our 'Twenty Golden Dates' tour, we had realized that we had something that was far too big and too precious to waste, and we had made a conscious decision to make one album a year and to tour Britain, and possibly overseas, at least every eighteen months, to perpetuate the name of the Shadows.

We have been true to that decision ever since.

1983 marked another reunion with Cliff Richard, this time to celebrate our silver anniversary in the business: twenty-five years and still going strong. We celebrated with a series of concert appearances in London and Birmingham, where we were seen by 100,000 people in just nine days, and the demand for tickets for the shows was unbelievable. A spokesman for the Wembley Arena, where we appeared, said that they had never had such a massive response for tickets in such a short space of time, not even for a Cup Final. Our *Shadows Silver Album*, which again was TV-advertised, went on to sell 300,000 copies through mail order alone. And we were also honoured by our peers with the Ivor Novello Award, the official Oscar of the British music industry, presented by the British Academy of Songwriters, Composers and Artistes, to mark our contribution to the music industry for over a quarter of a century. We were deeply touched.

The following year our world tour took in engagements across Europe, Singapore, Bangkok and Hong Kong, and for the first time in over sixteen years we went back to tour Australia and New Zealand. One newspaper wrote: 'And twenty-five years on the boards has taught them what Elton John knows . . . that is, the paying customers like to be entertained. The Shadows looked like five old mates who had just found 2,500 new friends in the audience.'

The Shadows have always been at their best when they are on stage. It is our great strength and what we came into the business for in the first place. We are now able to do concerts as something we all enjoy. It's all very well recording and writing, but as musicians one of the first motivations we had was playing together in front of an audience, where there was an immediate feedback. Recording is great fun, but if you are in the studio all the time, you cannot get that empathy that exists between the artiste and his audience. It becomes too clinical and you can lose touch with reality. With an audience there is an atmosphere and an immediate response. Even with a number like 'Apache', which we must have played a thousand times before, we can still add something extra to its performance because we know the audience want to hear and enjoy it. The adrenalin starts to flow and we know that *they* haven't heard it a thousand times.

Perhaps it was that tour of 1984 that inspired Hank Marvin to leave Britain and go and live in Australia, although he never discussed it in any detail with Brian and me, and the reason he left in 1986 is still a bit of a mystery to us both. He just announced one day that he was going, and emigrated shortly afterwards. Today he lives in Perth with his wife, Carole, his children, and his mother and father, and he has built a new life for himself in idyllic surroundings. A few days before he left, I looked out my old badge from Rutherford Grammar School and had it framed especially for him to take with him as a little reminder.

Hank's departure certainly put the brake on the career of the Shadows, although we have attempted to tour once a year since then. But we have to plan far in advance these days to accommodate him, as Hank doesn't like to tour for more than eight weeks at a time, which makes me discontented because it seriously inhibits the group in terms of career development.

If Hank was still living in Britain, I'm sure we would have developed more than we have. We would have been far more adventurous in the type of music we play, and would have experimented and broken new ground, but as it is we play safe and go for the middle way.

However, Hank has found contentment in Australia with his family and his religion, to which he has devoted himself completely, and I think it's marvellous for him. He is known as one of the legendary rock 'n' roll guitar heroes, and quite rightly so – loved by the public and respected by fellow musicians. Yet to me, he is the greatest waste of natural talent I have ever come across, and he knows I mean that in the nicest possible way, because we have often discussed it.

Hank has a God-given talent. I don't mean he plays 500 notes a minute, or blinds you with fast runs, but his style and playing technique are so unique, and he has developed them to such an extent, that they are instantly recognizable. But he won't exploit his talent any further; he won't develop it any more than he already has. He's contented with his lot and feels his music should come second. People love him in the same way they loved Eric Morecambe and Tommy Cooper, who, like Hank, were naturally gifted men and endeared themselves to the public – it's called star quality. Cliff has it. He looks and acts the part, and there has never been anyone like him at all. But Hank just shrugs his shoulders and smiles.

I think his attitude to the business has affected both Brian and myself. I feel we should do more, and I would certainly like to perform more – I am at my happiest when I am on stage. I envy people like Eric Clapton, Mark Knopfler and Phil Collins, who occasionally come together to tour. They find the time to go out on the road and make good music with each other. They are great buddies and do it for the fun of it all, but it's easy for them, they are such fantastic musicians. I would have liked to do something similar, but I realized I wasn't talented enough. Sure, I'm good with the Shadows, but I never became a consummate musician, like Hank and Brian. Other things got in the way.

I have never had a desire for a solo career, either. I have always resisted recording albums on my own. Hank and Brian have recorded several but I have always felt that my ability isn't good enough, and I have never had anything I wanted to say enough to put on record.

My strength is being part of a unit – on stage, entertaining – and when the Shadows unite, there is nothing quite like it in the world. Even if we've not performed together for over a year, once we pick up our guitars it all comes flooding back and falls into place, like yesterday . . . and I miss that.

12

'THE BEST YEARS OF MY LIFE'

In the spring of 1958, when Hank and I took our first tentative steps in the music business as wide-eyed naïve youngsters, all we knew was that we had a burning desire to be part of it. Maybe it would last for two or three years, maybe not. We were consumed by this new music. Here we are, thirty years later, still playing and enjoying it even more.

At that time anyone over the age of twenty-five was an old man; people of thirty seemed ancient to me. I couldn't imagine anyone playing rock 'n' roll at the ripe old age of forty, or beyond – that was outrageous. It was a young man's music, the product of a youth culture. It was the private property of the young, and the older generation had no right to interfere.

Times change.

Chuck Berry, one of the founding fathers of rock 'n' roll, celebrated his sixtieth birthday in 1986. Two years later Fats Domino reached the same milestone – and in 1987 Carl Perkins turned fifty-five. (If they had lived, Elvis would have been fifty-four, Buddy fifty-three.) Today they are still going strong, playing the music they pioneered, and sharing the stage with so many of the young musicians they inspired.

From such small and humble beginnings in the 1950s music has developed into a multi-billion-pound concern, affected by changes in technology, the media, fashion, politics and economics . . . and the ideas and inspirations of the musicians themselves who keep it going. It has found its rightful place in society. Yet despite everything it is still as exciting for me now as it was when I first started. The rewards are far greater, however. The record deals are certainly more lucrative for the artistes, the percentages are relatively high, and advances for the established stars can be phenomenal. In 1984 I heard that EMI had paid David Bowie an estimated advance royalty of $12 million for an album deal, the first of which, *Let's Dance*, sold over 5 million copies around the world. The record company recouped their money on the first album and still had more to exploit. It makes a mockery of our first contract. Big business has taken over.

After the initial explosion of the 1950s which inspired us all to become musicians, the music industry, such as it was, reluctantly accepted the role rock 'n' roll was playing in society, but tried to clean it up and keep it wholesome. It was no longer the music of a frustrated generation, just another arm of show business.

It was the sixties that saw the most changes to music and to society in general, and after the arrival of the Beatles in 1963 nothing was ever quite the same again. The media grew and took control, motivated initially not by the music itself but by the mass hysteria it was creating. For perhaps the first time in history men from all classes became liberated and were the peacocks in society, as fashion was now aimed very firmly in their direction: some of the fashions, like the music, were outrageous. Everything became freer and more open. Morals went to the wall. The old values changed – people started to ask questions and demand answers. Mass communication opened up the world, and we were all caught up on an amazing tidal wave. Music helped break down the barriers of class and colour and age.

The sixties spawned many diverse musical cultures, which all took root in a changing world – and went on to develop even further.

The folk rock boom, inspired initially by Bob Dylan in the USA, established groups like the Incredible String Band, Pentangle, Fairport Convention and, later, Traffic, who entered into the realms of drug-induced psychedelia. It was followed by the progressive groups and bands, of which Pink Floyd, with their own roots in folk rock, led from the front. They started their career in the studio by recording conventional three-minute pop songs with 'See Emily Play' and 'Arnold Lane' in 1967, and developed into a much more free-form style of musical exploration. Unlike the Stones or the Beatles before them, Pink Floyd never stamped their identity on the general public, to whom they were faceless, nameless musicians. Certainly not four mop-tops. But it was the music that counted anyway. Through their music they went on to sell millions of records all over the world, and pioneered a new art-form with great albums like *Dark Side of the Moon* (which I am told was fantastic to listen to smoking a 'jazz woodbine'), *Wish You Were Here* and *Animals*. A combination of harsh electronic technology and blistering musicianship, their music left the day of the three-chord trick a long way behind. But it was more than their music – Pink Floyd pioneered striking visual effects and spectacle in live performances to enhance what they were playing even more.

In total contrast, Tamla Motown emerged, with a gentle shove in the right direction from the Beatles, to give the world classic songs which developed out of the black rock 'n' roll groups of the fifties. The music, which was great to listen to, and even better to dance to, was perpetrated by brilliant studio session musicians and inventive producers and artistes like the Four Tops, the Temptations, Marvin Gaye, Diana Ross, Smokey Robinson and Stevie Wonder. The songs were sophisticated, with mature lyrics; the ballads had great depth and sensitivity. With Motown's help, soul music, another derivative form of rhythm 'n' blues, traded the sophistication of Tamla for raw energy and sexual excitement and saw artistes emerge such as Aretha Franklin, Otis Redding, Wilson Pickett, Arthur Conley and James Brown. It led in the seventies to the studio-created 'Philadelphia Sound' of the Three Degrees, to funk and jazz funk.

Soul music gained the acceptance of mass audiences particularly in Britain, and opened the gates for other more ethnic black music to gain a wider foothold, such as ska and the reggae of Peter Tosh, Jimmy Cliff and Bob Marley, who used it for their own political ends. The Police later took aspects of the reggae rhythm for the development of their own unique style, and, like rock 'n' roll before it, they cleaned up the harsher elements and turned it into a highly popular form of music. Their strength was in their musicianship and the songs they wrote and recorded, like 'Message in a Bottle', 'Every Little Thing She Does is Magic', 'Don't Stand So Close' and 'Every Breath You Take'. When I first heard that number, I couldn't believe that it was so ordinary.

I was disappointed, and yet it grew on me and I could see just how powerful it was.

From out of the British blues boom emerged the guitar heroes; for the first time, guitarists enjoyed as much status and cult following as singers, and in many cases more. They were good, too, yet a million miles removed from Hank Marvin, not in their ability but in their style. Eric Clapton led the charge, but he was in good company and there were some quite brilliant technicians: Alvin Lee, Richie Blackmore, Peter Green, Jimmy Page and Jeff Beck were in the initial wave. Ironically, it was the likes of Eric Clapton and the white British rhythm 'n' blues stars who inspired the great blues revival, not in Britain, but in America in the late sixties. They picked up on the black music of America, honed it with commerciality in Britain, and took it back across the Atlantic where they introduced it to the mass white audiences, who swallowed it up, never realizing for one moment where its true origins were. Yet the blues-inspired British groups who toured extensively across America, with their stage acts dominated by the raw, unharnessed excitement and attack of rhythm 'n' blues, were always gracious and ready to acknowledge just where the music they were playing, and the inspiration to play it, had come from. They were quick, too, to point the finger in the direction of the indigenous black American bluesmen like Muddy Waters, Jimmy Reed, John Lee Hooker, and the most consistent name of them all, B. B. King, and to give them all long and overdue recognition for their outstanding achievements, from an audience that had previously been quite willing to ignore them. In turn American audiences began to take stock and set about searching out the true origins of the blues for themselves. They discovered a rare and precious culture of their own, and a generation of original and authentic black musicians who had been playing the blues all their lives.

Jimi Hendrix had to come to Britain to establish himself. He emerged from the blues boom and went on to do something no other black musician had ever done before him. He became the first black teen idol, opening the way for later singers like Terence Trent D'Arby, Prince and Michael Jackson. I wasn't a great fan of Hendrix, but nevertheless I could appreciate great talent when I saw it. He was a magnificent showman, and although I wouldn't rate him as highly as Eric Clapton as a guitarist, he was certainly imaginative in his playing. He was technically brilliant, and laid the foundations for the heavy metal explosion that followed in his wake in the seventies and the eighties. For such a distinct personality on stage, he was a quiet and polite man and very humble away from performing, nothing like his image.

The Beach Boys had been around for a year or two before the Beatles made it, singing about the all-American dream of surfing and California girls. They were good, catchy songs and captured that wonderful essence of sand, sun, sea and surf, and having a good time, which epitomized the American West Coast. Being a family – Brian, Dennis and Carl Wilson were brothers and Mike Love was their cousin – they had that marvellous vocal blend and superb harmonies. Brian Wilson was their guiding light, and an inventive musician. Even at the height of Beatlemania, 'Good Vibrations', the song he created, was far ahead of its time. It stood out from all the rest, and stopped me in my tracks when I first heard it. It almost made me want to give up the business completely, because it was so clever and so original. The Beach Boys were one of the first groups to use their vocal prowess on record to dominate the instruments, following on from the Four Seasons in the development and popularization of falsetto harmony. The group's major contribution to the sixties came in the form of a spectacular album called *Pet Sounds*. It was their definitive offering, and took music on to another plane, although Brian never received the true credit the album deserved. But it contained one of the classic songs of the sixties, 'God Only Knows'. Unfortunately Brian got fired by his own inventiveness, and he took his music to extremes, stifling commerciality into self-indulgence. It all became a bit too clever and contrived. The follow-up album, *Smile*, was a disaster.

With the arrival of the Beatles, the major record companies were eager to find another teen sensation like the four Liverpool lads to exploit in a young market, and this led to the formation of the Monkees in the USA. It was after seeing the Beatles' movie, *A Hard Day's Night*, that Don Kirshner was inspired to adapt director Richard Lester's zany approach to filming and devise an American TV series on the same lines around the antics of a crazy pop group. The four members of the group were chosen not for any musical ability they might possess (though Peter Tork and Mike Nesmith had already established their names in the folk field) but as teen idols in the mould of Fabian, Frankie Avalon and Brian Hyland. For once, the music came second to clean-cut image and forceful personality, and has continued to do so ever since.

The Osmonds provided all the American razzmatazz and professionalism we had come to expect from Hollywood and Las Vegas. They were quite brilliant on stage, with well-choreographed routines and show-business sparkle. Squeaky-clean and sterile. The kids loved them, because unlike the rock 'n' roller of a generation before, whose music was based on wild aggression, the Osmonds posed no threat. David Cassidy enjoyed his moment of stardom and built a career on a pleasing personality and a pleasant voice, as did Andy Gibb. Britain's answer came in the form of groups like Herman's Hermits and the Bay City Rollers, who were hailed as 'the new Beatles' in 1975 following their two No.1 hits, 'Bye, Bye Baby' and 'Give a Little Love'. They provoked scenes of mass hysteria wherever they appeared, like Cliff Richard and the Shadows in the old days. Yet they never actually played on some of their records. Our keyboard player Cliff Hall and other session musicians played on most of the Rollers' hits. It was the *image* that mattered most, and when that faded, so too did the group. They had little else to offer. Cliff Hall and his colleagues played on so many records by different artistes that they would often ask before they started work, 'Who are we supposed to be today?' Cliff has probably played on more hits than the rest of us put together.

The history of rock music has shown that the life-span of all teeny-bop artistes is a very short one, because the market they are pitched into is the most fickle of all. Their appeal is aimed very definitely at young, pubescent girls between the ages of eight and fifteen, whose tastes and attitudes to life are changing all the time and subject to so many whims, and who ultimately grow up and move on to other things. The list of pop casualties is long – Mud, Adam and the Ants, Haircut 100 among the many. Ultimately the same fate could befall the likes of A-ha, Brother Beyond and Bros, if they don't move on to explore other aspects of the business and expand on the talent they have. The biggest teen idol of all, however, destined to go down in history as one of the greatest stars the world has ever seen, is Michael Jackson, yet he has transcended all ages. Quite honestly, I rate Elvis Presley, the Beatles and Michael Jackson as the three *biggest* influences of all time in the music industry. The rest are merely supporting players. Jackson, whose influence will be long felt throughout the 1990s, is possibly the finest entertainer we have ever seen. He is an amazing artiste: a brilliant dancer, a tremendous singer who gives a truly imaginative stage performance. He works hard at his trade. He has been performing since he was five years old – I first saw him when he was only eight and he was brilliant even then. He is a total performer, a prodigious talent, and has been all his life. He is quite simply the most exciting performer I have ever seen – *pure* Hollywood – and he has gained the respect and admiration of many of the great names in show business, for example Gene Kelly, Elizabeth Taylor, Fred Astaire and Katherine Hepburn, for his talent, which is something very special. Whenever I see him performing he inspires me tremendously. Michael is almost an old-fashioned song-and-dance man, a Fred Astaire in a modern musical world. I hope we haven't seen the last of him in live performance. He is far too good to take a premature retirement.

Towards the end of the 1960s the musical attention was taken briefly away from London and Liverpool, and focused sharply on San Francisco, as flower power gripped the world. It was a reaction to the Vietnam war; teenagers wanted to make peace, not war, and love was the message of hope. The music was the vehicle to voice their passive protest. Scott McKenzie's 'San Francisco (Be Sure to Wear Flowers in Your Hair)' led this peaceful rebellion, followed by groups like the Mamas and the Papas, Grateful Dead and Buffalo Springfield. But the reality of Vietnam was all too vivid, and the protesters buried their heads in the music and the drug culture that inevitably followed, as an escape. When they found they couldn't change the world, they retreated into their inner visions. Yet out of the San Francisco culture came community rock, which indirectly led to a spate of outdoor rock and pop festivals during the late sixties, of which Woodstock in 1969 was the most memorable.

The seventies woke up with a bang and brought the heavy

duty, heavy metal bands of Led Zeppelin, Deep Purple, Motorhead and Iron Maiden to the fore. At the same time, music in Britain drifted into three very distinct camps: the teenage pop idols, whose appeal revolved around the three-minute single; the singer-songwriter social commentators; and the more progressive groups who started to think about their music and built long-lasting careers around the album market, like Yes, Emerson, Lake and Palmer, Jethro Tull, and Moody Blues.

Show business returned to the music scene at the start of the decade in the form of Glam rock, which was so typically British. It brought flamboyance and spectacle into rock 'n' roll, with Gary Glitter leading the gang himself. I knew Gary back in the fifties as Paul Gadd, when he used to hang around the 2i's. He was joined by Alvin Stardust (the reincarnation of Shane Fenton), Slade, Sweet, Cockney Rebel, Suzi Quatro, Mott the Hoople, Wizzard and, of course, Marc Bolan.

Bolan gained a cult following through Tyrannosaurus Rex, a folk-inspired, almost Tolkienesque duo, and later attracted an army of teenage girl fans who turned him into another teen idol. Unlike so many of his contemporaries, however, he was an innovator in one sense because of his ability to write songs for the market he was aiming at, highly catchy pop melodies with meaningless lyrics like 'Ride a White Swan', 'Telegram Sam' and 'Get It On'.

Glam rock essentially brought the fun back into rock 'n' roll, at a time when we were all in danger of taking ourselves far too seriously.

Elton John emerged around the same time as one of the world's most eccentric rock stars, and although he dressed up in outrageous stage outfits for his live performances, he was definitely *not* a part of the Glam rock brigade. Far from it.

Elton John was one of the new breed of singer-songwriters, a superb musical craftsman, inventive and expressive, who had absorbed all the influences from rock 'n' roll's heritage and created something original of his own. With lyricist Bernie Taupin, he brought the great melodies to rock without the slush and sentimentality, through such endearing ballads as 'Candle in the Wind', 'Your Song', 'Goodbye Yellow Brick Road' and 'Sorry Seems to be the Hardest Word'. And yet he could rock with the best of them with 'Crocodile Rock', and 'Saturday Night's All Right for Fighting'. Curiously for one so talented, Elton succeeded in America long before he was acknowledged back home in Britain. He was one of a long line of British performers who have had to make it in America first, before acceptance comes at home. It happened to Olivia Newton-John, Steve Winwood, Peter Frampton, Chris Rea, Supertramp and Foreigner. I thought Elton's first British release, 'Lady Samantha', would become a hit, but it sank without trace, and it wasn't until a few months later that I heard about this brilliant young British musician who was causing all kinds of sensations in the Troubadour Club in Los Angeles. He established his name in America with 'Your Song' in 1970, a whole year before he made any kind of impact whatsoever in Britain, but we knew it was only a matter of time.

I remember first hearing of Elton in 1969, when I was searching for new material for Olivia Newton-John to record. My old buddy Jerry Lordan played me some demos of his new songs. When I asked him who the singer was, he shrugged his shoulders: 'Some fat little kid called Reg.'

Another great storyteller from that era who rivalled Elton, but in a totally different way, was David Bowie. He had his first taste of chart success in 1969 with 'Space Oddity', which, rumour had it, was one of the first records to be blatantly *hyped* into the chart. It was at the start of the seventies, however, that he established himself through his alter ego, Ziggy Stardust, and brought a theatrical element to the music industry, which was something Kate Bush was to expand upon during the next decade. Bowie was always one step ahead of the rest, anticipating musical trends and very often dictating styles and fashions of his own through his often complex words and music. His influence has inspired such talent as Iggy Pop, Lou Reed, Gary Numan, Human League, Roxy Music, Japan and David Sylvin.

The decade also saw the birth of Euro-rock through the talents of Boney M, and of course Abba. They developed their song-writing to an art. They came from Sweden and at first had difficulty mastering English, so they wrote the lyrics to their songs phonetically, using simple words and phrases to convey their message. This simplicity of style was to prove very effective. In a short space of time they managed to sell almost as many records worldwide as the Beatles. Shortly afterwards, the disco boom exploded on the scene, through the success of movies like *Saturday Night Fever*. The main protagonists in this direction were the Bee Gees, who had taken the style and sound of the Beatles one step further in the sixties, with such hits as 'Massachusetts', 'Words' and 'I've Gotta Get a Message to You'.

For some reason, over the years the Bee Gees have been much maligned in the industry for their image and style, which is totally unfair. They are very accomplished writers and have succeeded through three decades. To be able to come up with something as fresh and original as 'You Win Again', in 1988, takes tremendous talent.

Their career has succeeded through many different guises. The Bee Gees were the first people I came across using forty-eight track recording techniques long before they became generally available. They simply took two twenty-four track machines linked together, using one as a slave unit to drive the other, and recorded the music in the same way that George Martin had recorded *Sgt Pepper*, on four-track machines years before, mixing down from one machine to the next.

Then, in the mid-seventies, the whole music industry was thrown into total chaos through the new wave revolution of punk, which was the reaction by the kids to the over-excesses of the music industry. Rock music seemed to be moving away from the very audience for which it was created. It was becoming too self-indulgent and introspective – inward-looking instead of progressive. Artistes became far more interested in the financial rewards than in the music. Multi-track recording was with us with a vengeance, which meant that rock stars could spend up to six months in the studio laying down a single track. Some albums took as much as two years to make. It was excess gone mad and over the top. Johnny Rotten summed up the industry by calling the people involved 'boring old farts'. In many cases, he was right.

Punk rock emerged to break down the barriers even further and get back to basics. It proved that you could still make music without spending vast amounts of time in the recording studio, or huge sums of money. Rock had become part of the establishment, and out of touch with reality.

Punk had bags of energy, created by kids for kids. But it was a throwback to what rock 'n' roll had done twenty years before. It was the music of rebellion. Punk spawned outrageous fashions of its own, leaning towards bondage gear. It was a parody of pornography. Hair was shaved close to the bone, or featured spiky, Mohican cuts, dyed in bizarre colours. Make-up – white faces, black lips – was worn by both sexes, and clothes were often made out of dustbin liners or plastic bags. Jewellery included zips, chains, razor blades and safety pins, many stuck through ears and noses. Self-mutilation was an important part of the cult, and the trade in tattoos increased considerably. They also devised their own dance, pogo-ing, which was simply jumping up and down on a fixed spot, nearer to head-banging than anything else.

Punk became synonymous with the Sex Pistols, who were obnoxious and degrading. They were also totally talentless, but maybe that was the attraction. Everything the Stones claimed to be in the sixties, the Sex Pistols emulated. But the Stones had talent; the Sex Pistols had none. They went on television with one aim in mind, to shock, and they succeeded. In an interview on Thames Television's *Today* programme they were invited to be outrageous by the presenter, Bill Grundy. They obliged by unleashing a tirade of the most offensive four-letter words imaginable . . . at peak viewing time. They were made overnight – the legend was sustained by the tabloid press. It was a good story.

The Sex Pistols became the spokesmen for a new teenage culture which the record companies hoped to exploit. In the end they were exploited themselves. The Pistols were manipulated by their manager Malcolm McLaren, who carefully plotted to rip off the all-powerful record companies and then proceeded to do so. He took three of them for a pasting to the tune of £250,000.

I couldn't believe how bad the Sex Pistols were and how gullible the major record companies were to get involved. The music was terrible. They couldn't play their instruments, and did nothing more than re-hash established rock 'n' roll and rhythm 'n' blues standards into tuneless, mindless rubbish. Yet they had substantial hits: 'God Save the Queen' was the fastest-selling single of the year. The group's album, *Never Mind the Bollocks . . .*, topped the chart – it was acclaimed by the music press as 'brilliant' and certainly the album of the year. The great rock 'n' roll swindle was an apt title.

What punk did achieve was to bring music back down to street level again, to regain its credibility. Like skiffle before it, it gave everyone a chance to get up and have a go for themselves. You didn't need to be a rock star to play rock 'n' roll. Out of the punk explosion, a lot of groups established themselves and went on to make major contributions to music in the seventies and eighties, like the Police, Boomtown Rats, Elvis Costello, the Damned, Buzzcocks, the Jam, Tom Robinson, Siouxsie and the Banshees, Undertones, Stranglers and XTC – and the music industry was a better place for them. Some of the names of emerging punk groups left a lot to be desired – the Slits, Throbbing Gristle, Vibrators.

I met Johnny Rotten and Sid Vicious at the Rainbow one evening. I had gone there to watch a band and I was standing at the back of the theatre when the two punks came in. Rotten put his hand on my backside in a provocative manner. My immediate reaction was to hit him, and I threatened to push him through the theatre wall. Then I suddenly realized that if I caused a scene like that . . . it was just the kind of publicity they were looking for. So I didn't bother. He wasn't worth it.

Several major groups who arrived in the seventies have gone on to enjoy outstanding success throughout the eighties, including Genesis – so rich in originality – although Phil Collins is the exact opposite to what the record companies would class as a pop superstar. He is a most unlikely-looking pop star, and yet he has endeared himself to millions of people with his cheeky sense of humour and very expressive voice. A great musician.

Dire Straits emerged from a South London pub, almost as anti-heroes, and certainly didn't fit the image of conventional rock stars. Yet Mark Knopfler has become the definitive singer-songwriter of the eighties – a very perceptive and descriptive writer, who uses words extremely well. He observes and comments on life through his writing with great flair. He is also one of the greatest guitarists in rock.

Another completely original band were Queen, who in 1975 pioneered the use of the very first video on television. After they recorded the magnificent 'Bohemian Rhapsody' as a single, they could not promote it in the normal way because they could not re-create the superb studio sound on stage. They didn't want to mime to the record either. So they created a video of themselves performing the song. It was a very effective idea and sent the rock business off on another direction, from which it has yet to recover.

These days, the rock video has become all-important as far as music is concerned and the 1980s have become very much the product of the video age. It seems that sometimes it doesn't really matter how bad a record is, as long as the video is good. 'Great video, shame about the song.' The video industry has now sprung up alongside the music business and emerged as a multi-million-pound concern in its own right. In many cases a good video will certainly help to generate record sales – a prime example was A-ha's black-and-white graphics video for their No.1 hit single, 'Take On Me'. The more the video was seen, the higher the record climbed. And when Jackie Wilson topped the charts with 'Reet Petite' in 1988, the record sold on the strength of a superb and inventive stop-go video.

These days, record companies are actually signing up artistes whose talent lies in their ability to look good and relate to videos, while their musical ability is of secondary importance. The emergence of video has meant that artistes don't need to tour – or ever appear in concert again. Videos can reach so many more people than artistes could do by charging round the country on a one-night-stand tour. That was why Hollywood was so big – the movies reached millions of people all over the world. Video is the modern equivalent.

Video has ensured that many groups don't have to perform live any more, and the use of pre-recorded tapes means that backing groups are almost a thing of the past. Bananarama, who employ both, have become one of the biggest-selling girl groups of all time on the strength of catchy pop songs . . . and good corresponding videos. The Pet Shop Boys have become huge stars and set themselves up as one of Britain's most exciting recording acts without ever playing live to my knowledge. Now, of course, they don't need to.

The divide between the singles market and the album market has remained throughout the eighties. Recently the singles chart has been dominated by teeny-bop girls like Kylie Minogue, Sabrina, Tiffany, Belinda Carlisle, Samantha Fox, Kim Wilde,

Debbie Gibson and Tracey Ullman, who have all made their names in Britain with, for the most part, lightweight pop music that is instantly dispensable and aimed directly at the image-conscious teenage audience of girls – little girls wanting to be like them, to look like them and to wear the same kind of clothes.

Madonna, who, along with Whitney Houston, is probably the most successful girl singer of all time, has been very clever. She has managed to manipulate the media, in the main, for her own ends, and has built a career on a limited amount of talent. She has cultivated the Marilyn Monroe look-alike cult, the vulnerable 'tramp', very effectively. And, despite all that, she has managed to make some very good pop records.

So where do we go from here?

The music business is bigger than ever and it seems to be growing all the time, which is no bad thing. Despite the fact that people have been bemoaning the decline and fall of record sales now for many years, records are still very much to the fore. They keep telling me that singles are only made these days to promote album sales, from which a record company can make a lot of money. But singles are still selling. Most record companies would expect to feature three hit singles from each new album, and yet our first LP did not have 'Apache' on it. Michael Jackson's *Bad* has had five singles taken from its track-listing, while Genesis's *Invisible Touch* had four. New acts are still established through the singles charts.

I doubt very much, however, that the black vinyl single will be with us much longer because the quality is simply not good enough. The age of the compact disc and digital audio tape (DAT) is upon us. People have realized just how good the quality of CDs compared to conventional records has become. The compact disc has revitalized all album sales, particularly classical music, which sounds magnificent.

Entertainment as a whole will grow as we all come to terms with more leisure time. With the advent of modern office technology, like computers and facsimile machines, and modern telecommunications, people will no longer need to have offices situated in the major cities, they will be able to work from home, giving them much more leisure time in which to relax. So entertainment will be aimed directly at this new found freedom; it has already started with satellite and cable television. The day of the global village is upon us.

It's all very exciting. But is it exciting for rock 'n' roll?

Years ago the music industry was run by the musicians themselves, alongside the old professionals from show business, whose roots were steeped in entertainment. Today, as money seems to have taken over, the business is run by accountants and lawyers in more and more positions of importance. It's a sign of the times to note that of the top concert promoters in Britain, four of them are former accountants. Still, it can't be a bad thing if it benefits the musicians. One would hope that the horrendous publishing and recording deals of old are a thing of the past – and that artistes are given much better contracts.

The industry seems more concerned with making money than making music. Music has become a product, marketed like a bar of soap a lot of the time. It's all down to figures on a balance sheet at the end of the day – the 'bottom line' – instead of great songs and superb performances. The music industry should be encouraging new talent to grow and develop, but the cost of breaking new acts is enormous.

Looking back, I am totally amazed that we have survived so long. None of us would have dreamed it was possible in the early days. So many people have fallen by the wayside.

Cliff Richard – the eternal 'Young One' – goes from strength to strength. He is quite simply the greatest singing star Britain has ever produced. Over the years he has improved immensely from the kid I first saw performing down at the 2i's. He has learnt his craft over thirty years – found his limitations and played to his great strengths. He is an excellent singer. He has great pitch and a good ear, and he looks terrific. It has paid off. Who would have thought that at the end of 1988 – the year Cliff celebrated his thirtieth anniversary in the business – he would go on to top the British album and single charts simultaneously, enjoying a monster Christmas success with 'Mistletoe and Wine', and to head the CD and video charts as well?

The Shadows, too, have their place and have survived the great diversification of the rock industry – and we have continued to flourish. Our audience has grown with us, and has remained extremely loyal, and as long as there are people who like to hear what we do we have no intention of retiring.

Despite everything, I still consider myself to be a Shadow first and foremost, and I am intensely proud of what we have achieved. I have never had the time to become a full-time record producer because of my commitment to the Shadows, and my music publishing business can virtually look after itself, although I am constantly on the look-out for new songs. I have always had an ear for a good song and I pride myself on being able to spot talent, although I couldn't handle management – I am not very good at being told 'no'. I am totally the wrong kind of personality for a job like that.

I should write more songs. I used to be prolific, writing with John Rostill, Brian Bennett and Hank Marvin, but now that Hank lives in Australia it's not very easy to pop round to his house and sit down and compose. Most of my big hits were co-written, and I like to work with someone I can bounce ideas off. I've got very lazy in my old age. I think you get out of the habit of writing. I believe I need to be asked to write specific projects in order to be stimulated. Self-discipline can be very hard.

I still get a tremendous buzz from the industry even after all these years, and when I see groups like Dire Straits on stage I am inspired. It brings it all back to me, like starting over again. I haven't lost my feeling for the 'oldies' either, such as Elvis and Buddy. I still tingle when I hear 'Hound Dog' or the introduction to 'That'll Be the Day'. I can appreciate the technology of the eighties and how it has developed, but there will always be a place in my heart for the great pioneers of this business.

By nature, however, I have become quite cynical, I guess. I am on the side of pessimism these days rather than blind optimism. Despite all the success over the years, there is a great sadness in my life, especially with the recent failure of my marriage to Lynne, which I had hoped would endure.

I realize that there are many thousands of people like me who were born illegitimate, but, having grown up without the strength of parents, I always vowed to myself that if I had children of my own, things would be different. It was not to be. We all have to learn to live with our mistakes. However, like most fathers, I am immensely proud of my only son Dwayne, who is making his way in the record industry, not as a performer but on the business side of things. My own career has meant so much to me. It has given me fame, a nice lifestyle and all the trappings that follow success. I have travelled the world through my ability to play three chords (in any key). My job has been a labour of love. Had I not become a musician, I do not know what I would have done with my life, although I am almost certain I would have gone to sea or travelled, I was so desperate to get out of Newcastle.

In 1975 a young Australian singer called Kevin Johnson sang a song, 'Rock 'n' Roll – I Gave You the Best Years of My Life', which really sums up my own. For over thirty years my life has revolved around music . . . and I wouldn't want it any other way.

I can still remember when I bought my first guitar . . .
And my family listened fifty times to my two-song repertoire . . .
Rock 'n' roll – I gave you all the best years of my life
All the crazy, lazy young days, all the magic, moonlight nights,
I was so busy on the road, singing love songs to you,
While you were changing your direction and you never even knew
That I was always just one step behind you . . .

DISCOGRAPHY

SINGLES – the Drifters

Feelin' Fine/Don't Be A Fool With Love DB4263
Jet Black/Driftin' DB4325

SINGLES – the Shadows

Saturday Dance/Lonesome Fella DB4387
Apache/Quartermaster's Stores DB4484
Man of Mystery/The Stranger DB4530
FBI/Midnight DB4580
The Frightened City/Back Home DB4637
Kon Tiki/36–24–36 DB4698
The Savage/Peace Pipe DB4726
Wonderful Land/Stars Fell on Stockton DB4790
Guitar Tango/What a Lovely Tune DB4870
Dance On/All Day DB4948
Foot Tapper/The Breeze and I DB4984
Atlantis/I Want You to Want Me DB7047
Shindig/It's Been a Blue Day DB7106
Geronimo/Shazam DB7163
Theme for Young Lovers/This Hammer DB7231
The Rise and Fall of Flingel Bunt/It's a Man's World DB7261
Rhythm 'n' Greens/The Miracle DB7342
Genie with the Light Brown Lamp/Little Princess DB7416
Mary Anne/Chu-Chi DB7476
Stingray/Alice in Sunderland DB7588
Don't Make My Baby Blue/Grandfather's Clock DB7650
The Warlord/I Wish I Could Shimmy Like My Sister Arthur DB7769
I Met a Girl/Late Night Set DB7853
A Place in the Sun/Will You Be There DB7952
The Dreams I Dream/Scotch on the Socks DB8034
Maroc 7/Bombay Duck DB8170
Tomorrow's Cancelled/Somewhere DB8264
Dear Old Mrs Bell/Trying to

Forget the One You Love DB8372
Slaughter on Tenth Avenue/Midnight Cowboy DB8628
Turn Around and Touch Me/Jungle Jam EMI2081
Let Me Be the One/Stand Up Like a Man EMI2269
Apache/Wonderful Land/FBI re-release DB8958
Run Billy Run/Honourable Puff Puff EMI2310
It'll Be Me, Babe/Like Strangers EMI2461
Apache/Wonderful Land/FBI re-release EMI2573
Another Night/Cricket Bat Boogie EMI2660
Love de Luxe/Sweet Saturday Night EMI2838
Don't Cry for Me, Argentina/Montezuma's Revenge EMI2890
Theme from The Deer Hunter/Bermuda Triangle EMI2939
Rodrigo's Guitar Concerto/Song for Duke EMI5004
Riders in the Sky/Rusk EMI5027
Heart of Glass/Return to the Alamo EMI5083
Equinoxe (Part V)/Fender Bender POSP1048
Mozart Forty/Midnight Creepin' POSP187
The Third Man (The Harry Lime Theme)/The Fourth Man POSP255
Telstar/Summer Love '59 POSP316
Medley: Imagine/Woman/Hats Off to Wally POSP376
Treat Me Nice/Spot the Ball POSP439
Theme from Missing/The Shady Lady POSP485
Diamonds/Elevenis POSP629
Going Home/Cat 'n' Mouse POSP657
On a Night Like This/Thing Me Jig POSP694
Moonlight Shadow/Johnny Staccato POSP792
Dancing in the Dark/Turning Point POSP808
Theme from *EastEnders* and *Howard's Way*/No Dancing POSP847
Pulsaki/Change of Address POSP886
Theme from *The Snowman*/Outdigo POSP898
Mountains of the Moon/Stack-it PO47
Shadowmix/Arty's Party PZ61

SINGLES – Bruce Welch Solo

Please Mister Please/Song of Yesterday EMI2141

SINGLES – Marvin, Welch and Farrar

Faithful/Mr Sun RZ3030
Lady of the Morning/Tiny Robin RZ3035
Marmaduke/Strike a Light RZ3048

THE ALBUMS – the Shadows

The Shadows SCX3414/FA3061
Out of the Shadows SCX3449/AVM9001
Dance with the Shadows SCX3511/DL1092

Sound of the Shadows SCX3554/DL1092
The Shadows: Greatest Hits SCX1522
Shadow Music SCX6041
More Hits – the Shadows SCX3578
Jigsaw SCX6148
From Hank, Bruce, Brian and John SCX6199/BG0 LP20
Shades of Rock SCX6420
Rockin' with Curly Leads EMA762
Specs Appeal EMA3066
Live at the Paris Olympia EMC3095
Twenty Golden Greats EMTV3
Tasty EMC3195
String of Hits EMC3310
Another String of Hot Hits EMC3339
Change of Address 2442179
Hits Right Up Your Street POLD5046
The Shadows Live at Abbey Road/Life in the Jungle (Double Album) SHADS1
XXV POLD5120
Guardian Angel POLD5169
Moonlight Shadows PROLP8
Simply Shadows SHADS1
Steppin' to the Shadows SHAD30
At Their Very Best POLD8415201

COMPILATION ALBUMS

The Shadows SE8031
The Shadows: Walkin' MFP1388
The Shadows: Somethin' Else SRS5012
The Shadows: Mustang MFP5266
The Shadows Live (Double Album) MFP1018
Rock On with the Shadows MFP50468
The Shadows Collection (6-album boxed set) World Record Club
Rarities NUT2
The Shadows at the Movies MFP50347
The Shadows Vocals EG-2600751
The Shadows EP Collection SEE246
The Shadows Silver Album TELLY22
Compact Shadows (compact disc only) 8230802
Another String of Hot Hits and More CDMFP6002

THE ALBUMS – Marvin, Welch and Farrar

Marvin Welch and Farrar SRZA8502
Marvin Welch and Farrar Second Opinion SRZA8504
Step from the Shadows SEE78

SOLO TRACKS ON CLIFF RICHARD ALBUMS

Cliff SX1147
The Young Ones SCX3397
Summer Holiday SCX3462
Wonderful Life SCX3515
Finders Keepers SCX6079
Aladdin SCX3522
Cinderella SCX6103
Established 1958 SCX6282
Thank You Very Much EMTV15

THE VIDEOS

The Shadows Live MUR9900512
Thank You Very Much (With Cliff Richard) PM0003
Together (With Cliff Richard) MVP9910082
The Young Ones (With Cliff Richard) PES-38075
Summer Holiday (With Cliff Richard) PES-38073
Wonderful Life (With Cliff Richard) PES-38076
Rhythm 'n' Greens

THE EPs – The Shadows

The Shadows SEG8061/ESG7834
The Shadows to the Fore SEG8094
Spotlight on the Shadows SEG8135
The Shadows No.2 SEG8148
The Shadows No.3 SEG8166
Wonderful Land of the Shadows SEG8171
The Boys SEG8193/ESG7881
Out of the Shadows SEG8218/ESG7883
Dance On – The Shadows SEG8233
Out of the Shadows No.2 SEG8249/ESG7895
Foot Tapping with the Shadows SEG8268
Los Shadows SEG8278
Shindig with the Shadows SEG8286
Dance with the Shadows SEG8342
Rhythm 'n' Greens SEG8362/ESG7904
Dance with the Shadows No.2 SEG8375
Aladdin SEG8396
Dance with the Shadows No.3 SEG8408
The Sound of the Shadows SEG8459
The Sound of the Shadows No.2 SEG8473
The Sound of the Shadows No.3 SEG8494
Alice in Sunderland SEG8445
Those Talented Shadows SEG8500
Thunderbirds Are Go SEG8510
The Shadows on Stage and Screen SEG8528

INDEX

FOR THE BEST IN PAPERBACKS, LOOK FOR THE 

BIOGRAPHY AND AUTOBIOGRAPHY IN PENGUIN

Jackdaw Cake Norman Lewis

From Carmarthen to Cuba, from Enfield to Algeria, Norman Lewis brilliantly recounts his transformation from stammering schoolboy to the man Auberon Waugh called 'the greatest travel writer alive, if not the greatest since Marco Polo'.

Catherine Maureen Dunbar

Catherine is the tragic story of a young woman who died of anorexia nervosa. Told by her mother, it includes extracts from Catherine's diary and conveys both the physical and psychological traumas suffered by anorexics.

Isak Dinesen, the Life of Karen Blixen Judith Thurman

Myth-spinner and storyteller famous far beyond her native Denmark, Karen Blixen lived much of the Gothic strangeness of her tales. This remarkable biography paints Karen Blixen in all her sybiline beauty and magnetism, conveying the delight and terror she inspired, and the pain she suffered.

The Silent Twins Marjorie Wallace

June and Jennifer Gibbons are twenty-three year old identical twins, who from childhood have been locked together in a strange secret bondage which made them reject the outside world. *The Silent Twins* is a real-life psychological thriller about the most fundamental question – what makes a separate, individual human being?

Backcloth Dirk Bogarde

The final volume of Dirk Bogarde's autobiography is not about his acting years but about Dirk Bogarde the man and the people and events that have shaped his life and character. All are remembered with affection, nostalgia and characteristic perception and eloquence.

FOR THE BEST IN PAPERBACKS, LOOK FOR THE 

Warhol: The Biography Victor Bockris

'For the definitive documentation of the man's life, the discerning reader should go for Victor Bockris's biography' – *Time Out*

'By far the most revealing parts of Bockris's book (I doubt if there will ever be a better one, given that Bockris has been hard-working, questioning, and a friend) concern Warhol's origins in industrial Pittsburg. The origins of so much that was to come – the star-worship, the insularity, the snobbery, even the soup-cans, it seems – can be traced to those tough early years . . . Makes increasingly clear that far from being a weirdo-outcast Warhol was in fact a pretty accurate personsification of his country . . . Warhol emerges as a shy, nervous, vulnerable man who hid his nervousness behind a carefully constructed façade of cool detachment' – *Guardian*

'This is the kind of book I like: it tells me the things I want to know about the artist, what he ate, what he wore, whom he knew (in his case . . . everybody), at what time he went to bed and with whom, and, most important of all, his work habits' – *Independent*

The Big Wheel Bruce Thomas

Imprisoned in hotel rooms and hustled onto tour buses from Perth to Peru with nothing but a bass guitar, a bottle of wine and a paperback for company, Bruce Thomas rode the Big Wheel of international success with The Attractions.

The gruelling schedules of whistle-stop US tours, the attentions of fans, places half-glimpsed in states of exhaustion or brain-numbed repetition, early morning bicycle rides in strange cities – Bruce Thomas provides a witty and myth-free account of life on the road.

Combining travel, autobiography and perceptive and dazzling reportage, *The Big Wheel* describes Bruce's ways of surviving the lunatic excesses of The Drummer, the legendary temperament of The Singer – and the licence to behave badly issued by the tour manager along with the day's expenses.

The Penguin Encyclopedia of Popular Music
Edited by Donald Clarke

'There has been a desperate need ... for a quality reference book on popular music covering the huge terrain of 'non-classical music this century'. In 1,000 pages and just over 3,000 entries, this book goes a long way towards satisfying that need ... the entries are well chosen, considered and informative' – *Observer*

From Abba to ZZ Top via James Brown, Artie Shaw and Frank Sinatra, *The Penguin Encyclopedia of Popular Music* is a comprehensive, fascinating and often surprising companion to all styles of modern music. Featuring performers, songwriters, musicians and record labels it is a mine of information on today's music the world over.

'A wealth of arcane learning ... the book doesn't cleave purely to the letter but often also to the spirit behind the music' – Mat Snow in *Q* Magazine.

'Fact-packed ... well researched ... I really am impressed by Clarke's achievement' – Tim Rice in the *Literary Review*

Rock of Ages: The *Rolling Stone* History of Rock and Roll
Ed Ward, Geoffrey Stokes, Ken Tucker

Here, at last, is the complete story of the artists, the industry and the social forces that gave life to rock and roll and shaped it into the most vital music of our time. From the rockabilly rhythms of Elvis Presley, Bill Haley and Jerry Lee Lewis to the soulful rhythm and blues of Little Richard and Sam Cooke; from the British invasion in the Sixties – the Beatles, the Rolling Stones, The Who – infusing rock with a new energy and fanning the flames of social protest, to 'glam rock', punk, 'new wave' and the hard rock extremism of heavy metal; right down to today when performers like Bruce Springsteen and Michael Jackson have helped enshrine rock and roll as a mass art form ...

Rock of Ages discusses them all with a passionate enthusiasm, a wealth of intriguing facts (did you know, for instance, that Keith Moon was in a surf band called the Beachcombers before joining The Who?), and a vigour and vitality that make this a book no serious music lover should be without!